The New Book of
LOSTWITHIEL

Cornwall's Medieval Capital

BARBARA FRASER

HALSGROVE

First published in Great Britain in 2003.
Revised and reprinted 2012

Copyright © 2003 and 2012 Barbara Fraser.

This book is dedicated to my four youngest
grandchildren, Francesco, Chiara,
Sophia and Imogen.

British Library Cataloguing-in-Publication Data.
A CIP record for this title is available from the British Library.

ISBN 978 0 85704 179 1

HALSGROVE
Halsgrove House,
Ryelands Business Park,
Bagley Road, Wellington, Somerset TA21 9PZ
Tel: 01823 653777   Fax: 01823 216796
email: sales@halsgrove.com

Part of the Halsgrove group of companies
Information on all Halsgrove titles is available at: www.halsgrove.com

Frontispiece photograph: *Bodmin Hill in Edwardian days.*

Printed and bound in China by Everbest Printing Ltd

Foreword

*T*he *New Book of Lostwithiel* tells the story of the people as much as the place where important events have occurred since the town's beginnings after the Norman Conquest. Key historical buildings have become integral features of the town throughout its development and are testament to Lostwithiel's rich heritage. What characterises this fascinating book is the firm idea of a sense of place and, as Barbara describes, the impact that the town has had on the lives of those who have lived in Lostwithiel and who in turn have contributed to the character of the town.

I was brought up in Lostwithiel and believe that the people and the place have contributed to and greatly influenced my life. I attended Lostwithiel Primary School from 1982 to 1987 and until I was taught history by Derek Taylor, I couldn't really see the point in going! Then, at nine years old, a whole world of history opened up before me with tales of kings and queens, of intrigues and mysteries and of faraway places and cultures. Derek brought history alive and running out of school at the end of the day I couldn't wait to return. His enthusiasm for the past shaped my future, leading me to an archaeology degree at Cambridge and now a career in museums. This might never have happened if I had lived anywhere else.

Being surrounded by history in such a place as Lostwithiel can often be taken for granted, which is why it was with great pleasure that I read the first book that Barbara wrote about Lostwithiel. *The New Book of Lostwithiel* is a longer version that extends the story of the characters, groups and institutions of the town, so that a real flavour of what it was (and is) like to live in this friendly Cornish town really shines through. One of the important aspects of the new book is the in-depth research and the number of different historical sources that have been used to describe the development of the town, including interviews with local people. *The New Book of Lostwithiel* captures these stories for the enjoyment of future generations of the town and it is thanks to Barbara that they will not be lost.

Corrina Faye Bower,
MA (Hons Cantab), MA (UC London).

Medieval characters, carnival parade, 1988. Left to right, back row: *Sheila Edwards (peasant), Lesley Bower (Black Prince), Mike Edwards (serf), Corrina Bower (Princess Joan, wife of the Black Prince), Peter Turner (serf holding banner), Marian Chanter (serf kneeling), Ian Chanter (serf), John Pegg (serf), Richard Marks (sleepless knight holding baby Rosie Marks), Richard Bower (all three castle ghosts);* kneeling in front: *Charlotte Richardson, Toby Chanter, Wayne Dungey, Adam Richardson.* (LB)

Above: *Town stocks, now in the south porch of the church.* (SBC & IF)

Above right: *Approaching Lostwithiel on the Liskeard Road. Drawn by G.B. Lawrance, in the nineteenth century.* (RE-C)

Right: *Milestone at the original Lostwithiel borough boundary.* (IF)

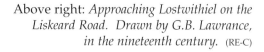

Below: *Watching the pageant, silver jubilee day, 7 June 1977. Were you there?* (CBu)

Contents

Acknowledgements

A sincere thank you to the many people who have helped with this book by sharing knowledge and information and generally supporting me, be it by chatting in the street, over a cup of coffee or by telephone, e-mail or letter, I am grateful to you all. I thank especially those who have contributed to the text and I have acknowledged them individually in the book.

I am most grateful to John Keast, of Jefferys of Lostwithiel, who has generously sponsored the project and supported me throughout.

The library staff at the Lostwithiel branch has been gracious and helpful over many months and years, thank you.

Photographer of Lostwithiel and Fowey, Jonathan Barker, and Lostwithiel Museum have generously allowed me freedom to use their pictures. Ken Beard, in charge of museum picture archives, has made original negatives available to me and I have drawn on the collection of the late Cyril Bunn (which now belongs to the museum). My husband Ian has taken new pictures and scanned many of the others for me, thank you all.

For the new edition, the publishers are indebited to Mike Rushworth; The *Cornish Guardian*; Debbie Curtis; Matt Connolley; and Victor May.

I thank the following who kindly gave permission to reproduce material (acknowledged in the captions by initials): *Ptolomy's Map of Britain* Ref. Maps cc.111.d.3, copyright British Library (BL); *The Caneing in Conduit Street*, Ref. 8826, copyright British Museum (BM); the Royal Archives, Windsor (RAW); the National Trust (NT); the Cornwall Records Office (CRO); the Cornwall Archaeology Unit (CAU); the Royal Institution of Cornwall (RIC); the Cornwall Centre Collection, Redruth (CCCR); Cornwall Archaeological Society (CAS); the Devon and Cornwall Record Society (DCRS); the Lostwithiel Town Council (LTC); the Lostwithiel Museum (LM); the Rector and PCC, St Bartholomew's Parish Church (SBC); A.D.G. Fortescue (ADGF); Jonathan Barker (JB) and Ian Fraser (IF).

From their collections: Jean Ashton (JA); Christine Barnicoat (CB); Lesley Bower (LB); Meg Breckon (MB); Ron and Doreen Brown (RB); Daphne Bryant (DB); the late Cyril Bunn (CBu); Patrick Chudleigh (PC); Richard Edward-Collins (RE-C); Matt Connolley (MC); *The Cornish Guardian*; Debbie Curtis (DC); the late Charles Day (CD); Donald Dunkley (DD); Pauline Dustow (PD); Barbara Fraser (BF); the late F.M. Hext (FMH); Vivien Hony (VH); Jim Jeffery (JJ); Rachel John (CRJ); John Keast (JK); Sandra Knight (SK); Wendy Liddicoat (WL); Bruce McDonald (BMc); Jude Martelli (JM); Angela May (AM); Victor May (VM); Claire Mitson (CM); Ralph Motton (RM); Florence Netherton (FN); H.J. Offord (HJO); Donald Parsons (DP); Gill Parsons (GP); John Pegg (JP); Betty Rawlings (BR); Myrtle Redmond (MR); Malah Rundle (MRu); Mike Rushworth) (MRus); Leslie Stephens (LS); Desmond and Eileen Talling (D&ET); Sheila Tyacke (ST); Margaret Wabeke (MW); Iona Wilton (IW); Pat Wilton (PW) and Margery Worden (MW).

Thank you to the staff at Halsgrove for smoothing the way for me.

Finally, thank you to all my family for patience and forbearance, especially to Ian. The book has been part of our lives for much of the past year and I could not have managed without him.

Barbara Fraser.

Introduction to the Original Edition

It has been a privilege to have this opportunity to write *The New Book of Lostwithiel*. I have aimed to tell the story of the generations of people who have inhabited these few acres of land over almost 1,000 years, who have, through good times and bad, gradually developed the town into the very special place it is today.

I have tried to search out the true facts and to be fair in any assessments I have made. I apologise sincerely for any mistakes and for the omissions; time and space are finite, whereas the stories of Lostwithiel are infinite!

I want to express my gratitude to my friend Daphne Bryant, who first urged me to take up the challenge to write about Lostwithiel nearly 12 years ago. I have been 'hooked' ever since. The bonus has been the many friends I have made along the way.

One of the fascinations in researching local history, is to discover the different language and thought processes of past times, which are illustrated in the documents and newspaper cuttings and other records that have been preserved. Here I want to pay tribute to Oscar Morse and Jonathan Barker, of our local newspaper, the *Cornish Guardian*. They are reporting, in words and pictures, the history of Lostwithiel as it happens. Their work is building up a substantial record, which will enable future generations to experience the true feeling of life in the town as we know it today, and will, no doubt, be a great help to future local historians!

Meanwhile, I hope my readers will enjoy this book as much as I have enjoyed writing it.

Barbara Fraser.
June, 2003

Left:
*By-law
poster,
1822.*
(LM)

BOROUGH
OF
LOSTWITHIEL.
BY
A BY - LAW,
MADE BY THE
*Mayor, Aldermen, and Assistants, of the
said Borough,*
The **24th Day of October, 1822,**
IT IS PROVIDED,
THAT IF ANY
**WAGGON, CART, CARRIAGE,
or HORSE,**
Shall be left standing and remaining within the Streets or Roads of the said Borough, unattended by any Driver, or other Person under whose care the same ought to be, the Owner shall forfeit and pay for every such Cart, Carriage, or Horse, any sum not exceeding
TEN SHILLINGS,
AS THE MAYOR SHALL ADJUDGE
That no Person may plead Ignorance of this Law, it has been thought advisable to make it thus Public, as the Mayor strictly intends to enforce it.
By order of the Mayor,
BENNETT, Town - Clerk.
Dated Lostwithiel, October 24, 1822.

Liddell and Son, Printers, Bodmin.

Right:
*Wherry's
garage
advert,
1930s.*

Telephone : Lostwithiel **26.**

W. J. WHERRY

Garage Proprietor.

**MOTOR - CYCLE, Cycle
and General Repairer.**
(Any Make Supplied).

CARS FOR HIRE.
PETROL, OILS, &c. STOCKED.

Queen Street, Lostwithiel

Above: *Lostwithiel Bridge, 1911.* (DB)

Right: *A cow waiting at the railway crossing.* (DB)

Above: *Lostwithiel seen from the bridge, 2002.* (IF)

Right: *Men of the Sherwood Foresters billeted in Lostwithiel, 1915.* (LM)

Chapter 1

THE PLACE AT THE TAIL-END OF THE FOREST

Lostwithiel – a natural place for a settlement to develop. This engraving dates from 1813. (DB)

Lostwithiel is proud of its rich heritage. In medieval times the most important port and the centre of administration for Cornwall and the tin industry, it owes its existence to the wealth of tin deposits in the area at that time and to its unique position on the River Fowey. Now a quiet, friendly town, it can look back on a millennium of constant change. Its buildings bear testimony to its fluctuating fortunes over more than 700 years. Throughout the centuries the people of the town have, with their hard work, courage and determination, enabled it to survive. This is the story of the people of Lostwithiel.

The compact little town nestles in the valley, surrounded by the 'loveliest inland scenery in Cornwall'. This was the verdict of travel writer Arthur H. Norway in his *Highways and Byways of Devon and Cornwall* in 1897, and it still holds good. Quite apart from its beauty, it is clear that here was a natural place for a settlement to develop, situated at the upper tidal reach of the river, six and a half miles inland from the estuary, where the river was

originally navigable by seagoing ships. Here the valley, narrow higher upstream, opens out to provide a few acres of level land, protected on all sides by well-wooded hills. It was on this land, the site of a small settlement, that Lostwithiel came into being as a town, planned and developed by private patronage, after the Norman Conquest. Below the confluence with the small tributary stream the Cober (which now runs under South Street in a culvert), the river meanders through water-meadows and on through richly wooded country to the sea.

How the town acquired its name has long been a mystery and subject for debate (it has been spelt in a variety of ways). The sixteenth-century historian, Camden, claimed that the town derived its name directly from the Roman 'Uzella', which translated as 'Les Uchel' in Cornish. Carew, in the seventeenth century, thought the name, translated from 'Lost' (a tail) and 'Withiel' (a lion) described the town as 'the tail of the lion' (the lion being the powerful lord who lived in the castle). This idea was treated with

Right: *Below the town the river meanders through water-meadows and on to the sea.* (IF)

Below: *Lost Gwydeyel – 'the place at the tail-end of the forest'.* (CAU)

scorn by Davies Gilbert, another historian, a century later. Suggestions such as 'Lost-within-the-hills' and 'Lost-withal' are treated with similar scorn in the twenty-first century.

Current thinking is that the name derives from two Old Cornish (or even pre-Cornish) words: 'Lost' and 'Gwydeyel' meaning 'tail' and 'wooded area'. This has been interpreted as 'the place at the tail-end of the forest'. If this is so, it was most probably the name given to the tract of land and small settlement in the valley (where Lostwithiel was later built) by the inhabitants of a pre-Roman fort up on the hill, near to the site of Restormel Castle and Lostwithiel would have been identified as a place nearly 2,000 years ago, long before it became a town.

Aerial photographs of a spur above Restormel Castle, taken in 1968 (for English Clays Lovering Pochin & Co. Ltd) revealed an earthwork consisting of three concentric rectangular enclosures with rounded corners. The inner enclosure measures 77 by 64 metres. This is believed to be Uzella, the pre-Roman hill-fort, which was probably occupied into the Romano-British period. Scraps of Roman pottery have been found in the area. Uzella was identified on Ptolemy's map of the second century AD sited west of the River Tamar. (Ptolemy was a Greek scholar and cartographer.) As it is likely that tin from Bodmin was being shipped to the coast from Restormel in those days it is conceivable that the hill-fort was used as a base, before and during the Roman occupation, from which operations were overseen. Perhaps one day more will be known – this site is waiting to be excavated.

There is evidence of human habitation in the hills surrounding the town, going back at least 3,000 years. The tumuli at Boconnoc were the burial-grounds of Bronze-Age people, who lived in hill settlements. Merchants from the Mediterranean are thought to have come to Cornwall to buy tin in those far-off days. It is likely that the river was already being put to good use, both for transport and as a source of food.

Castle Dore, on the west bank of the River Fowey between Lostwithiel and the estuary, is the best local example of Iron-Age occupation. Ralegh Radford wrote:

The fortified village can only have contained a small community not exceeding 150... It flourished during the first century AD but did not survive to the end of that century.

The eighteenth-century historian Borlase believed that there were two Roman roads into Cornwall from Exeter, one passing via Stratton to Bodmin, and a southerly road by way of Horsebridge, the Hurlers and Braddock Down, fording the River Fowey below Lostwithiel en route west. F.M. Hext, in 1891, recalled that workmen cutting a canal at Pontsmill in

the nineteenth century 'laid open the arched work of a bridge and a road of Roman construction' which would support this theory. Borlase mentioned:

... a stone causeway between Lostwithiel and Bodmin, the remains of which existed about midway between the two towns, and which tradition ascribed to the Romans.

'The Giants Hedge', parts of which remain, may have been a Roman road, although some historians believe it was a later defensive earthwork. Extending from Looe to Lerryn it was in parts 7 feet high and 20 feet wide and had a ditch on either side. Roman coins have been found at Lerryn. The Romans maintained several small forts in Cornwall from which officials kept an eye on the tin trade. The settlement at Nanstallon, Bodmin, is thought to have been occupied for about 25 years. At this time Bodmin was the centre of the tin industry.

After the Romans left Britain, around AD400, there began a period known as the Dark Ages. Legends flourished, kept alive through the centuries by troubadours and minstrels. The legends of King Arthur have long been associated with Cornwall, most often with Tintagel, but the Lostwithiel area may have played a part in this distant history – it has been suggested that the area is connected with the birth of King Arthur. It is believed that Castle Dore was reoccupied in the fifth century and developed into a palace, which may have been the Castle of Gorlois, a Cornish king married to Igraine. Legend has it that Uther Pendragon fell in love with Igraine and pursued her to her home. Gorlois was murdered and Pendragon then seduced Igraine. This was the begetting of Arthur. Might it all have happened so near to Lostwithiel?

Another legend told down the centuries was the tragic love story of Tristan and Isolda. This story is believed by many to have been set at Lantyan, 'The Cold Valley'. There is still a place called 'Castle' in the valley, which may have been the site of King Mark's palace (there is no other explanation for its name). The woods by the river, known as Tristan's Woods, could be where the lovers kept their secret trysts.

There is also a theory that Castle Dore later became the site of King Mark's palace. A stone now standing beside the road into Fowey is inscribed, *'DRYSTANS HIC IACET CUNOMARIS FILIUS'*. It is said that the sixth-century stone records the death of Tristan, son of Mark. Old manuscripts tell of King Mark attending the Church of St Sampson at Golant with his Queen (Isolda) mentioning that the Queen gave her best dress to the church, which was displayed on feast days.

During the Dark Ages, Britain was invaded and settled by adventuring hordes from Europe. The Celts in Cornwall constantly resisted invasion of their land and held out against the Saxons until well

Below: *Restormel earthwork,*
a pre-Roman hill-fort, based
on a drawing in the Cornish
Archaeological Journal. (CAS)

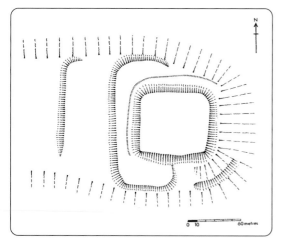

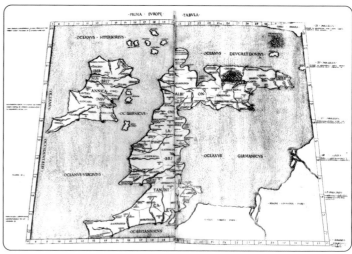

Above: *Ptolemy's map showing Uzella in the second century* AD. (BL)

Above: *Castle Dore, first-century*
Iron-Age fort. (CAU)

The Tristan Stone records the
death of Tristan, son of King
Mark, in the sixth century. (IF)

Celtic cross in St Nectan's
churchyard, one of several in
the area. (IF)

into the ninth century. It was another 100 years before the Saxon King Athelstan finally controlled the whole of the peninsula. As the Saxons penetrated Cornwall they developed the manorial system, superseding the Celtic way of life. The Celts had organised the land into parishes and lived and farmed independently in scattered hamlets, ruled by local chieftains. The hamlet surrounding the Parish Church was known as the 'Churchtown', as can still be seen in the nearby Lanlivery Churchtown. The Saxon lord of the manor claimed ownership of the land and most of the inhabitants, and took responsibility for their safety. The men on the manor worked for their lord and farmed small plots of land for themselves. The original Celtic scattered smallholdings obviated the need for the strip system used elsewhere in England. The priest farmed his glebe (allotment of land) in return for his services. The reeve acted as magistrate representing the people. There were rules and laws and regular 'moots' or courts, where justice was seen to be done.

Before 1066 there was an important manor in the parish of Lanlivery, west of the River Fowey, including the land where Restormel Castle and Lostwithiel were later built. The river was much wider then and its course was further west. The first solid ground would have been where the church stands. It is likely that there was a ferry crossing and possibly a ford at low tide. If there was a chapel or hermitage at the river crossing, as tradition believes, it was most likely on, or very near to, the site of the present church. There were homesteads in the valley, belonging to the manor, a quay at Restormel and a number of tracks leading off into the hills and beyond. The Saxon lord's name was Grim and his manor was known as Bodarther or Bodardle.

Chapter 2

THE FOUNDING OF A NEW TOWN

Restormel Castle in a print by S. & N. Buck, 1734. (DB)

The Norman Conquest changed England for ever. William I had his own harsh methods of subjugating the people he had conquered. He divided and subdivided the country, rewarding his loyal knights by giving them each an area to govern. These knights usurped the Saxon lords, taking over important manors and building castles as a show of strength. The castles were built quickly, in the first instance using wood. At the same time William organised the building of cathedrals, abbeys, and priories, to which he appointed French 'alien' clergy, sympathetic to his will. In this way he aimed to control both the physical and spiritual lives of the population.

Two decades after the Norman invasion William ordered a great census to be undertaken throughout the land and all details were recorded in the Domesday Book. At that time the town of Lostwithiel did not exist, but the manor of Bodarther (Bodardle) was recorded. (There is still a Bodardle Farm, towards the top of Bodmin Hill.) William had given lands in Cornwall to his half-brother, Count Robert Mortain, creating him Earl of Cornwall. In 1086 Bodardle Manor belonged to Robert Mortain. The manor was held for Mortain by Turstin, one of three powerful barons in Cornwall, who held many manors. It was recorded that Grim, the Saxon lord, had paid tax for one virgate of land at Bodardle (this

was a varying measure, thought to be about 30 acres). There was, however, one hide (sufficient land to support one free family and dependants, usually up to 120 acres). As acres were not the same then as now it is difficult to estimate the true size of the manor.

There was land enough to utilise 8 ploughs, each plough needing a team of 8 oxen, but there were 4 ploughs there. There were 7 serfs (slaves with no rights), 10 villeins (men bound to the manor, who could only attain freedom if they ran away and remained free for a year and a day) and 24 bordars (smallholders who paid their rent by labouring). The manor included 20 acres of woodland, 30 acres of pasture, 2 cobs, 1 bull and 17 sheep. Bodardle had formally been valued at 35s. and was, by 1086, worth 20s.

It is probable that Baldwin Fitz Turstin, son of Turstin, started to build the castle at Restormel before the end of the eleventh century. The earliest construction was a circular earthwork, with a quadrangular bailey to the west. Baldwin's original keep was probably built of wood. The earliest stone building was the gate tower, the base of which survives. It dates from about 1100. A bridge over the river below the castle was known as Baldwin's Bridge. Here also was a chapel or hermitage, dedicated in honour of the Holy Trinity, and a quay, the river being tidal and navigable up to this point.

Above: *Recesses in the south wall of the church, said to be the tombs of Robert Cardinham and his wife, Isolda.* (IF)

Right: *The church from the south-east, photographed in 1903.* (DB)

Left: *Twelfth- and thirteenth-century 'tin route' from the Port of Fawi.* (IF)

Right: *The streets of the town were laid out on a grid pattern, as shown in this nineteenth-century map.* (LM)

The remains of Cardinham Castle. (CAU)

The Martyrdom of St Bartholomew, patron saint of tanners, depicted in a medieval painted alabaster carving rediscovered in the church and restored in 1839. (SBC)

At about this time, the Cardinham family was building a castle five miles north-east of Restormel. The Cardinhams are said to have descended from Bertrand de Dinant, one of two brothers, Norman knights, who accompanied William I to England. Some years later, it seems, the Norman lords had taken possession of their lands in their own right, and a female descendant of Turstin's married into the Cardinham family, enriching and increasing their power by joining the two estates, and opening up enormous opportunities for the Cardinhams. They abandoned their castle and came to Restormel. It is still possible to follow tracks between the two castles.

In the twelfth century Devon and Cornwall were the only known sources of tin in the western world. Tin was used in the manufacture of bronze, for which there was great demand in London, Europe and beyond. Bodmin was the centre of the tin industry in Cornwall and was the main market for refined tin, which was shipped from the quay below Restormel Castle. The lords, now the Cardinhams, realised how much they stood to gain by developing a port a mile downstream, where the land opened out, and the river was wide – at 'the place at the tail-end of the wood'. Here more ships could be accommodated, and trade could be expanded. The town was conceived and developed as a commercial venture, some time between 1086 and 1189.

Many workers would be needed – craftsmen in wood, stone, metal and leather – as well as labourers to fell trees, quarry stone and transport material, more men than Bodardle could provide. It is likely that craftsmen came over from Brittany and it is possible that some labourers were escaped villeins. There must have been a great influx of people and surge of activity over a number of years to establish a new town, 'a plant of exotic growth' as the historian Charles Henderson described it. The first buildings were probably temporary wooden constructions, followed, as the town was established, by more permanent stone buildings. At some time during the twelfth century, as the little town developed, it must

have been referred to as Lostwetall or Lostwidiel, harking back to the ancient name. It was also known more officially as the Port of Fawi, together with the other smaller ports, Golant, Bodinnick and Polruan (the town of Fowey not having been established at this time). Bridging the river prevented ships from reaching Restormel Quay and the new port flourished.

A regular tin route was developing from here to Oleron, an island in the Bay of Biscay. From Oleron tin was distributed to La Rochelle, Bayonne and Bordeaux. It was also shipped to Barcelona, Genoa, Messina and the Levant (the eastern Mediterranean).

Soon after the Norman Conquest, the Benedictine St Andrew's Priory was set up at Tywardreath. St Andrew's was a daughter priory to SS Sergius and Bacchus, at Angers in France. The Cardinhams, now patrons of this 'alien' priory and of Lanlivery Church, built a daughter church, in their new town. This was dedicated in honour of St Bartholomew, the patron saint of tanners. The tanning industry developed alongside the smelting of tin, as it used the bark from the trees felled for charcoal. It is probable that tanneries were established in Lostwithiel in these early days. The design of the church with its lean-to aisles was common in Brittany (although rare in Cornwall), indicating a strong Breton influence. Two recesses found in the west end of the south wall are said to have been intended to be the tombs of Robert Cardinham and his wife, Isolda. Stories vary as to whether or not human remains were ever found in the tombs.

St Bartholomew's Church may well have had links with the Crusades in the twelfth and thirteenth centuries, situated as it was at a point of departure for the Mediterranean region. Crusaders from the West Country may have kept all-night vigils here, before setting out to fight in foreign lands.

The streets of the town were laid out in a grid pattern. This planning was not unique, other 'new towns' or 'planted towns' were developed in a similar way, both in Britain and France. Newtown on the Isle of Wight was one such settlement. The bishops of Winchester established six new towns between 1200 and 1255.

The configuration of the land helped the planning of Lostwithiel; the River Fowey ran north–south, and the Cober, forming the southern boundary, came in from the west. The east–west lie of the church fitted neatly into the scheme. However, a lane must have run north–south immediately west of the twelfth-century church, for when the tower was added some time later, the lane did not deviate, but became a right of way through the tower. The use of this passage continued though the centuries until the 1870s. The road now jinks round, west of the tower.

By 1186, Robert Cardinham, Lord of Bodardle, Restormel and Cardinham, had inherited through his wife, Isolda, daughter of Robert Fitzwilliam of Tywardreath, 71 knights fees, about 42,000 acres of land between the river and Tywardreath, and all the waters of 'Fawi' from the Haven to Respryn 'where 2 oxen yoked together could walk in the river bed.' Robert was indeed rich and powerful.

Nearly a century after the stone gate tower of the Restormel Castle was in place, the curtain wall of the circular keep had been built of stone. The church was established in the town, the river was bridged, a quay was in regular use by seagoing ships from many lands, and Lostwithiel was becoming a thriving commercial asset.

However, it needed a market. Robert applied to the King for permission to establish a market, paying 10 marks for the privilege. This was the time to keep the townspeople content by reiterating their rights and privileges and increasing their opportunities for trade. A Charter was granted which referred to a previous Charter, of which there is no record. This latter Charter, undated, but calculated to have been awarded around 1189, is the earliest surviving document relating to the town. It is the first time the town is officially called Lostwithiel. The translation is as follows:

Know all ye, as well present as to come, that I, Robert de Cardinhan, here given and granted and by this present Charter have confirmed to all my Burgesses and men of Lostwithiel, and to all those who hold burgage, tenements or land in the same town, all honours, liberties, dignities and quittances (as far as I can for myself and my heirs) which my ancestors gave them of old on the day on which they founded the town – To wit – every Burgess shall hold his burgage, tenement or tenements hereditarily by rendering for each burgage sixpence annually – To wit – threepence at Easter and the same number at the Feast of St Michael in discharge of all services and demands.

And at his death his testament shall be valid, but his heirs shall for a relief of twelve pence hold his hereditaments freely and hereditarily and possess them in peace.

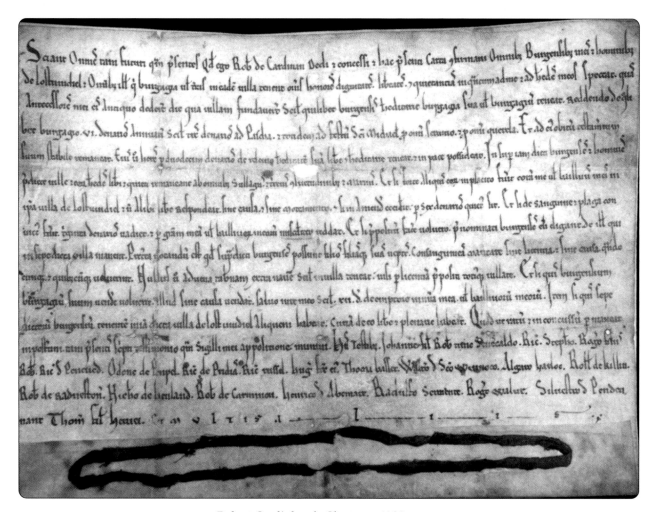

Robert Cardinham's Charter, c.1189. (CRO)

Moreover the aforesaid Burgesses and men of the aforesaid town and their heirs shall remain free and quit of all sullages and customs by land and sea.

And if by chance any one of them shall be impleaded he shall answer before me or my bailiffs in the said town of Lostwithiel, freely without cause or motion, and not elsewhere. And if he shall incur a fine he shall be quit for sixpence.

And if he shall be convicted of blood or wounds he shall give security for twenty pence and pay them as shall be mercifully allowed him by me or my bailiffs.

And if I shall wish to make a Provost, the aforesaid Burgesses shall elect from those persons who are resident in the often hereinbefore mentioned town. Moreover, it is to be noted that the above-named Burgesses may give their sons, daughters and kinsfolk in marriage, without licence or suit, whensoever and to whomsoever they will. But no stranger shall keep a shop out of a ship, that is to say, in the town, except by the permission of the Provost and the whole Townsfolk.

And if any Burgess should wish to sell his burgage tenement, he may do it without suit save my right – To wit – twelve pence from the purchaser (through my favour or that of my bailiffs).

Likewise if any of the oftentimes named Burgesses shall have any tenant in the said town of Lostwithiel, he may freely and fully hold a court for him.

That this may remain ratified and unshaken for the time to come I have strengthened it as well by the testimony of this present writing as by the affixing of my seal.

These being witnesses – John, son of Robert, then steward, Richard Stephan, Roger, sons of Robert, Richard of Pencoid, Otho of Penpol, and many others.

The privileges allowed to the men of Lostwithiel to be free men, having hereditary rights with regard to property, and rights to elect a Provost (Mayor) for the town, show how town life was progressing. In those feudal days such privileges must have given the people of Lostwithiel a feeling of pride, a sense of security and confidence in the future.

So fast was foreign trade developing that a few years on, in 1203–05, the returns of Winchester Assize Hall refer to 'the Port of Fawi' as the thirteenth port of the realm out of a total of 35, for the value of foreign trade, excluding tin, which was exempt from subsidy. If the value of tin had been included, Lostwithiel would have held seventh place. Its foreign trade was greater than all the Cinque Ports put together, and it was second only to Southampton, on the South Coast. Exports included tin, wool, fish and timber. Foreign ships brought goods to the

town, which they sold from their decks.

From the mid-twelfth century miners developed rights and freedoms, particularly the right of 'bounding', whereby a man might search for tin on any land. If he staked out his claim and registered it lawfully, he was free to keep the tin he found. There was no formal administration of the stannaries (tin-mining districts) except the collection of taxes for the Crown. In 1198 the King appointed a warden, De Wrotham, to organise the tin trade. King John granted a Charter to the miners in 1201 confirming their rights of bounding. Stannary courts were established at about this time.

Robert's wife must have died in about 1190, for there is a deed of that date from Hamlyn, Prior of Tywardreath, that makes reference to a Mass being said for her soul. Robert Cardinham was succeeded by his son Andrew between 1224–27 and at Andrew's death Restormel and Lostwithiel were passed to his daughter Isolda, who later married Thomas de Tracy of Barnstaple. The prior of Tywardreath held the estates for some time, probably in trust during Isolda's minority. In 1264, during the war between Henry III and the barons, Sir Thomas de Tracy signed a warrant to deliver the Restormel Castle to Simon de Montfort, who had taken up the barons' cause. This did not come about and Simon was killed soon afterwards at the Battle of Evesham.

For some time Richard, Earl of Cornwall, had coveted Restormel and Lostwithiel, seeing great potential in the small, thriving town. In 1268, possibly on the death of her husband, Isolda signed deeds of resignation and granted her lands to Richard, thus:

Know ye, present and to come that I, Isolda de Tracy, daughter and heir of Andrew de Cardinham, have given to Lord Richard, King of the Romans, my whole Manor of Tewington etc. Moreover, I have given and granted to the aforesaid Lord, the King, the Castle of Restormell, with villeinage in demesne, wood and meadow and the whole town of Lostwithiel, and water of Fowey with the fishery, with all liberties and free customs to the said water, town and castle belonging, whereof the water of Fowey shall answer for two and a half knights fee.

It seems that the part of Bodardle Manor to the west of the 'Via Regia which runs from Bodmin to Lostwithiel' was not included.

So it was that Restormel Castle, Lostwithiel and many acres of land reverted back into the possession of the Earls of Cornwall. It was during this period that Lostwithiel was to attain its greatest importance.

Left: *Copy of the Charter of Richard, Earl of Cornwall, 1269.* (CRO)

Below: *Eighteenth-century engraving of the Great Hall, or Duchy Palace, in ruins after the Civil War. The River Cober flows under the archway into the River Fowey.* (DB)

Left: *Duchy Palace buildings before they were sold in 1878. Note the tramlines to the jetties.* (DB)

Right: *The river still flows under the archway, now in a culvert beneath the flags.* (CBu)

Chapter 3

The Earls of Cornwall: Lostwithiel's Heyday

Richard, Earl of Cornwall, born in 1209, was already approaching 60 years of age when he received the lands which included Restormel and Lostwithiel from Isolda de Tracy. He was the son of King John, the younger brother of King Henry III, a man of poor physique, who never really enjoyed good health. Despite this he participated in a Crusade at an early age, and at 16 years old was knighted Count of Poitou. He was granted the Earldom of Cornwall when he was aged 22. As such he received dues on all the tin mined in Cornwall. Richard had a love of property and money, he was a good businessman and grew to be possibly the richest man in the realm, owning land and castles throughout England. He organised the wool trade, exported tin and imported corn. He supervised and financed the recoinage of the country, keeping a proportion of the profits for himself.

He had many Jewish friends and business associates, some of whom were probably involved in the tin industry in Cornwall. Jewish communities had been involved in smelting from the twelfth century. In the early days, the smelting furnaces near the mines were known as 'Jews' Houses'. Richard, however, did little to help his Jewish friends during the persecutions that took place at that time.

As Regent in 1254, Richard summoned the first full assembly of elected knights from the shires. This can be seen as an early model for Parliament. Although it failed, it was an important landmark, and the precedent was not lost. Richard's biographer, Denholm Young, claims that he had 'a real but not always acknowledged place in the history of Parliament.'

In 1256 there began the negotiations and intrigues by which Richard was made 'King of the Romans'. The title was granted after an election had taken place in Germany. After much negotiation, Richard was chosen to be a candidate by four out of seven princely and ecclesiastic electors. At the final election Richard was the only candidate. It had cost him a total of 28,000 marks to achieve this! He sailed across the Channel with a large retinue in 50 ships and was crowned at Aachen in great splendour by the Bishop of Cologne in 1257. Richard's reign as King of the Romans lasted fifteen years, only three years, nine months of which he spent in Germany.

Richard had a love of compromise and a zeal for arbitration, and was much involved during the troubled times of the 1260s when the barons were at odds with Henry III. Richard gave very many years of loyal support to his weaker brother Henry. He was taken prisoner at the Battle of Lewes in May 1264, and held in the Tower of London until September 1265. The Melrose Chronicle claims that his release cost £17,000 sterling, plus £5,000 of 'desirable gold'.

This then was the man who, although already owning Tintagel, Trematon and Launceston Castles, sought to acquire Restormel and Lostwithiel. Having had a lifelong interest in tin and the income from it, Richard, no doubt, saw the advantages of developing still further this small town, central in Cornwall, close to the tin-bearing lands of Bodmin Moor and Blackmoor and accessible to shipping. Lostwithiel was already the main port for exporting tin, but hitherto Bodmin had been the trading centre. Richard saw the good sense of bringing these two activities together and establishing Lostwithiel as the capital.

Very soon after acquiring the town Richard granted a Charter to Lostwithiel, dated 13 July 1269, extending the rights of the burgesses considerably. The following is a translation from a copy preserved among records in the Tower, the original Charter has been lost:

We, Richard, by the grace of God, King of the Romans, always Augustus have granted, and by this present Charter have confirmed to our Burgesses of Lostwithiel and Penknek in Cornwall, that our said boroughs of Lostwithiel and of Penknek be one borough, and that our Burgesses may have there a Guild Mercatory and free and civil customs and Sake and Soke, and Thol and Thegn and Infangenethof: we have also granted them for ourselves and our heirs, that all the said Burgesses be quit throughout all Cornwall, from giving toll in fairs, and in markets, and wheresoever they shall buy and sell, and from pontage, passage, lastage, tollage and stallage. We have granted unto them also that they shall not be impleaded in the Hundred or County Courts, nor on any summons go to plead anywhere without their borough of Lostwithiel and Penknek of any plea except pleas of the Crown of the Lord, the King of England belonging, which nevertheless are to be bound over by the same Burgesses until the coming of the Justices. We have granted to them also that they have once a year a fair in their borough. To wit – on the eve, on the day, and on the morrow, of St

Bartholomew – and a market in each week, and that they take distress for their money due, and not paid from their debtors. In testimony whereof we have caused our seal to be affixed to this present writing. These being our witnesses – Robert de Esthall, Archdeacon of Worcestor, our Clerk, Reginald de Boterill, Philip de Bodrigan, and others. Given at Wallingford the thirteenth day of July in the twelfth year of our reign.

The Merchants' Guild enabled the burgesses to regulate their commercial affairs. By means of 'Sake and Soke' they were allowed to hold their own courts. By 'Infangenethof' they were given jurisdiction over thieves caught in the borough. By 'Thol' they were bound to pay duty on imports, and by 'Thegn' they were allowed the status of freemen and landowners, but were bound to give military service, on demand, to the King or nobles. They were excused from all dues and tolls throughout Cornwall, except those to the Crown, and could not be summoned to courts outside their borough. The borough was enlarged to include Penknek (later Penknight) which adjoined Lostwithiel south of the Cober, in the parish of Lanlivery. Penknek was described as already a borough. Was there another lost Charter relating to Penknek?

Richard brought to Lostwithiel all the administration of Cornwall under the guidance of the Sheriff. He established the courts here, transferring them from Launceston around 1268. For a brief period the Assize Courts were held here, but these were restored to Launceston on payment of a fine.

It is not known whether Richard started to build the Great Hall (now known as the Duchy Palace). He certainly created a need for such a building, but four years after taking over Lostwithiel, he died and was succeeded by his son Edmund in 1272.

Edmund was a capable statesman, and for three years acted as Prince Regent for his cousin King Edward I, while the King was in France. Together with the Earl of Gloucester he put down a Welsh rebellion, for which the King gave him credit, saying he had served the Crown well.

Edmund was Earl of Cornwall for 27 years. During this time Lostwithiel became the undisputed capital of Cornwall. It is probable that Earl Edmund built the Great Hall, acquiring the land from local burgesses. An undated Charter in the *Cartulary of Earl Edmund* records that at some point before 1290 he acquired the house and grounds of one Ralph Wiseman, which occupied the corner at the confluence of the Cober and the Fowey. In 1292 William de London gave to Edmund all rights 'in a certain piece of land on which the steps of the Hall of the... Earl have been built.' Two years later Michael Quoynt conveyed to the Earl all his rights in the Great Hall.

The hall was comparable with Westminster Hall and with Dartington Hall in Devon. It had eight bays with a Gothic window set in each gable and a rose window set in the north gable. At its north end was built a smaller hall known as Convocation Hall. This building still stands at the corner of Fore Street and Quay Street. It was sold by the Duchy to a Mr Thomas in 1874. He sold it to the Freemasons, who renovated it in 1878. It is regarded by many as being one of Cornwall's most important buildings and greatest treasures.

The whole complex of buildings erected by Edmund was sited along the river, by the quay, and occupied about two acres between Fore Street and the River Cober, and between the Fowey and what is now Church Lane. It was never a palace, but rather an administrative centre, housing at the time of Edmund, the offices and treasury of the Sheriff and the courts. It was also the centre for the stannaries (the administration of the tin industry). Here were housed the stannary court, Exchequer and Convocation Hall, the Coinage Hall, assay buildings, smelting houses and stannary gaol. There was also a strongroom, 'the tynne porch' probably for the storage of tin. Accounts show that there were general security locks but there is no evidence that the Great Hall was ever fortified. There must have been accommodation for officials, as expenditure on 'the auditor's bed' is recorded.

This building became the heart of Cornwall from which all activity was generated. Here would be found the Sheriff, along with the steward, receiver (collector of revenue), feodary (supervisor of feudal affairs), havenor (supervisor of maritime affairs) and auditors who kept the accounts, all with their lieutenants and servants. Lawyers, judges and court officials were also based here.

Lostwithiel was the first 'coinage' town and, at times, the only one in Cornwall. Here, in the Great Hall the twice-yearly coinage of tin became a ritual. After the first smelting, the tin was moulded into blocks. A corner (coign or coin) was struck off each block, and the quality affirmed (assayed). The block was then weighed, stamped and stored ready for transportation. A record of each block, its weight, owner and duty paid, was kept in triplicate. Tinners brought their tin by packhorse and the coinage could take from two to ten days, depending on the quantity of tin. There were regular sittings of the stannary courts, and no doubt the stannary gaol was rarely empty – the temptation to cheat or defraud must have been great.

Throughout the year Lostwithiel Quay, 'the Port of Fawi', was the busiest in Cornwall, importing wine, salt, iron, garlic, corn, pitch and dried fruits and exporting cured fish, salted hogs, cheese, cloth and tin. From 1303–10 Lostwithiel had eight ships of its own bringing wine from Bordeaux.

There were annual fairs and weekly markets, when the 'shoppes' or market stalls around the Great Hall and along the quay would do a brisk trade. Foreign merchants, seamen, tinners, farmers, Duchy officials and itinerant entertainers were all regular visitors. Truly this busy, bustling, thriving little town was both the administrative and commercial capital of Cornwall.

The stone bridge was built during Edmund's time, the first reference to the 'Great Bridge of Lostwithiel' being in a deed dated 1280. It is believed that the original medieval bridge had nine arches. The foundations of the four most westerly of these have been uncovered from time to time under North Street, as far as the Globe Inn (during construction work on buildings and roads). The course of the river has changed over the centuries, when the bridge was first constructed the watercourse was further west and much wider. The rounded arches extending the bridge to the east were added at a later date.

The fourteenth-century octagonal font. (SBC)

The five remaining medieval arches of Lostwithiel Bridge. (DB)

The tower of the church was built in the thirteenth century. Much of the nave was rebuilt in the fourteenth century. (DB)

Above: *The keep of Restormel Castle, in 1952.* (DB)

The tower of St Bartholomew's Church was also built by Edmund, the octagonal lantern being added afterwards. During Edmund's time Lostwithiel became architecturally, as well as materially, rich. It is said that Edmund called the town his 'Lily of the Valley', 'Villa Regis' and 'Fairest of Small Cities'. He had reason to be proud!

Edmund is credited with having rebuilt the castle. There was no longer any need for a fortified castle, so Edmund built a splendid home for himself, one that befitted his royal station. It included a great hall, solar, kitchen, bed chambers and the chapel, which projected eastwards from the curtain wall. There were large windows in the solar, from which the deer park and woodlands along the valley to Lostwithiel could be observed. The dry moat surrounding the keep was 60 feet wide and 30 feet deep. Fresh water for use in the castle was brought from springs in the hills above via lead pipes. According to a survey of 1337, the bailey of the castle (now obliterated, except for a few bumps in the ground) had its own hall, chapel, chambers, kitchen, offices and stables. These buildings housed the servants as well as the men at arms.

Edmund further developed the amenities of his castle by the acquisition of more land east of the river to add to his deer park. He took great pride in this park, which had probably been set up by his father. Traditionally the Norman kings had preserved all hunting rights for themselves, although in Cornwall these rights were extended to the earls. However, to increase his revenue, Henry III had sold sporting rights, and Walter Bronsecombe, Bishop of Exeter, had enclosed woodlands on his manors of Lanner and Panton near Wadebridge, creating deer parks. This angered Edmund, and in 1274 there were violent clashes in the park at Lanner between Edmund's men and those of Bronsecombe. Master Jordan, a former Archdeacon of Cornwall was 'roughly handled, his horse mutilated, park fences destroyed and the authority of the Church flouted.' The knight who led the assault on the bishop's park was Sir Thomas de Kancia of Boconnoc. He and his fellow assailants were excommunicated. Despite all this the bishop dared not implicate Earl Edmund! It is recorded that a year later Sir Thomas knelt before the bishop as a penitent and offered 50 marks in compensation.

Edmund died childless in 1299. His bones were buried at Hailes, the Cistercian abbey in Gloucester founded by his father. Both his father and mother, Sanchia, were buried there before him.

According to the *Inquisition Post Mortem* of the revenues of the Earldom of Cornwall in 1301, there were 305 burgesses (men of property) in Lostwithiel at the time of the Earl's death. The town, now well established as the capital of Cornwall, had come a long way from its beginnings as a private, baronial venture. With the exception of Launceston it was the largest medieval town in Cornwall, and the most important. Richard and Edmund, rich, powerful and ambitious men, had given Lostwithiel this high status, bringing power, riches and opportunities to many of the people who lived there. Edmund also left us all a rich legacy in those buildings that still survive.

Edmund was the last Earl of Cornwall to reside at Restormel. His unhappy marriage had left him without an heir and there followed an unsettled time for the Earldom. Piers de Gaviston held the title for a few years until he was beheaded in 1312. The Earldom was revived between 1330 and 1336 when John of Eltham, the brother of Edward III held the title. He died in 1336 without an heir.

While Lostwithiel was enjoying its heyday as the capital and the only coinage town in Cornwall, there was much resentment elsewhere. Tinners and merchants clamoured loudly against the costs and time involved in transporting tin from all parts of Cornwall. So in 1305 a Charter was granted for the coinage of tin at four more towns: Bodmin, Liskeard, Truro and Helston. It confirmed the rights of bounding, freed tinners from ordinary taxes, confirmed royal pre-emption and outlined the jurisdiction and responsibilities of the warden of the stannaries.

Now it was Lostwithiel's turn to complain. Local officials accused the new coinage towns of exporting tin bearing false stamps and evading the King's dues, and petitioned for the return of sole rights of coinage.

In the year 1990, when Prime Minister Margaret Thatcher introduced the poll tax, Mr Fred Trull, living in Lerryn, claimed that the Charter confirming the rights of bounding and freeing tinners from 'ordinary taxes' had never been repealed. He staked a claim to a piece of land and declared himself to be a tinner, arguing thereby that he was not eligible to pay poll tax. He went on to invite others to buy a £1 share in his claim. This received national coverage by the media, and the Post Office was seriously embarrassed by the volume of post that arrived in the town. It is said he was inundated with over 1,000,000 application letters containing money for shares and several local volunteers

Royal Cornish Consols
United Tin Mines Cost Book Company

Nº 43213

SHARE CERTIFICATE

This is to Certify that **JOHN PEGG** of **LOSTWITHIEL**
is the Holder of One Share of One Pound
Sterling Cornish each and numbered as above in:—

Royal Cornish Consols United Tin Mines Cost Book Company

subject to the Regulations of the said Company and in accordance with the Ancient Rights Laws and Customs of the Cornish Stannaries and that there has been paid in respect of each said Share the full sum of One Pound Cornish.

RCC
UTM
CBC

Given under the Seal of the said Company this 28th day of February, A.D. 1990

Signed: *FRA Trull* Tinner,
Purser to the said Company.

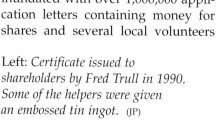

Left: Certificate issued to shareholders by Fred Trull in 1990. Some of the helpers were given an embossed tin ingot. (JP)

were engaged in helping Mr Trull to deal with it all. Of course, it made no difference to the applicants' eligibility to pay their taxes. The money disappeared without trace, Mr Trull has since died and the where-abouts of his fortune remains a mystery.

In 1312 King Edward II, who had borrowed money from the Florentine Bardi Society, as a favour to them, authorised a Genoese merchant, Antonio Pisano, to visit Cornwall and buy on his behalf all the tin coined here. Two years later the King granted Pisano the royal pre-emption to buy tin. Pisano, for his own convenience and economy, used Lostwithiel as his coinage town (and was probably behind the petition for sole coinage rights). However, Pisano was abusing his privileges, using his own balances for the weighing of tin, paying 42s. per thousand-weight for it and selling at 72s. Tinners complained bitterly! This was so uneconomic for them that their numbers fell from 3,000 to 500, causing a recession of trade. Exports fell and people could not afford to buy the imports of cloth, wine, iron and salt. Feelings ran so high that in 1315 a deputation came to Lostwithiel and assaulted Pisano's men. The next year the King revoked his grant. It was only a partial victory for the Cornishmen – they got rid of the rascally Pisano, but the King appointed a Steward, Richard de Polhampton, to reside at Lostwithiel, have custody of the stamp and supervise the coining of the tin, which was only permitted to take place at Lostwithiel.

From early in the fourteenth century Cornwall was represented in Parliament by two 'Knights of the Shire'. Their election took place in the Great Hall at Lostwithiel, bringing many people and much excitement to the town. This continued until 1832.

There was an incident, described by Canon E. Boger in 1887, which took place at Lostwithiel Bridge in 1314, and which must have drawn the crowds, caused local people some excitement and given them plenty to gossip about. Two years earlier there had been a dispute between the ordained and the secular clergy in the Priory of St Petroc at Bodmin. One of the canons, Odo Denisch, had wounded a secular clergyman 'even to the effusion of blood' (in other words, he had killed him). The priory and its ceme-tery were desecrated by this act, so no holy rites could be performed in them until they had been re-consecrated. Despite this, the community had continued to celebrate Mass and inter the dead, probably bearing in mind the cost of re-consecration, which they could ill afford, and thinking perhaps that they were far enough away from Exeter for their bishop never to find out. But find out he did, and the prior of Bodmin, Roger de Kilkhampton, was summoned to meet Bishop Stapledon at Lostwithiel Bridge on the Saturday after the feast of St Leonard (6 November) to account for the terrible occurrence and subsequent deception. Lostwithiel must have been agog – here was a great scandal concerning the town's great rival, Bodmin!

When Bishop Stapledon, founder of Exeter College, Oxford, made his visitation, splendidly attired and accompanied by his retinue of chaplains, cross bearers and attendants, he was met at Lostwithiel Bridge by an unhappy, guilty and humili-ated Roger de Kilkhampton and a sad little group of fearful monks. Here, publicly, they made a full confession. He dealt mercifully with them and visited their priory a week later. After a day in consultation with the Chapter, involving 'serious admonition' and a fine of £20, on Sunday 16 November he performed a service of re-consecration.

Under the stewardship from 1315, Lostwithiel continued to enjoy its status and to grow. In 1337 it was the third-wealthiest borough in Cornwall, after Truro and Bodmin. The number of burgesses had increased from 305 in 1301 to 391 in 1337 and some of these were very rich and powerful.

The *Caption of Seisins*, 1337, indicates that several Lostwithiel men (Crown officials) were leasing land from the Crown. Gerald Curtoys leased five acres at Penlyne and eight burgages (a house and surrounding plot of land). William Gill leased four and a half acres and one messuage (house, land and outbuildings) for 2s.6d, and Matthew Coombe leased three messuages, and 49 acres for 26s.4d. Matthew Quoynte (Mayor in 1346) and Alex Crantock leased the Moor of Penknek and Randolph Jolly, clerk, one messuage and ten acres for 6s. These rich men were speculators rather than farmers and the land was usually sublet.

A situation was developing where almost all holders of the largest amounts of land were Crown officials, merchants, burgesses, mining entrepreneurs or middlemen. They had almost complete domination over the non-peasant tenants who subleased their holdings. There were fewer and fewer peasant tenants, i.e. villeins farming land directly controlled by the lords of the manor. These men were still not free as they paid dues for permission to marry and 'chevage' for licences to live outside their native manor.

In 1337 King Edward III sought to reshape the administration, and created the Dukedom of Cornwall.

Above: *The emblem of the Black Prince can be seen on the gable-end of the Duchy Palace.* (JB)

Above: *The remains of a fourteenth-century chapel window in North Street.* (MW)

Below: *Restormel Castle before 1926.* (DB)

Chapter 4

THE BLACK PRINCE, FIRST DUKE OF CORNWALL

By the *Great Charter of 1337,* King Edward III created his eldest son, Prince Edward of Woodstock, the first Duke of Cornwall. Prince Edward was then seven years old. He was later known as the Prince of Wales and nicknamed the Black Prince, probably because he wore black armour in battle.

The Charter granted to the Duke 17 manors and a number of boroughs and towns in Cornwall, including Restormel and Lostwithiel (which are in the eastern division of the hundred of Powder). The privileges included the right to appoint the Sheriff of Cornwall, profits and havens, including 'wrecks and royal fishes', the rights of 'prisage and customs of wines', the profits of stannaries, revenue from the courts, most of the profits of the hundred courts, profits of all ports and stannary courts, the right to take duty of 40s. on each thousandweight of tin mined in Cornwall, revenues on farms and bailiwicks of stannaries, and poll tax from tinners working with shovels. He also had the right of advowson (the right to appoint clergy) of all churches, abbeys and priories. (Cornish possessions formed only part of the Duchy estates, other properties were spread across England.)

The Charter laid down that the Dukedom should be inherited at birth by the first son of the reigning monarch, and that in the absence of a Duke, the Dukedom should remain in the hands of the Crown. It was also decreed that the estates should remain intact. Edward III, however, did not adhere strictly to the Charter, and allowed the Prince to grant various of his manors to retainers and military veterans for the duration of their lives. (Over a century later, in 1453, the eight manors which had been leased were restored to the Duchy by Henry VI, Restormel being one of them.)

During the minority of the young Duke, Cornwall was governed from the Great Hall (later called the Duchy Palace) in Lostwithiel by a Sheriff, stewards and other Duchy officers and administrators. The maritime court for Cornwall was taken over by the borough of Lostwithiel, who administered it on behalf of the Crown. It dealt mostly with local cases of poaching, smuggling, rowdyism and disputes in the ports. On one occasion, the King's commissioners, seeking to impress ships for the war with France, ordered the town of Bodmin to provide four vessels.

The burgesses of Bodmin were in a quandary; did the commissioners not know that Bodmin was an inland town? As the vessels were not forthcoming, Bodmin's Mayor and several burgesses were thrown into gaol in Lostwithiel. Here they languished until a compromise was reached through the maritime court, whereby merchants of Bodmin agreed to send a ship, in which they had an interest, out from Fowey. In 1347, there were 47 ships and 800 men from 'Foy Haven' assisting the King at the Siege of Calais. Foy Haven included Lostwithiel, Bodinnick, Polruan, Golant and Fowey. The 800 men no doubt included some adventurers and runaway serfs.

The Black Death of 1348–49, which was carried throughout Europe by fleas living on rats, was brought across the Channel in ships, initially afflicting Dorset and the West Country, and quickly spreading to the rest of England. This pestilence, which killed over one third of the population of the country, left one third of the tenanted land of Restormel Manor without tenants. The land reverted into Duchy hands. Many lessees of the fisheries perished and no new ones could be found. For some time the fisheries could only realise 20s. a year in fees, and the weir fell into disrepair. John Dabernoun, the Duke's keeper of the fees, appointed on the Duke's behalf a new vicar for Lostwithiel and a new prior for Bodmin Priory, where all but two canons had died. Four years later, rents on mills, fisheries and all customs were reduced by half to help the town of Lostwithiel to recover.

Overall the effects of the Black Death were not so marked in Cornwall as in much of England. The tin-mining, fishing and port activities helped to offset the agricultural recession. The size of tenanted farms increased as there was less demand for land, and there was an increase in the amount of sheep rearing, leading to further development of the wool trade. Lostwithiel was an important centre for the collection and export of wool, so this helped its recovery. Having weathered the pestilence, the town, with financial help from the Duchy was able to re-establish itself gradually and continue its varied businesses of administration, exporting, importing and all the commerce of a port dealing with tin, wool, wine, fish, timber, corn, meat and salt.

Prince Edward, Duke of Cornwall, came of age in 1351. He had already been involved in the wars against France, showing great bravery at the Battle of Crécy, when only 16 years of age. He took the motto 'Ich Dien', meaning 'I Serve'. His short life was spent largely waging war, and for some time he lived in France, governing the conquered provinces, until a reversal of fortune and poor health brought him back to England.

He was very conscious of his position and responsibilities as Duke of Cornwall, and on coming of age, the Duke set about organising Duchy affairs. *The Black Prince's Register*, a daily log of his orders, shows the attention to detail with which he dealt with his affairs, and gives a clue to the many facets of his personality. No doubt, many of the orders were issued by officials of the Prince's household in London, but his character shows through.

Although he gained a reputation for cruelty as a soldier, and was stern in exacting all his royal dues, he showed concern and compassion for the less privileged of his subjects. Orders from the Prince were carried by a bailiff-errant riding from London to Lostwithiel at least once a week. Sir John Wengfeld was appointed Sheriff, Sir John Dabernoun was a steward, and John de Kendale became the Prince's receiver and constable of Restormel Castle. The Prince also appointed Brother Robert of the Hermitage of the Holy Trinity at Restormel to the chaplaincy of the Castle for life, to sing Masses for his royal ancestors.

Sir John Dabernoun was soon asked searching questions about the administration during the Prince's minority:

... to enquire how much tin has been forfeited, but not answered for, by whom it was forfeited and on what account, into whose hands it has come, and how and for what reasons such forfeitures may fall to the Prince, and to send the inquisition so taken to the Prince between now and the month of Easter next.

Many officials must have been sent scurrying when that arrived! At the same time came orders to repair 'the Hall wherein the County Courts are held' and to buy extra balances for the weighing of tin 'so that there be a pair of balances at both places of coinage' (Lostwithiel and Truro).

The Prince was concerned with keeping his properties in good repair and frequently sent orders with regard to his administration hall, castle, bridge, fisheries and mills at Lostwithiel. In July 1351 the Prince was interested in 'the repair and safeguarding of the Prince's Castle at Restormel, in this time of war.'

Towards the end of his first year in charge, the Prince enquired particularly about the state of his mills. When the burgesses of Lostwithiel had begun leasing the mills a decade earlier, the millstones and gear were all in good condition. Now, it seemed, the millstones were replaced with damaged ones of inferior local stone, the machinery was broken and the burgesses were grinding elsewhere. John de Kendale

was instructed to see that the mills were properly repaired at the expense of the burgesses and that the Prince's profits were secured. He directed John to go so far as to 'arrest all the corn and malt which he can find them grinding... at other persons' mills and keep the same safely.' In the same order the Prince commanded the receiver and the steward to take action to prevent poaching in the river 'Fawy' and 'put in guard any persons found trespassing'.

About 18 months later the Prince had been reassured that the condition of the mills was not a result of negligence, but of severe deprivation and loss of life during the plague. He showed his compassion by allowing a 50 per cent reduction in all rents for mills, fisheries and customs for the four years following the pestilence.

The Prince was concerned for his personal effects. He directed four of his top representatives in Cornwall:

... to make arrangements among themselves for hiring a well manned ship as cheaply as possible... to send wines... to the Prince at London with speed... if... there are at sea any special perils... they are to put on board the ship, at the Prince's cost, as many archers as they shall think necessary for securing the safe arrival of the wines. They are also to have the tuns... well and securely hooped and bunged, so that the Prince may not have so much loss as he had of the wines that were last sent him... [and] to appoint a definite person in whom they trust to take care of the wines and deliver them... to the Prince's butler at London, or to charge the master mariners to attend thereto on pain of forfeiting all they can forfeit.

Orders invariably contained the message 'with the least possible cost to the Prince'.

There was constant rivalry between Lostwithiel and Bodmin for the right to sell tin. Lostwithiel always claimed that it was more convenient for merchants to have the coinage, the market and the ships for transport all in one place. The tinners, on the other hand, found it expensive in time and labour to carry their tin to Lostwithiel. In June 1353 the Prince ordered the sale of tin to take place at his town of Lostwithiel 'unless too great damage will result to the common people, and especially the poor tinners, whose estate the prince would not wish to worsen.' At this time the Prince was enquiring as to the most profitable and convenient place for the preparation of wool, this being a growing industry in the area.

Early in 1354 Lostwithiel started to prepare for a royal visit. There were orders from London to repair all defects to castles, manors, houses, bridges and particularly the conduits for the water-supply to Restormel Castle. Instructions were received with regard to the fuel, food and wine required to cater for the large number of people expected to be at the castle, including courtiers, retainers, lords, knights and their servants.

The traditional way for earls to enter Cornwall was by way of Polson Bridge. John de Kelygren (sometimes Killigrew) held his lands in return for carrying out official duties, which involved receiving his lord on the threshhold of Cornwall, taking from him his great riding cloak and carrying it in his train for 40 days. The Black Prince, Duke of Cornwall, intended to keep up the tradition, so purchased a cloak for the sum of 3s.4d., in order that John de Kelygren might carry it.

On 20 August 1354 the Prince, preceded by heralds, priests, squires and noblemen, and accompanied by five knights of his household, crossed the newly repaired bridge at Lostwithiel and rode in splendour to establish his court at Restormel. Feudal lords, knights, tenants and burgesses from all over Cornwall came to pay him homage and swear fealty. Amongst these were John de Kelygren, Warin Vantort of Tregantle, John Laladroun of Laladroun and Gurron, and John de Inkepenne from the manor of Hauton, near Trematon, who promised the Prince that if the castle of Trematon were ever besieged, he would 'be therein with three men armed for the defence thereof, for forty days at his own cost, and forty days at the Prince's cost.'

An eighteenth-century engraving of Lostwithiel, seen from Restormel Castle. (JK)

The burgesses of Helston brought a petition to which the Prince gave his consideration. The friars of Truro paid homage, and were repaid by a promise of ten oaks from the park, suitable for constructing houses, and the Friars Minor of Bodmin received 20s. The court at Restormel lasted for two weeks. By 5 September it had moved to Launceston. On 11 September orders came from Exeter for the venison, fish and tin vessels left at Restormel to be sent by sea to Southampton!

Lostwithiel must have suffered a great anticlimax after all the preparation that had taken place and the excitement of the court. The town would have been busy for months in advance with extra officials, builders, carpenters and other workmen, as well as merchants and traders preparing for increased business, and the itinerant entertainers, who were always around when something was afoot.

The Prince made calls on the Duchy to service his wars in France. At one time he called for wine, oats, wheat and brushwood for fires, for use by 800 men-at-arms, waiting to embark at Plymouth. Then he wanted 104 score and 11 sheaves of arrows, plus 500 cod (300 dried, 200 powdered), 400 salted congers and 200 salted salmon to be sent to France.

Some years later John Dabernoun and John de Kendale were required to send to Aquitaine, chargers, trotting horses, palfreys, packhorses and cart-horses (80 altogether) as well as oats and hay to feed them on the voyage. Then, in September 1364, the Prince called for 4,000 shoes, and 150,000 nails in Gascony.

The Prince was impatient with inefficiency, and removed at one stroke six bailiffs from office, ordering John de Kendale to 'put other more able persons in their place.' He was, however, generous to those who served him well. He sent a 'pipe of wine' to his auditor of accounts and a doe each to five of his senior officials before Christmas. He granted the ferry at Saltash, with all profits for life, to a loyal servant and porter who lost an eye at Poitiers. He also granted John Dabernoun a manor for life, free of rent, after many years of loyal service.

Although the townspeople of Lostwithiel were enjoying freedom and many privileges, those born 'in bond' to a lord of the manor were still bound by feudal laws. The Prince received a petition from the Lord of Tywardreath saying that one of his bondsmen had married a bondswoman of Restormel and had two sons by her. He claimed that these belonged to the Lord of Tywardreath and not to Restormel, where they were living.

Two entries in the *Prince's Register* in 1356 suggest that all was not well in Lostwithiel. One was a petition from a tenant for permission to remove the iron, stones and timber from an abandoned mill, between Restormel and Lostwithiel, which had fallen into decay and not been repaired since the pestilence. The other was much more serious. It was a petition from Abraham Lestymour, a tinner, who had worked all his life with 300 men in the royal mines, paying his dues. He had been assaulted at his mine by a number of armed officials. With the Sheriff's permission, he had been forcibly taken to Lostwithiel and imprisoned, together with 30 of his servants, until each had paid a 20s. fine. Thereafter he had been made to agree to a very heavy toll of white tin to the value of 20s. for every 12 days of work completed by each worker in the mine, to be paid for ever. Abraham asked that a remedy might be found, so that they may be governed in accordance with the Tinners' Charter.

The problem was that Abraham was streaming tin on moors that were drained by tributaries of the River Fowey. The streaming caused sand and rubble to be carried down into the Fowey which was rapidly silting up, particularly where it met the tidal flow, thus interfering with the working of the mills and fisheries, and making it impossible for some of the seagoing ships, which had hitherto sailed up to Lostwithiel Quay, to reach the town. Boats of shallower draught had to be used and much of the tin had to be carried by packhorse along rough tracks to small quays downstream. The Prince's instruction was to ascertain the cause of the nuisance. If it proved not to be caused by the miners, 'see to it that Abraham and his fellows are allowed to work therein in a proper manner' otherwise 'cause them to be utterly removed therefrom'. Six months later mining on Redwith and Respryn Moors was discontinued 'as the Prince's mills of Lostwithiel and the Haven of Fawey are well nigh ruined thereby.' During the centuries since the 1350s the river has silted up in the same area.

All was not well in the blowing house either. There were complaints from merchants that pieces of false metal were being inserted into the tin. These were to be dealt with 'in such a manner as shall be a warning to others.'

Almost half of the orders issued to Cornwall were directed to John de Kendale and only on one occasion was there a hint of displeasure with him. This angry outburst must have come as a shock to John:

The Prince is amazed and moved with anger against him for having shown letters recently sent to him under the Prince's seal, which ought to be kept secret, to those who sued for them; and would have him know that if any such fault is found in him again, he will have him chastened that others will take warning from him not to disclose their Lord's counsel in future.

Nevertheless, eight days later orders were coming through to John as ever, with never another reference to the misdemeanour.

The Prince visited Restormel Castle on two more occasions and the town experienced again the frantic preparations and excitement of the royal court. In November 1362 notice came from Plympton that 'the Prince intends to come presently to the Castle of Restormel and stay there for Christmas.' Then on board ship in Plymouth Haven in June 1363, he ordered payment to be made to John de Kendale of £12.8s.10d., 'which he expended by the Prince's order between St Matthias Day past and Easter following, while the Prince was staying at the Castle of Restormel.' By this time the Prince was married to Princess Joan of Kent, and was about to take up residence in Bordeaux as Governor of the newly created Princedom of Aquitaine.

While he was abroad the Prince's Council managed the Duchy on his behalf and the officials here still received regular orders. John de Kendale handed over his office of receiver to his son Richard in 1365.

By this time the extent of the silting up of the river was serious indeed and so the mining of tin, which had been the source of Lostwithiel's growth, prosperity and high status, brought about the town's gradual decline. The Prince, whose health had suffered as a result of his military career, returned to England and died at the early age of 46 years. Restormel Castle was leased out together with the surrounding land. It was never again used as a royal residence and gradually fell into disrepair. Lostwithiel is proud of its association this highly respected medieval prince.

Chapter 5

THE MIDDLE YEARS, DECLINE & DEVELOPMENT

Following the death of the Black Prince in 1376, Richard II granted the town another Charter confirming the liberties, privileges and responsibilities it already held. Lostwithiel was sometimes referred to as the royal borough or 'Villa Regis'.

The port had declined, losing its seagoing trade to Fowey and other ports nearer the estuary. Goods to and from Lostwithiel were carried by boats drawing no more than 7 feet of water. Later, barges were used on the river and this continued into the first decades of the twentieth century. Lostwithiel retained its rights over the river and the town was entitled to dues from all ships using its ports, until the formation of the Fowey Harbour Board in 1870. The Mayor held jurisdiction over the maritime courts and, for some time, the title of Admiral of the River. This ancient privilege, which had become merely a formality by the seventeenth century, was symbolised by the silver oar given to the town by Silas Titus, MP from 1663–79.

During the fourteenth century, block houses had been built at Fowey and Polruan, and a protective chain slung between them to protect the river from French marauders who continually harried the South Coast. A century later the men of Fowey Haven were engaging in piracy on their own account, terrorising foreign ships in the Channel and seizing their cargoes. In 1449 Sir Hugh Courtney of Boconnoc was involved with three others in seizing a Spanish vessel that had been sheltering in Plymouth Sound. They put the Spaniards ashore, brought the ship to Fowey and sold off the cargo. This sort of piracy was difficult to control as it was sometimes the case that the local men dispensing justice were involved in piracy themselves.

Some 25 years later this lawlessness still prevailed and the exasperated King Edward IV sent his own commissioners to restore order. They arrested all the mariners, masters and victuallers of ships in Fowey, Polruan and Bodinnick and imprisoned them in Lostwithiel Gaol. They also tricked the

merchants and burgesses of these towns into coming to Lostwithiel (as they thought on business) where they too were held in custody. Ships, gear and goods were all confiscated. Many dire punishments were meted out and a Captain Harrington was hanged at Lostwithiel. As a final act of retribution, the defensive chain across the harbour was removed and given to Dartmouth. Richard Carew of Antony, telling the story, wrote, 'their wonted jollity transformed into a sudden misery, from which they strived a long time to relieve themselves.' The gallows at Lostwithiel had been set up by Earl Edmund. Tradition has it that the site of this was the small plot of land at the top of Bodmin Hill, the upper end of which was known for centuries as Gallows Hill.

Throughout most of the fourteenth and fifteenth centuries Lostwithiel was the only tin-coinage town in Cornwall, although it shared coinage with Truro for a short period. From early times there had been a stannary parliament or convocation, which met from time to time in the Great Hall at Lostwithiel. Convocations, called by the warden of the stannaries, were made up of 24 stannators. Six stannators were nominated to represent each of the four stannaries (mining districts) and in the early days the stannators were all miners. They were nominated by the Mayor and burgesses of the four stannary towns: Launceston, Lostwithiel, Truro and Helston. Lostwithiel chose the stannators for Blackmore Stannary, the mining area between Bodmin and St Austell. The business of the parliament covered all aspects of stannary affairs, mining, trading, maintenance of standards, abuses of liberties, disputes and the protection of miners from exploitation.

Throughout the centuries there was constant smuggling. All classes of men used every ingenious method they could devise to avoid paying the tax. Stannary laws were passed at various times to combat this. Coinage had to take place at the lawful time in the lawful place, before any tin could be sold; all smelting had to be completed by Michaelmas; tin had to be transported by the shortest route and never at night; tin was never to be bought from

Centre: The stamp on the tin-coinage hammer. (FMH & RIC)

29

an unauthorised person and smelting houses were required to use an official stamp. Assayed tin was stored in the tin porch until released by the warden. Sometimes there were four coinages in the year, taking place at Lady Day, midsummer, late August and Michaelmas. At other times there were only two, depending on the amount of tin to be coined.

Meetings of the parliament took place in private. Stannators had the power to question any arrangements made by the Duke of Cornwall or the sovereign, concerning the stannaries. However, decrees of the stannary parliament had to be signed by the stannators, the warden and the Duke, in order to become law. So, in effect, the stannators could be overruled. It is doubtful whether they ever represented all classes of tinners, chosen, as they were, by mayors and burgesses, who had an interest in stannary affairs and keeping the Duke and his administrators happy.

As time went by, mine owners and merchants appeared among the stannators, until by the seventeenth century, members of the Cornish landed gentry were elected stannators. In 1674 each stannator was allowed to choose a non-voting assistant, in order to be kept informed of the opinions of 'lower class tinners', so it was recognised that the parliament was out of touch with the workers. Soon even assistants were being chosen from the gentry class! The need for a stannary parliament gradually diminished and the last one was held in 1752.

The stannary courts, controlled by a steward, assisted by bailiffs and with a jury of tinners, dealt with all legal disputes relating to tin, until coinage was finally abandoned. During the sixteenth century the Star Chamber Court of Henry VIII had a right to hear appeals from the stannary courts.

Back in the fifteenth century the Great Hall (Duchy Palace) was very much the centre of power in the tin industry, and between 1460 and 1470 major repairs to the roof were undertaken. Renovations to the complex had been ongoing since 1351. The Duchy retained three master craftsmen, a carpenter, a tiler and a plumber and employed a number of local men. Wood for repairs came from Restormel Park, while most of the stone came from local quarries. Freestone for tracery and mouldings came from Pentuan by boat, slates were brought from Delabole and lead from Tavistock. The emblem of the Black Prince was erected at the apex of the north gable of Convocation Hall and in the early-seventeenth century a stone low-relief carving of the Cornish emblem was set in the north wall. It can still be seen in 2003.

During the fifteenth century the Duchy of Cornwall could be likened to a Palatinate – a locally based administration of government, a little state within a state, with its own hierarchy of officials in London and active administration in Cornwall, centred on Lostwithiel. So perhaps 'Duchy Palace' is

The Cornish emblem was set in the north gable of the Convocation Hall in the seventeenth century. (JB)

a more accurate description of the building than modern usage of the language would indicate.

In 1496, by Act of Parliament, Henry VII had new weights and measures made for Cornwall, to be kept and used in Lostwithiel. It is understood that for hundreds of years these were part of the town's treasure. (The weights and measures currently held in the Mayor's Parlour are stamped with the borough emblem and dated 1741.)

For centuries tin had been bought for the manufacture of pewter (between 80 and 85 per cent tin, combined with lead or copper depending on the use for which it was intended) and there would always have been pewterers amongst the traders buying tin. As the production of tin increased in the late-sixteenth and early-seventeenth centuries, pewter became more fashionable, and began to replace wood as a material for making domestic utensils. The use of pewter tableware indicated a family's social status. There were pewterers working in Lostwithiel.

The increase in tin production, however, was in the west of Cornwall and, unfortunately for Lostwithiel, it coincided with a sharp decline in tin produced from Blackmore and Fowey Moor, both of which had been mined for centuries. Miners were moving west to find richer lodes. By the beginning of the seventeenth century only 15 per cent of tin was being produced in the east, so Truro took over from Lostwithiel as the primary coinage town.

By this time, however, Lostwithiel merchants were investing directly in mines, as were other merchants and landowners throughout Cornwall. This involvement led to the more efficient organisation of the industry and helped to speed up its modernisation. In 1639, John Haymen of Lostwithiel coined 98,778 pounds of tin, eight per cent of the total output for that year. Richard Edgcumbe, whose family was later to become so involved with Lostwithiel, coined 21,292 pounds of tin. Agents from London, the traditional 'middlemen' in the trade, gradually gave way to the smelters, who took over their role, growing rich and becoming part of the developing middle class. Carew, however, writes in 1601 of the wretched living conditions and great poverty of the labourers in the mines, who earned at that time about 8d. a day – not enough to house, feed and clothe a family.

The tin industry still occupied many of the townspeople at all levels, but as this declined the woollen and tanning industries and crafts associated with them grew in importance. Pottery also developed as a local industry. Bodmin Hill was called Crockerne Street at that time, while Queen Street was known as Ducken Street. This name derived from the ducking pond at the south end of the street, where nags and scolds were punished!

Many poor men had more than one job, some supplementing their income by weaving. Their wives and daughters were the carders and spinners. Women also worked on the farms and in the markets. Lostwithiel was very much involved with farming, and most people relied on the weekly markets for the necessities of life, both the buying and selling of fresh produce for the table as well as livestock, wool, hides, pottery goods, yarn, cloth, ropes, tools and harnesses. Men worked in the mills, the tanneries and slaughterhouses, they fished, salted and cured meat and fish, they loaded and unloaded boats, plied their craft up and down the river, and worked as masons, tilers, carpenters and plumbers.

Lostwithiel was always one of the less impoverished of Cornish towns, being at the centre of good farming land, although this did not extend very far, 'Downend' about a mile to the east, indicated the extent of the farm land. The appearance of the land surrounding Lostwithiel was gradually changing. There was a move towards the enclosure of tenant holdings. These usually consisted of a house, outbuildings and land up to 30 acres, around which high hedges were built. First, ditches were dug and the earth piled up alongside. The high banks were planted with hawthorn, hazel, ash and oak, making impenetrable hedges and affording shelter for animals and a source of fuel for households. These ancient hedges remain a feature of the Cornish landscape and can still be found in the area. A form of 'mixed farming' developed, rotating crops of oats, barley, rye and peas. Barley was widely used for bread making. Cattle, sheep, goats and pigs were reared and oxen, horses and raunceys (packhorses) kept as work animals. Raunceys and riding horses were the only means of land transport, the tracks were unsuitable for wheeled vehicles. Animals were kept by the townspeople in sheds and linneys (lean-to buildings) beside their houses and were grazed on common lands belonging to the town.

Mature Cornish hedge, Bodmin Hill, Lostwithiel. (IF)

In the fifteenth century there were no officials holding tenancies of Duchy land, a reversal of policy after the death of the Black Prince. As a result there was a growing number of yeoman peasants leasing holdings directly from the manors and passing them to their sons when they died.

Life on the manor was still not free for some, but the feudal system was breaking down and greater numbers of manorial tenants were paying a fee for permission to live elsewhere. In 1438 there were eight unfree tenants from Stoke Climsland and one from Helstone-in-Trigg living in Lostwithiel. These people, no doubt, found work other than farming.

In 1437 Lostwithiel Bridge was badly in need of repair, and a Bishop Lucy granted an Indulgence of 40 days to all those who contributed to the repairs. In those days people paid a penance for their sins. The penance was decided by the priest after the sinner had made a confession. It could be fasting, flogging or other painful punishment, over a period of days. A system developed whereby a remission (forgiveness) could be bought for money. This was called an Indulgence and the sale of Indulgences became common. In this case it was used as a bribe!

In 1490 a dispute arose between the townspeople of Lostwithiel and Richard Curteys of Pill, who claimed ownership of two moors beside the river. A rich merchant, Walter Wooley, had given these lands to the town, and they were held in trust. Revenue from them was used for the upkeep of the church and the bridge. Richard had enclosed about four acres of these moors with hedges, which had enraged the townspeople. They drove their beasts into the enclosure, where they 'did eat up and befoul the grass'. Richard thereupon impounded the cattle and proceeded to St Bartholomew's Church, where he confronted the populace and announced what he had done. It was eventually agreed that he would release the cattle in return for a promise never to attempt to graze them in the enclosure again. That was not the end of it, however, as the townspeople were sure it was their land and the Mayor brought an action against Richard in the Star Chamber Court.

It is significant that Richard made his announcement from the church, which was central to the life of the town. Throughout the Middle Ages the Church held great spiritual power over the people. At all levels of society there was a great fear of the Lord, as interpreted by priests and prelates. Religious beliefs were mixed with superstition, which in turn was exacerbated by ignorance.

The Reformation brought a desire for knowledge and access to it for an increasing number of people, creating a new atmosphere and greater freedom of thought within the Church. This must have had its effect upon the people of the town, once they had overcome the initial confusion, fear and anger attendant upon the implementation of Henry VIII's Act of Supremacy of 1534. These were disturbing times indeed. From being a daughter church of Lanlivery, paying revenues to St Andrew's Priory and owing unquestioned allegiance to the Holy Father in Rome, St Bartholomew's Church became a Parish Church in its own right. Its congregation was required to recognise the King as supreme head of the Church of England and an English translation of the Bible was used for the first time. Peter Waryson, the first vicar, who had been a chantry priest at Liskeard, was probably appointed by King Henry himself, Lostwithiel being a Duchy living, and there being no Duke.

Peter found himself in charge of the smallest parish in Cornwall (about 112 acres of land). These were bewildering changes for people of a small Cornish town, as an aspect of their lives that they had believed to be unchangeable had been redefined.

There followed another turbulent period when the English translation of the Book of Common Prayer was introduced, Divine Services were conducted in English and there were changes in the Mass. The medieval Chantry of St George, a small chapel at the eastern end of the south aisle of St Bartholomew's, was dismantled in accordance with the Courts of Augmentation. The chantry had been administered separately from the main church and had its own priest, John Halwell being the last. Members of the Guild of St George had paid for the upkeep of the chantry and the Guild-owned lands.

Altar stone from the Chantry of St George, placed outside the south porch of the church. The seventeenth-century tomb of the Taprell family can also be seen. (IF)

There were bitter disputes before the land was confiscated and the altar stone was removed and placed on the floor of the south porch of the church, where it would be forever desecrated. It is believed that the marble slab, 2.2 metres x 1 metre wide, which lies across the approach to the south porch, is that altar stone, moved into its new position during the 1878 restoration of the church. Lady Howe, Mayoress of Lostwithiel in 1958, would never tread on the stone and always made a point of stepping around it. However, it is understood that the stone had been deconsecrated, so we can walk over it without fear of irreverence.

The Cornish language was still spoken by some people around Lostwithiel into the seventeenth century, but because it had always been a cosmopolitan town with a high proportion of incomers and much coming and going, English was more commonly used. The use of Cornish died out here earlier than in the west of Cornwall.

Norden in the late-sixteenth century and Carew in the early-seventeenth century, visited Lostwithiel and described a ceremony which took place each year on Little Easter (Low Sunday) and which was already reputed to be an ancient custom. Freeholders of the town assembled and chose from amongst their number one to act the part of the 'Prince'. Dressed in 'brave apparel', crowned and carrying a sceptre the Prince was mounted on a horse. Accompanied by all the others, also on horseback, and with a sword borne before him, he proceeded along the main street to the church. He was received at the church gate by the priest wearing his best vestments and escorted into the church, together with his attendants, to hear Divine Service. After this, the Prince and his retinue remounted and made their way to an appointed house, where a feast had been prepared. Seated at the head of the table the Prince received homage and acts of fealty from those present, after which they all enjoyed the feast and later returned to their homes. This custom was still being enacted late into the nineteenth century. It is recorded to have taken place on 10 October 1884, by torchlight, watched by nearly 1,000 people.

The original reason for the custom is unknown, but it certainly seemed to involve the more wealthy members of the community. It may originally have been a means of reminding the people of their absent Dukes, while providing an excuse for public festivity.

The landowning gentry in Cornwall were not as rich and powerful as their counterparts in the rest of England, owing to the Duchy holding so much of the land. Nevertheless they were the local ruling class, as they held positions of power in the Duchy administration. The smelters, mill owners, boat owners, tanners and merchants were becoming richer and their lifestyle was changing, becoming more refined.

It is believed that there were 22 taverns and inns in Lostwithiel catering for the needs of townspeople and visitors during the sixteenth century, but it would seem that despite all the commercial activity, the new middle class spent little money on the upkeep of buildings. Leland, making an official survey of Cornwall for Henry VIII between 1533 and 1540, was appalled at the state of its buildings and in the latter year an Act of Parliament was passed requiring repairs and the rebuilding of derelict houses in several Cornish towns, including Lostwithiel. Apparently nothing was done about this. Consequently, 45 years later Norden wrote of Lostwithiel:

This town was famous and glorious, but since it was deprived of the Duke's presence it hath lost also her beauty, as appareth by the ruins of many decayed houses.

Restormel Castle fell into disrepair during the fifteenth century. Leland wrote of the dilapidation of the castle describing the bailey as 'sore defaced', the chapel 'now unrofid' (unroofed) and using the terms 'dissolute', forsaken' and 'forlorn'. He reported 'tynne works and good wood in the park, a Chapel of the Trinity in the park'. Henry VIII 'disparked' Restormel and stopped the singing of Mass in the Chapel of the Trinity. Deer and timber were sold off at this time. In 1559, the castle and manor of Restormel were leased to the Earl of Bedford by Queen Elizabeth I and land was sublet to tenant farmers. Little interest was taken in the castle building. John Norden, in 1585, was very impressed with the dimensions of a ruined oven, four yards in width,

The castle fell into disrepair. (DB)

which he saw as testimony to the generous hospitality afforded in the past. He contrasted this with his view of modern (Tudor) ostentation, '... great halls and little meat, large chimneys and little smoke.'

In 1601 Richard Carew of Antony wrote of more positive destruction:

The conduit pipes taken away, the roof made sale of... the planchings rotten, the hewn stones of the windows, durns and clavels [doorways and chimneys] pulled out to serve private dwellings... only there remaineth an utter defacement to complain upon this unregarded distress...

The castle was patched up and used briefly as a garrison by the Parliamentary Army during the Civil War, until it was taken by Sir Richard Grenville for the King. For the next three centuries it was left to decay, taken over and hidden by trees, shrubs and creepers. Towards the end of the 1920s the Office of Works enclosed the castle grounds and started to clear the site and preserve what remained of the building.

Mr Bruce Netherton was appointed assistant custodian in 1946 and on the retirement of Mr Rowe he became custodian and was largely responsible for the development of the castle grounds. He was awarded the Queen's Silver Jubilee Medal in 1977 for his services. It is now cared for by English Heritage, and Bruce's daughter, Mrs Carol Woodward, is the custodian at the time of writing. By tradition, Lostwithiel residents have the privilege of free access to the castle, perhaps in recognition of the interdependence between the people of the castle and the people of the town many centuries ago. It is said to be our place of refuge in times of danger.

By its Charter Lostwithiel was obliged, in time of need, to muster men and arms for the defence of the realm. During the unsettled years of dispute with foreign powers, muster-rolls were drawn up in readiness. In 1569 there were 37 men of Lostwithiel on the roll, which consisted of 13 archers, 16 bill men (armed with bill hooks), 7 harquebusiers (carrying portable guns) and a pikeman. Names on the list included

Kendal, Swete, Hellyer, Hendye, Tonkyn and Collyns.

Tinners, by their own Charters, were exempt from these demands, so in 1588, when there was a real threat of attack by the Spanish, Sir Walter Raleigh, then Lord Lieutenant of Cornwall, warden of the stannaries, called a stannary parliament at Lostwithiel. By custom, tinners supported the Crown and provided men-at-arms when directed by their own parliament. As a result of tinners coming forward, and a good response from the towns, Cornwall's certificate of muster in 1588 included 5,560 men, 1,395 shot, 633 corselets, 1,956 bills and halberds, 11,528 bows, 4 lances and 96 light horse.

By the end of the sixteenth century there had been an improvement in the quality of life, both in the town and the surrounding countryside. There was more food to eat and material progress had been made. People were more self-reliant and the changes brought about by the Reformation had encouraged people to think for themselves on religious issues. None of this was reflected in Carew's description of Lostwithiel. He was most disparaging when he wrote:

... despite its mayoralty, markets, fairs and nominations of burgesses for Parliament, its coinage, keeping of stannary gaol and County Courts... yet all this can hardly raise it to a tolerable condition of wealth and inhabitance.

Civic pride must have been at a low ebb and the fabric of the town sadly became run down.

In 1609 the Charter of Incorporation reorganised the government of the town. There was to be a Mayor, six capital burgesses and 17 assistants (these 24 people were the only ones allowed to vote in elections). There was to be a recorder (a borough magistrate) who held this position for life and a court of record (magistrates' court). The first recorder under the new Charter was Sir Reginald Mohun of Boconnoc. Courts of 'pye-poudre' (a corruption of *pieds pudreux*, meaning 'dusty footed' travellers) were instituted, to be held on market and fair days. These dealt with petty crime. The population of Lostwithiel was about 900 at this time.

Chapter 6
LOSTWITHIEL & THE CIVIL WAR

By the 1640s this small market town still retained some of its Duchy and stannary importance, although the Duchy Palace buildings were in need of attention. Several influential landowning families lived within a few miles of the town and some towns-people were members of the rising middle class – Duchy officials, owners and managers of tanneries, mills, smelting houses, etc. However, by far the most numerous of the population were the men and women who worked for these employers and strug-gled to live decently in poor housing and with inad-equate income.

This was the time of England's greatest political upheaval, which culminated in the execution of the King and 11 years of Commonwealth rule. In the early days of disagreement between Charles I and Parliament, some local landowners could see the rights and wrongs of both, but when it came to war they were forced to take sides, which led to some families being split. This inevitably caused great distress.

Lostwithiel was represented in the Short Parliament of 1640 by Richard Arundel of Trerice and Nicholas Kendal of Pelyn. Later that year John Trevanion took Kendal's seat. All these men were staunch Royalists, as were the Mayors of the town in the early 1640s. It is probable, however, that opinion amongst the townspeople was divided, and they were not too well informed. Little news reached them of the goings-on in London. There had been a hint of Protestantism in the Church when, in 1633, John Davy signed registers as 'minister' rather than 'vicar'.

Lostwithiel first saw action in January 1643, when Lord Ruthin Gray of the Parliamentary Army marched his men into Cornwall and took up a posi-tion on the high ground near to the church at Braddock, hoping that Lord Stamford would join him with reinforcements.

Further west, Arundel, Beville Grenville and Sir Ralph Hopton waited near Bodmin, ready for action, with a smaller Royalist force, many of whom were Cornishmen.

Sir Ralph Hopton wrote in the *Narrative of his Campaign in the West* that on hearing of the enemy approach, the Royalists 'advanced that night without cannon or baggage to Boconnoc Park.' Next morning, 19 January, according to Hopton they 'advanced,

determined to find the enemy wheresoever he was.' 'They came upon 'the rebels' at Braddock and positioned themselves within sight of them on a hill to the west, the valley between them. Hopton was invited to command the troops that day, which he willingly did. He arranged his men on foot in the middle, flanked on each side by horsemen. Then public prayers were said for all to hear. The Roundheads, observing this, passed word around that they were saying the Mass and mocked them. After the prayers, two small brass guns, minion drakes from Boconnoc, were 'speedily and secretly' placed on the left flank and the Royalists were ready first. The rebels were in position for battle but were still manoeuvring their five cannon into position. Hopton fired off the drakes into the midst of the rebel troops, taking them completely by surprise. He followed this up rapidly with a charge by both foot and horse, down the valley and up into the enemy ranks, forcing them into utter confusion. They dropped their arms and scattered, heading off towards Saltash. The Royalists were merciful, they did not kill indiscriminately, but took 1,200 prisoners, the five cannon and all the ammunition and arms. 'They marched that night to Liskeard, where they rested the men and gave public thanks.' This was the Battle of Braddock Down, a resounding victory for the Royalists, who then chased the rebels out of

Prayers before battle. Re-enactment of the Battle of Braddock Down, 1982. Left to right: Revd Miles Brown, Jan Liddicoat, Mayor Paul Brewer, members of the Sealed Knot Society. (CBu)

Cornwall. Royalist sympathies would be riding high in Lostwithiel after such a victory, but it is likely that the wounded Parliamentarian soldiers would be carried back and cared for here with compassion.

Life settled down again after this skirmish, although soldiers continued to pass through Lostwithiel, and recruiting officers constantly looked for more men.

Lord Robartes of Lanhydrock, a respected Parliamentarian, formed the opinion that the Cornish people would favour Parliament's cause if its Army were here. He succeeded in persuading the Earl of Essex that it would be an easy matter to take Cornwall. Essex, against his better judgement, brought his Army of 10,000 men over the Tamar on 20 July 1644. Sir Richard Grenville's Army, including Hopton, retreating before him, retired to Truro.

On 2 August, Essex took Lostwithiel and set up his headquarters in the town. He then occupied the peninsula, taking Fowey and the harbour. Thus he held a good central position in Cornwall, with a reliable access for supplies from Plymouth, a Parliamentarian town. These could be shipped under the protection of the Parliamentary Navy. Essex garrisoned the two towns, Restormel Castle, Respryn Bridge and Lanhydrock House, where he himself resided.

This was the beginning of Lostwithiel's misery. Officers and men, who vastly outnumbered residents, took over the town. Every spare room,

parlour, kitchen, linney, every outlying farm, barn and building, all were commandeered for the Army's use. The soldiers helped themselves to the town's food, and made free in the taverns. There were 2,500 horses to be fed, watered and housed – some of them were stabled in the church.

Essex now summoned Cornwall to rally to Parliament's cause, but everything went wrong for him. The King decided to pursue Essex, and warning his soldiers to abstain from plunder, he crossed into Cornwall meeting up with Prince Maurice and his Army on 31 July.

News that the King was in Cornwall fired the Cornish with Royalist zeal. Richard Symonds, an officer in the King's Army, wrote a diary of the events in August. Grenville moved up towards Bodmin with 800 men. He sent a message to the King saying that he was 800 strong and desired His Majesty to make haste towards him. The King replied that he was coming with all possible speed with an Army of 10,000 foot soldiers, 5,000 horsemen and 28 pieces of cannon. By 8 August the King was at Braddock Down and had made his headquarters at Boconnoc. On 9 August, Prince Maurice sent a letter to Essex, carried by a trumpeter (said to be Essex's nephew) inviting him to join with the King and work towards peace.

Left: *Lord John Robartes, Parliamentarian, painted by Sir Godfrey Kneller.* (NT)

Below: *The Parliamentarians garrisoned Respryn Bridge.* (CBu)

King Charles I, 1600–49. (IF)

The next day came back the reply:

My Lords, in the beginning of your letter, you express by what authority you sent it. I, having no authority to treat without the Parliament who have entrusted me, cannot do it without breach of trust. Your humble servant, Essex.

There was frequent skirmishing in the hills between Boconnoc and Lostwithiel but no major action. St Nectan's Church suffered badly in the crossfire, losing its tower, which has never been replaced. One day an unusual challenge to battle was received by the Royalist Colonel Digby, from Colonel Straughan and 100 young Roundheads, all 16–20 years of age. Digby and a similar group of Royalist youths took up the challenge. The protagonists formed up against each other on a hill at Boconnoc, near to the Liskeard road. It is said that Col Straughan wore only a hat and a shirt, although his men were well armed for combat. Digby and his 100 youths advanced to meet their adversaries, but tragically they fired their pistols before they were within range. Straughan's men then moved in fast, firing amongst them at close range, killing half of them within minutes and badly wounding the other half. This sad and gratuitous waste of young lives was recorded by three eye witnesses: William May of Digby's Royalist Army, and Joseph and William Upcott of Straughan's. The site of the battle is marked by a monument erected in 1896, on which is written:

On this hill Once the site of Druid Idolatry and civil bloodshed, this ancient symbol of the Holy Redeemer is erected in grateful acknowledgement of a pure faith and a peaceful country.

Left: *Monument erected in 1896 on the site of the pre-arranged battle, in the grounds of Boconnoc estate.* (IF)

It refers to the belief that druids flourished there, and to this pre-arranged and tragic battle. It is not known why Col Straughan brought about this battle. Perhaps the inactivity and scarcity of food were causing serious disciplinary problems amongst the young soldiers in Lostwithiel, and this was his way of dealing with it.

Meanwhile, Grenville and Hopton's Armies were closing in on Lostwithiel from the north and west. The rebels garrisoning Respryn saw that they would be surrounded, so abandoned the bridge and consequently left free passage between the two Royalist Armies. The Royalists took Lanhydrock, giving strict orders that there was to be no plundering. A few days later, a soldier was hanged for disregarding this order. However, it must be told, Robartes' silver was stolen to be melted down in the Royal Mint!

The King's Army had fortified the eastern bank of the River Fowey. At Hall View and Polruan guns trained on Fowey and the harbour entrance prevented supply ships from landing. The weather also helped, as Cornwall was lashed by cold winds and rain throughout August. The King, inspecting the fortifications at Cliff, narrowly escaped death when a shot from Golant killed a fisherman within yards of him.

Sir John Astley, in charge of these fortifications, captured a consignment of two butts of wine and much tobacco, together with horseshoes and other equipment intended for the rebels. This shipment of luxuries would indicate that Essex had expected his Army to live easily off the land. This was not the case, here the land was mostly unproductive downland, the farms providing enough food to feed the small population. This food was very soon devoured by the vast numbers of soldiers and there was a great shortage of anything to eat. The King's men were also foraging for food as far back as Liskeard as they too were getting hungry. Essex was trapped, besieged in Lostwithiel and the Fowey peninsula, and the squeeze was getting tighter as Royalists moved in, taking St Austell, St Blazey and Par.

St Nectan's Church was caught in the crossfire and its tower was never replaced. (IF)

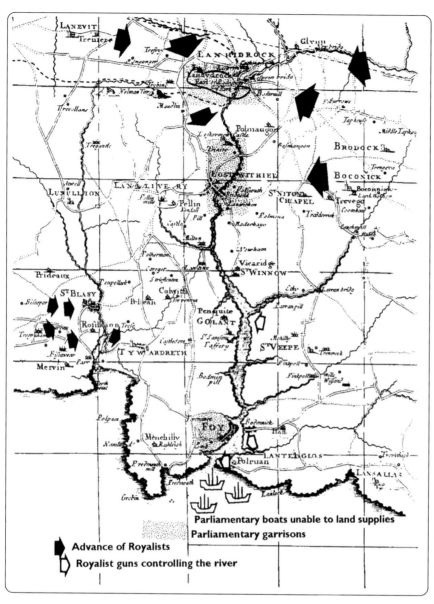

The siege of Lostwithiel (based on Gascoyne's map).
Essex's Army was trapped by Royalists. (IF)

Parliamentary boats unable to land supplies
Parliamentary garrisons
Advance of Royalists
Royalist guns controlling the river

was set alight and badly damaged, losing all its ancient documents. Homes were plundered and food, animals, cloth, leather, wood, tools stolen. The local population, vastly outnumbered, were helpless, and within three weeks they had lost everything except their anger. Indeed, they fought their corner wherever they could, particularly the women. It was said by a soldier occupying the town, that the townswomen were more to be feared than the enemy Army!

Lostwithiel suffered too at the hands of its friends. On 21 August the Royalists, firing into the town, set the cottages in Bridgend ablaze. At the same time, Grenville surprised and took Restormel Castle from the west, capturing 30 men and several barrels of salted beef – this was a prize indeed. The Parliamentarians had blocked up the three-light window over the altar in the chapel, strengthening the wall to support a gun trained on the valley below.

That night the King's men dug a redoubt (gun emplacement) at Boconnoc, 20 yards square, from which to bombard the town. The Patronal Feast Day of St Bartholomew was 24 August, and on this day the tower of the church was damaged by Royalist cannon fire. It is hard to imagine the effect on parishioners of this 'unkindest cut of all'. They must have despaired.

The Royalists had scattered papers on the hillsides above Lostwithiel offering pardon to any rebels who joined the King's ranks. Many men defected from Essex's Army, bringing stories of great hunger and hardship.

With all the food in Lostwithiel and the peninsula gone, and no supplies getting through by sea, everyone was starving, soldiers and civilians alike. The exceptional insanitary conditions caused by so many people, the rain and the mud, led to an outbreak of plague. The inactivity of the besieged Army under these conditions must have driven the men to desperation, and the violent and destructive behaviour of the soldiers may well have been their reaction to hunger, boredom and incipient fear.

Willful damage was done to the church and its valuable records destroyed. Acts of sacrilege took place – for example a horse was christened at the font and was given the name Charles! The Duchy Palace

Essex, who had been cut off from food, ammunition supplies and communication for almost a month, finally decided to take action and organise an escape. His only option was to attempt to send the cavalry through the Royalist position towards Saltash, a very dangerous manoeuvre. Sir William Balfour was made responsible for this. Essex proposed to take the infantry to Fowey and escape by sea to Plymouth. The Royalists had advance warning of the moves planned for the cavalry. They garrisoned a cottage on the Lostwithiel–Liskeard road with 50 fusiliers, and the Armies in the hills were alerted and put on guard. Nevertheless, under cover of darkness and heavy fog, on the night of 30/31 August, having bound their horses' feet with cloth, 2,500 Parliamentarian cavalry slowly and silently made their way through the Royalist territory unmolested! The fusiliers in the cottage were asleep or drunk, and the Army 'on guard' were straggled abroad foraging for provisions.

Only the Earl of Cleveland with 100 horsemen faced the enemy on the hill, but with so few men he dared not attack. Later, when the King arrived with the Queen's Regiment, Cleveland attacked their rear. This, however, came too late to make much impression. The rebel cavalry escaped to Plymouth.

There were bitter recriminations to follow, but now the King mustered what infantry he could 'which God knows were very few' and at 7 o'clock in the morning marched into Lostwithiel with 1,000 men. The rebels were already retreating to Fowey, having mined the bridge to hinder the Royalist approach. Luckily this had been observed, and the mine was defused in time to prevent any damage being done.

Even as they retreated, the rebels found time for vandalism. Two Royalist gentlemen, imprisoned in St Bartholomew's Church, had climbed into the tower and were mocking the retreating soldiers. Angered, the rebels tried to smoke them out, by burning damp hay, then fired muskets at them from inside the tower. As neither of these brought the men down, they ignited a barrel of gunpowder inside the church. This damaged the roof but the prisoners remained unharmed.

The Royalists chased the rebels from field to field through deep mud along the river valley and there was bitter fighting all the way to Castle Dore. Here Essex made a stand. His men were weary and disheartened and it came to nought. The King spent that night in the shelter of a hedge with his men. Meanwhile, Essex and several of his officers, including Lord Robartes, slipped quietly away and escaped, probably by boat from Polkerris, leaving General Skippon to surrender. The Royalists' conditions for surrender were generous: officers were allowed to keep their arms, and the sick and wounded were left to be cared for in Fowey. The 6,000 fit men were to march under escort to Poole, and there were instructions that the prisoners were not to be plundered. Symonds describes the exodus on Monday 2 September: '... it rained extremely as the Varlets marched away... pressed all of a heap like sheep, so dirty and dejected it was rare to see.'

The escorts, even with drawn swords, could not prevent the Royalist soldiers from mocking and robbing the prisoners, but this was as nothing compared with what awaited them in Lostwithiel. The angry townspeople, and especially the women, after weeks of starvation and degradation at the hands of the Parliamentarians, attacked them 'tooth and nail', mocked, abused and stripped them of their clothes and their boots, before driving them across the bridge, defeated and disgraced. Only 1,000 of the 6,000 men reached Poole. A few escaped to Plymouth, but most died of exhaustion or plague, or were set upon and murdered on the way. The King

A house built after the Civil War, which has since been converted into a shop. (IF)

left Cornwall on 5 September saying 'Dear Mr Sheriff, I leave Cornwall to you safe and sound.'

He left Lostwithiel filthy, shattered and starving, and prey to a pestilence that killed many of its people. The surrounding land from Liskeard to St Blazey, from Fowey to Bodmin, was trampled and broken, with nothing left to harvest. It took many years for the area to recover.

Gradually the markets and the industries revived. In 1649 Cromwell's Survey sought to take away the rights of the Duchy, and the fishing rights from Fowey Haven to Respryn Bridge were given to Lostwithiel. St Bartholomew's was tidied up and the roof, tower and spire were eventually repaired. The Duchy Palace never recovered completely, although parts of it were repaired and used again. Only the Convocation Hall remained intact. Domestic buildings were put up on land which had been part of the Duchy Palace complex. Other domestic buildings in the town were patched up where possible, until people could afford to build new houses.

Over the next few decades a number of modest but substantial houses were built. Some were later converted into shops. These seventeenth-century buildings can be seen all over town, in Fore Street, North Street, Tanhouse Lane, Church Lane, Malthouse Lane and Monmouth Lane, in Queen Street, Castle Hill and on Bodmin Hill. Some have date stones on the walls, some have outbuildings and small plots of land, and may have been smallholdings. In 1688 a piece of land on Terras Hill was leased to Melchisedek Woen, a husbandman of Lostwithiel, who probably built Mount Pleasant. The Star of David is still to be seen on the eastern gable-end. Towards the end of the century a window tax was levied, which would account for the blocked up windows in this house.

'Tangier' was the original name of Castle Hill, Lostwithiel. It became part of the borough when the boundaries were altered in 1934–35, and was included in the parish of St Bartholomew in the late 1940s or early 1950s. It was about this time that the name was changed to Castle Hill. The old blue and white enamelled street sign was taken down, and is now in the museum. Why was the name changed and how did it get this name in the first place? To discover the latter, we must go back to the reign of Charles II (1660–85) which is about the time the houses were built. Charles received Tangier as part of a wedding dowry on his marriage to the infanta, Catherine of Braganza. It was hoped that Tangier would become an important base and rich trading centre in the Mediterranean. A great artificial harbour was built, said to be the most ambitious work that English engineers had ever undertaken. It was under constant attack by the Moors and a garrison of 3,000 men was needed to hold it.

One story told in Lostwithiel is that men from the cottages just beyond the town boundary were 'press-ganged' into serving in Tangier, thus giving the lane this name. Press-ganging was a method of forcing (kidnapping) men, for service in the Navy. However, recruitment would be for soldiers not sailors, so this is unlikely.

It is more probable that as Tangier was a post trading in tin, and as soldiers were needed to replenish the troops in Tangier, they may well have been legally recruited from Lostwithiel and other towns and villages on the Fowey river, and travelled out to the Mediterranean on the trading ships. During the 1660s the area was still recovering from the devastation caused by the Civil War, so poor and unskilled men may have been glad of the opportunity to take their wives and families overseas to make a fresh start. When, in 1683, the troops and their families were repatriated from Tangier, it is possible that people originating from these parts sailed back into

Seventeenth-century houses on Castle Hill, formerly 'Tangier'. (IF)

Fowey harbour, and came upriver to find work, settling in the newly built cottages on the hill, which became known for nearly three centuries as 'Tangier'.

Lostwithiel was being repaired and rebuilt, industries were being re-established in the town and by the 1680s the economic outlook was brighter than it had been for four decades. Society was developing and retail shops were beginning to appear. The town looked forward to better times.

Chapter 7

GEORGIAN LOSTWITHIEL

King George III ascended the throne in 1760 at the age of 22. In 1783 it was written of him:

Never did prince ascend the throne of his ancestors with greater éclat than this young monarch... Such was the tide of popular affection, that addresses flowed in from every part of the kingdom... Indeed the people seemed to vie with each other in expressions of loyalty and affection to their new sovereign.

It would appear that it was very fashionable at this time to write to the sovereign.

George took a great interest in British domestic politics and attempted to exercise control in government. However, his influence declined following a number of bouts of mental illness, which started to occur in middle age. It was on his recovery from one of these illnesses in 1789 that a group of local citizens wrote him the following letter:

Encouraged by the example of our fellow subjects, and influenced by our own feelings We, the Mayor, Recorder, Capital Burgesses, Assistants and other Principal Inhabitants of the Borough of Lostwithiel in the County of Cornwall, assembled at the Town Hall this twenty eighth Day of March one thousand seven hundred and eighty nine, beg leave to approach your Royal Person with our congratulations and heartfelt joy on your Majesty's happy recovery from your Late indisposition.

The general sorrow that appeared in the countenances of your loyal subjects during your Majesty's illness and the universal joy expressed by all ranks of people on your recovery are Evident marks of the duty and affection that a grateful people bear to the best of Kings.

King George III, 1738–1820. (IF)

Impressed with a conviction that your Majesty's Endeavours are uniformly designed To promote the welfare of your Kingdom's and that your chief glory the happiness of your people We cannot sufficiently express our deep and awful sense of the goodness of divine providence in Rescuing the nation from despondency, and giving us an opportunity of laying at the foot of your Throne this tribute of our joy and gratitude to the Almighty for his gracious Mercies, which we pray May be long continued to your Majesty and your Kingdom's.

James Baron	*John Bennett*
Chas Rashleigh Mayor	*Jas Bower*
Richd Whetter	*Mount Edgcumbe, Recorder*
William Blewett	*R. Edgcumbe*
Philip Carnsew	*Thomas Blewett*
Nevil Norway junr	*F. Gregor*
W. Symons	*John Harper*
Sam Hext	*Edm.d Goude*
John Wainwright	*? Bennett*
Thos Strong	*Wm Fortescue*
Wm Burgess	*Simon Bone*
Thos Hext	*Chas Kendall*
Wm Hicks	*Chas Colliver*
Edwd Freeman	*Jno Knight*
Thos Daniel	*Humy Westlake*
Walter Lukes	*Edmd May*
Nevil Norway	*Richd Lanyon*
Nicholas Knight	*Wm Westlake*
Richard Foster junr	*Jas Rowe*
Jno Baron	*Nich Hugo*
Edmund Facey	*Philip Blewett*
*John Macg_*	*William Hamley*
Joseph Maynard	*James Philp*
William Netherton	*Thomas Geoffrey*
Reuben Nanjulian	

This document was found on the internet by Bruce McDonald during the course of his research. The original is in the Public Records Office in London. The occupations of some of the signatories were found in the 1791 *Universal Directory of Traders*. They are as follows:

James Bower, mercer and draper
Thomas Blewett, shoemaker
Edmund Goude, auctioneer

W. Symons, cooper and victualler (London Inn)
Thos Strong, shoemaker
Wm Hicks, glazier
John Knight, carpenter
Richard Lanyon, surgeon
Richard Foster junr, tanner
Nicholas Hugo, merchant
John Bennett, attorney
William Blewett, blacksmith
William Hamley, saddler
Wm Netherton, victualler
Nevil Norway, merchant
? Bennett (possibly steward to Lord Camelford).

The Prime Minister in 1789 was William Pitt, the Younger. He was first cousin to Thomas Pitt, the first Baron Camelford of Boconnoc. George III reigned for over 50 years. His son took over as Regent in 1811, but George III survived until 1820.

Before the Turnpike Act of 1751, whereby users paid a toll towards the upkeep of roads, there was very little wheeled transport west of Plymouth. Although stagecoaches had been carrying passengers between London, Exeter and Plymouth for 100 years, the uncomfortable journey over rough roads took several days, and travellers into Cornwall had to ride on horseback or walk over the rough tracks. Goods were carried by packhorse or boat and barge. Following the introduction of 'toll roads' the quality of the roads improved, and the system was gradually developed in Cornwall. The first stagecoach between Torpoint and Truro called at Lostwithiel in 1796. After this, Lostwithiel was soon established as a staging post. In November 1806 the first Royal Mail coach from Plymouth to Falmouth, via Lostwithiel, was ferried over the Tamar, loaded with letters. The toll-house at Bridgend still stands but the one west of the bridge on North Street was demolished during the late-twentieth century.

Towards the end of the eighteenth century, travellers to London could go by 'Russell's Waggon' which passed through Lostwithiel in each direction once a week. This was a huge carriage upon four very large wheels, 'arched over with canvas like a bower' and drawn by eight horses. Each horse carried neck bells to advertise their approach and the carrier walked beside them dressed in a smock of coarse linen. Progress was very slow, the journey to London taking about three weeks. Passengers carried their own bedding and slept overnight in the vehicle. Goods to be carried were heaped on top of the coach, under the canvas. There were many hazards to be encountered on a journey, including unsafe bridges, ford crossings, highway robberies and sickness. It was common for travellers from Cornwall to make a will before setting out!

In the West Briton newspaper of 15 February 1811, notice was given by Joseph Norway (the clerk), of a meeting of the turnpike trustees, to consult about

Bridgend at the beginning of the twentieth century, showing the old toll-house facing the road. (DB)

the erection of a toll-gate at Polscoath (Downend) between Lostwithiel and Liskeard. They also needed to consider compensation to occupiers of land at Penpillick, Pelyn and Scrations Lane, through which 'the turnpike road has been lately made'. There were problems with the building of new roads then, as there are now!

Very soon towns along the route came to rely on the coaches for news from London, which they received regularly. This was especially important during the war with France. The Royal Cornwall Gazette reported Lostwithiel's reaction to news of peace on 16 April 1814:

The populace... went forth in crowds... to meet the mail, and draw it by hand into the town... Every individual in the place wore a white cockade and all the houses were decked with laurel and many with flags.

Unfortunately, in the excitement two men were run over by the coach and badly injured.

In 1832 the 'reformers' were waiting to meet the coach bringing news of the passing of the Parliamentary Reform Act. It reached Lostwithiel at 4a.m., whereupon 'a band of music made the valley resound.' The improvement in the roads increased opportunities for trade, and the inns and taverns did good business.

From the early-nineteenth century coastal vessels carried limestone as ballast from Plymouth to Fowey. It was then barged upriver to Lostwithiel kilns alongside the quay, to be converted to lime for agricultural use. Iron ore, leather, meat and fish were sent downriver to be shipped from Fowey.

In the mid-nineteenth century proposals were made by Richard Foster Esq. for the construction of a ship canal between Golant and Lostwithiel, to allow passage of vessels of up to 200 tons. The scheme included the construction of a lock below Golant, and was to ensure that only tidal water from the seaward end would be used to feed the canal. Estimates showed that the canal would be uneconomic, particularly as it was realised that there would soon be a railway coming this way, and the project was abandoned.

Towards the end of the eighteenth century the difference between rich and poor people became more marked. The price of bread increased threefold between 1792 and 1812, and there were a few destitute people in the town who, under the Poor Law, were the responsibility of the parish. A Vestry Book, kept for many years in an iron chest in the church (and now in the Cornwall Records Office), recorded the parish's care for the poor between 1781 and 1825. Parishioners who could afford to do so paid a 'poor rate' and overseers were appointed to manage the money. The first entry in the book records that on 17 April 1781 there were seven women and six children receiving between 1s. and 2s. a week each. At this time there was no 'poorhouse', but by 1784 the parish officers were looking into the possibilities of finding one. The Vestry Book indicates the nature of discussions: '6 May 1787. Margaret Treleaven shall be allowed in future 2s. a week... She appearing to us to be an object worthy of such pay.' Parishes usually accepted responsibility for those born in them:

16 May 1784. We... agree unanimously that Grace Roberts and Alice Roberts, two paupers of this parish, now lodged in Padstow Workhouse (for divers reasons), shall be fetched home.

This probably meant that they must walk home under escort.

By 1790 there was a poorhouse: '... that 2s.6d. a week be allowed to Thomas Williams, a pauper, now in the poor house.' Clothes and tools were issued. For example, '3 February 1793. Peter Treleaven be supplied with a coat, waistcoat, breeches, stockings and shirt.' In 1820 John Vane received a new spade, but it remained the property of the parish until he had paid for it. Nancy Leavers was not so lucky. She applied for an oven, flour and fuel to start up a 'penny pie business'. However, as many ratepayers were in that same line, it was judged that 'an injury could be done to them by granting it.'

In 1798 Richard Foster, a wealthy tanner, negotiated to buy the poorhouse, which was near to his residence, and to provide another, some distance away. It seems the 'boghouse' was becoming a nuisance to him!

The children of paupers were put out to apprenticeships. To make this more attractive to prospective masters, a sum of money went with them. On 12 May 1800 it was agreed at a Vestry meeting to give £4 with a boy and £6 with a girl, to any tradesman taking an apprentice. People of lower status, taking apprentices, were to receive £2 'to clothe the child'. On that day two girls and three boys were bound – two went to tailors, three went with £2.

The distribution of the poor rate applied only to Lostwithiel Parish. People living south of the River

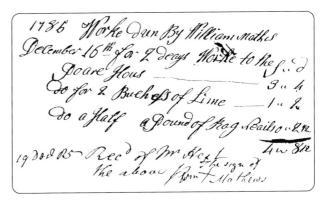

Receipt for work done on the poorhouse by William Matthews, 1785. (CRO)

Cober, in Summer Lane (Summer Street), Tangier (Castle Hill) and the Moors (Park Road), were in Lanlivery Parish and were therefore not entitled to help from St Bartholomew's. This was the poorest part of the borough and received little, if any, help from its own parish.

By 1800 the stannary gaol was being used for debtors. It was housed in the Duchy Palace complex, where there is a private house at the time of writing. The iron bars can still be seen in the windows on the top storey. The prison was visited in 1805 by an official, James Nield, and described as being 'very dirty, not having been whitewashed for nearly thirty years.' One of the last debtors to be imprisoned here was a St Agnes man, Salathiel Harris, who had no money and whose wife and family were too far away to bring him food. No food was provided, so to save the poor man from starvation, during four months in prison, the gaoler brought him down to an iron-grated window by the street, 'there to solicit the casual charity of passers-by, by means of a shoe suspended by a cord with which the keeper had humanely provided him.'

No sooner was Lostwithiel celebrating peace in Europe, than soldiers of the 28th Regiment were marching through the town from Pendennis Castle to Plymouth to embark for America. The *West Briton* of 26 August 1814 reported a local tragedy, the murder of the town sergeant and a bystander, which took place on Sunday 21 August 1814. The story of the event was told by witnesses at the trial. After the military baggage had gone through the town, four drunken soldiers 'loitered behind the main body', two of them incapable of walking. Between one and two o'clock on the Sunday afternoon, John Sims and Richard Rogers, drunk but not incapable, applied to William Hicks, the constable, who lived on Market Street, for a cart to convey their two companions to the next town. The constable refused to let them have one unless they paid for it. The drunken men went away muttering angrily, but returned to ask how much a cart would cost, and were told 12s., in advance. The soldiers became abusive and sat together on a doorstep a few doors along the road. James Netherton, who lived across the road, saw and heard all this from his house. A small crowd had gathered, attracted by the shouting, but they were quiet, perceiving the mood of the soldiers. Sims was heard to say that he would have someone's blood before he left the town, and he loaded his musket, fixed his bayonet and threatened to shoot. He then assisted Rogers in priming and loading his gun and Rogers fixed his bayonet and went a few steps down the street pointing his gun at the crowd and muttering abuse. One soldier fired, but the powder only flashed in the pan. The soldiers turned into Fore Street. Meanwhile the town sergeant, Joseph Burnett, had been called out. He was a man of 42 years, a well-respected member of the community, a heel and patten maker by trade. He arrived, wearing his official cloak, saying he would 'take into custody him who fired'. Sims replied 'I'll shoot you first' and fired twice. The second ball hit Burnett in the side. It is said that it passed through Burnett's body, striking another man, Walter Davies. It is more likely that either the first shot hit Davies, or in the commotion another shot was fired. Burnett staggered into the Town Arms next to the Guildhall (now Ann's Gallery) and from there was carried to his home across the road, a cottage which stood on the site of Boseglos House. Spectators secured the soldiers. Joseph Burnett died within half an hour, leaving a widow, Grace, and nine children, the youngest only ten weeks old. Walter Davies died three days later, leaving five children.

John Sims and Richard Rogers were taken to Bodmin Gaol and committed on a charge of willful murder. To the astonishment of everyone attending the trial, Richard Rogers was acquitted. John Sims was found guilty and the judge, Sir Robert Graham, immediately pronounced sentence of death and ordered that he be executed on the Friday following, and his body given for dissection.

Sims requested his wretched mother, whom he saw three times after being sentenced, to write to his brothers, also in the Army, and entreat them to avoid the evils of drink, to which he attributed his own miserable end. He was hanged on 31 March 1815 at Launceston. It was reported in *The Star* that '... he conducted himself with becoming resignation and fortitude, and was launched into eternity a few minutes after twelve o'clock on Friday last.'

Joseph was buried in the churchyard – his stone is leaning against the churchyard wall very close to where his cottage stood. Shortly after Joseph's death, the lease on the cottage passed from Grace Burnett to Charles Rashleigh of Duporth. The town sergeant's cloak is now in the museum.

During the year 1812 corn was scarce, prices were high and there was much hardship. A local scheme was introduced to subsidise the sale of barley. Thomas Hext made an interest-free loan to the overseers to buy barley, for resale to the poor at a cheaper rate. It seems 70 families, about a quarter of the population, benefitted. Some of these were on 'poor relief' but most were labourers, craftsmen and even shopkeepers, struggling on the brink of poverty. When all the corn was sold there was a deficit of just £27, which was borne by the poor rate. There was satisfaction that the scheme had worked so well.

After the Napoleonic Wars the level of unemployment was such that the Lostwithiel Vestry could barely cope with the requests being made. A scheme was set up between 1819 and 1822 and again in 1825–29 whereby unemployed men worked in the town quarry on Terras Hill. They received very low wages but this was seen as preferable to being idle and miserable on parish support. The venture lost money, tools had to be provided, the men were initially unskilled, and there were few markets for the stone during the depression. In six years £97 had been spent and income had been £53.6s.1½d. However, the money spent was offset by the non-payment of relief. The men had been occupied and paid for their labour, and once again the overseers were satisfied

In 1812, driven by hunger and hardship, the men of St Neots came one night to Lostwithiel and destroyed the salmon weir, which lay above the bridge. They believed this weir prevented the fish from reaching their part of the river. In 1990, during construction of the golf course, broken granite blocks and mangled iron bars were found beside the river. These were the remains of a night's destruction nearly 200 years ago.

In contrast to the poverty was the leisurely life of the rich. In the summer of 1800 Mr Thomas Staniforth of Liverpool travelled in his own carriage to Lostwithiel, changing horses frequently en route, and making many social calls. His journey took nine days. He described the road between Liskeard and Lostwithiel as 'fine but very narrow'. Mr Staniforth was a ship owner and merchant, who traded in whales, seals, oil, ivory, iron and slaves. He was well respected in Liverpool and was elected Mayor. His daughter had married John Hext of Lostwithiel and Mr and Mrs Staniforth came to spend four months with her at Restormel House. In his diary Thomas Staniforth wrote:

Saturday 16 August. Morning very bright, hot sun. At 10 Hext and I set out on horseback for Boconnoc, the seat of Lord Camelford.
Wednesday 20 August. Entered my journal and amused myself in reading. Mr Tho. Hext came and dined and drank tea with us.

On 27 August there begins a sequence of entries illustrating that even the rich could not buy good health. Thomas' diary reveals that John Hext's father Samuel:

... was in a very alarming state, in consequence of a suppression of urine. Dr Hall of Bodmin came over at 8.

Samuel passed a most painful day without any evacuation, not having had resolution to undergo the operation of catheter, though he attempted it more than once, which distressed us all very much for fear of an inflammation, which might deprive us of so good and valuable a man in the course of a few hours. Dr Hall sleeps there.

During the week Samuel's condition deteriorated. He was unable to resort to a catheter and the doctors could do nothing to save him, although attending him constantly. He died after eight days of suffering and the funeral took place at midnight of 8/9 September 'according to the custom of the country when any person of consequence is buried.'

On Sunday 9 November Mr Staniforth experienced something which still occurs in Lostwithiel occasionally, although since the 1970s to a lesser degree.

... tremendous night of wind and rain... the river has overflowed the moor, the bridge and ground before the house [Restormel House]*... the current which ran down was so dreadful and every reason to fear the bridge would be carried down... the bridge at Lostwithiel impassable... Mr Baron, the clergyman confined to his house, a strong current running through the house* [30 Fore Street].

Between the extremes of rich and poor came the majority of Lostwithiel's solid citizens, who paid the poor rate and from amongst whom came the church-wardens, overseers, and 'assistant councillors'. They included shopkeepers, innkeepers, smallholders, and craftsmen, masons, shoemakers, carpenters, tailors, coopers and blacksmiths. There are records of a potter, John Courtis (also spelt Curtys) working in Lostwithiel in the 1730s–'40s. The steward at Lanhydrock bought earthenware from him. He also provided eight 'creasts' (ridge tiles or finials?) for repairs to the market house in 1743.

The Grammar School was founded by the Corporation in about 1770 and was probably housed originally in the Guildhall. There were no endowments, but the Corporation paid £20 a year towards costs, and nominated six boys for free education.

In 1781 the new Market Hall was built, the upstairs area being intended for an assembly room. This, however, became the Grammar School. A succession of masters taught in the school, most of them clergymen, for an annual salary of about £50. One of these was the Revd John Mousley, who deputised at Morning Service on 9 November 1800, when the Revd Baron was confined to his house by flood waters, and who was later to become the first Archdeacon of Madras. A writing master was also employed, for £20 a year. The school closed in 1842. A commercial school, using the Guildhall as a base, moved into the Grammar School premises and continued into the 1880s.

Early in the nineteenth century, iron ore was found in the hills to the north and west of the town. The development of the Restormel Iron Mine brought work for everybody in Lostwithiel. In the early years the ore was carried down to the quay by horse and cart, but in 1836 when the mines were at their zenith, tramlines were laid to Lostwithiel wharfs. This meant horses could pull several trucks at once, making transportation quicker, easier and cheaper. The tramlines came down, parallel to Restormel Road, through the mine's yard where the administrative offices were sited (later the cattle market and, in 2003, the car park), across North Street, along Monmouth Lane (still called Tram Lane by many people), and along Quay Street to the common (Coulson Park) and the loading jetties. The ore was barged from here to Fowey. On 16 September 1836 an advertisement appeared in the *West Briton*:

... to be sold 14 strong useful horses, from constant work in drawing iron ore, which will now be brought down by a railroad. They are young, staunch and in good working condition.

The success of the iron mines gave a great boost to the economy. People were attracted to the town not only to work in the mines, but to trade and pursue their crafts. In the decade between 1831 and 1841 the population (including Bridgend) is estimated to have increased by 66 per cent, from 1,110 to 1,850. Speculative builders were at work putting up rows of cheaply built 'workers cottages'. These had two rooms upstairs and one downstairs, only one exterior door, tiny windows, no plumbing and no garden. They were named after their builders, hence the names Eveleighs' Row, Knights Row, Philp's Court, Mason's Row and others. They were insanitary and overcrowded. Many were pulled down before the end of the nineteenth century, the last were demolished after the Second World War. In the late 1820s cottages had been built at 'Goosey Town' along the river, to house the limekiln workers, the bargees and the sawyers who worked there. These houses had small plots of land and a few still survive, modernised and cherished.

Several substantial houses of the period, built or restyled for the more wealthy residents were later converted into shops. The architectural refinements beyond and above the shops are seldom suspected by the casual shopper. Those which are still dwellings retain their early-nineteenth century dignity.

For many decades Commander George Bell Lawrance RN was forgotten in Lostwithiel. There are tablets near the north-west door in St Bartholomew's Church in memory of him and his family, which would indicate that he was a man of importance in the town, and has a place in its history. In 2003 more is known about Commander Lawrance and it is possible to put together something of his life story.

45

On the right of the picture are Georgian town houses in North Street. At the top of the street is the first Bank Methodist Chapel. (DB)

Mr Peter Turner, of 11 Bodmin Hill, saw in the deeds of his house that it had been bought by Lieutenant G.B. Lawrance in the early-nineteenth century. Peter connected this name with the memorial he had seen in the church, so decided, with the help of his friend Robert Bulgin of Port Isaac, to find out more about the Lawrance name. They consulted documents held at the Public Records Office, as well as documents in Mr Bulgin's possession.

Mr Richard Edward-Collins has in his possession a book of paintings by G.B. Lawrance, with a note pinned to the front page, saying 'Will Mr & Mrs Foster give this old scrapbook a home before being destroyed? M.E. Lawrance, August 15th 1910.' Miss Margaret Emma Lawrance was the daughter of George, and Mr and Mrs Foster were the grandparents of Mr Edward-Collins. It is believed that Miss Lawrance had been a governess to the Foster children at Lanwithan, so that could be why she turned to them, in her old age, to look after her father's precious 'scrapbook', there being nobody in her own family left to whom she could give it.

G.B. Lawrance attended Exeter School; his scrapbook contains watercolours painted while he was there. From *The Memorandum of the Services of George Bell Lawrance* (his service record) last dated 17 December 1811, we find that he entered the Navy on 1 March 1797, aged 21, as master's mate to Captain Bartholomew James, with whom he served on board the *El Corso* and the *Canopus*. From September 1799 to July 1800 he sailed as master's mate with Captain William Bligh on the *Director* (this was 12 years after the notorious episode on the *Bounty*). He was commissioned as lieutenant on 8 September 1803. In 1805, Lieutenant Lawrance, who for some time had command of the *Gypsey*, schooner of a dozen guns, captured a privateer of four guns off Trinidad. From 10 July 1806 until 15 July 1808, he served with the late Sir Samuel Hood on board *Centaur*. His last appointment was 5 June 1810 to the *Cadmus* under Captain Thomas Fife, with whom he served off the coast of France until 17 December 1811. He retired with the rank of commander on 4 May 1836. He died on 9 April 1846.

Lieutenant Lawrance was 35 when he completed his active service. There is no account of his life after he came to Lostwithiel. We know that he asked for the hand in marriage of Miss Dorothy Bullock Bennett, and that her father, Richard (recorded as 'gentleman of Lostwithiel') agreed to the marriage on condition that he provide a suitable house for her. He bought 11 Bodmin Hill and the marriage took place in Lostwithiel Church on 17 January 1814. They were recorded as being 'both of this parish'. George and Dorothy had four children, George Bennett, born in 1815, two little girls who died in infancy in 1820 and Margaret Emma born in 1822.

George was a prolific painter – his scrapbook contains many watercolours of ships, foreign coastlines and naval engagements, painted during his years of service. After he settled in Lostwithiel he

Paintings by G.B. Lawrance

Gypsey schooner of 12 guns, commanded by Lieutenant G.B. Lawrance and painted by him, c.1805. (RE-C)

Fore Street, showing G.B. Lawrance's house on the right, painted by him in 1825. (RE-C)

View of Fore Street, painted by G.B. Lawrance in 1825. (RE-C)

painted local scenes and subjects. The pictures best known are the views he painted looking up and down Fore Street.

It was usual in those days for the Navy to 'axe' officers at times when there was less need for them at sea, while still retaining them on half pay. It is not known whether George supplemented his pension during those early years of marriage, but it is possible that he gave drawing lessons, and even lessons in the 'three Rs' to small groups of children, using a front room of his house as a schoolroom. This was common practice, there were no State schools, and the children of those families who could afford it were educated privately.

That George had already established himself as a teacher while at 11 Bodmin Hill is quite probable, because in about 1825, by which time he was approaching 50 years of age, he moved to a much larger house, where there is some evidence that he ran a boarding-school where skills in seamanship were taught.

George painted a view of Fore Street, showing this house, No. 32, to good advantage. The house in the painting looks very new, but the evidence in the building itself suggests that it was a major development incorporating some older property. This again was common practice at the time. (The next-door properties in the painting were yet to be further developed.) It is probable that this development was designed specifically for Lieutenant Lawrance, to provide a comfortable dwelling-house for his family and accommodation for a school, having a strong element of seamanship in the curriculum, possibly for about 12 boys.

The main house was spacious and the Georgian staircase elegant. The top floor was (and still is) approached by both a narrow internal stair and an external stair leading directly from what would be a square yard. This provided the dormitory accommodation. The yard (now the garden) would have been where the boys did their 'drill' or physical training. This was connected by a doorway to the long, two-storey building (now a dwelling in Bassett's Yard), which was most likely used as a boat-house, and by a covered passage (now a barber's shop) to Parade Square and so to the river.

There is no evidence to suggest that this school had any official connection with the Navy. Information from the Royal Naval Museum in Greenwich suggests that in the days before Dartmouth College was founded, such 'academies' were run privately by retired naval officers. The curriculum would include the usual subjects of English, mathematics, Bible studies, physical training, and drawing as well as the crafts of seamanship. Drawing was important in the days before photography. No doubt the boys would have attended church regularly on Sundays.

As the iron mines developed, Lostwithiel must have been a noisy, dusty, busy town, but it was thriving, and it is likely that Lieutenant Lawrance ran a very successful establishment. He did not sell his house on Bodmin Hill until 1843. From the memorial in the church we know that he died in 1846, aged 70, his wife having died just a year earlier aged 60. They are buried in a family vault in the church. George Bennett Lawrance, son of George Bell, entered the Navy in 1829 and was promoted to the rank of lieutenant in 1843. He served on the West Indies and North American stations and died of yellow fever at St Croix in 1853, aged 38.

Margaret Emma never married. She lived to the age of 90 and died at Bridgend and was buried in St Winnow churchyard in 1912 (new flooring was laid in the church in 1870s, sealing off the family vaults). There are tablets in memory of George Bennett and Margaret Emma together with the one they had put in place, in memory of their parents. Another tablet, in memory of Dorothy's parents and the two little girls, was removed some years ago and has not yet been replaced. This seems to be the end of their story.

The family had its own coat of arms, made up of the Lawrance coat of arms, incorporating the 'shield representing the heiress of the Bennett family'. A plaster cast of this was found at 32 Fore Street. It had been part of the ceiling decoration in one of the front rooms of the house. Mr Adrian Daniell (not related to Henry John Daniel, *opposite*) remembers that it was still there when the premises were used as a fried-fish shop in the 1940s. It was thought at that time to be the coat of arms of the private girls' school which he remembers occupied 32 Fore Street in the days before the fish shop. There was a 'Ladies' School' in Fore Street run by Miss Rebecca Baron in 1862, and a 'Ladies' School' called 'Raglan House' in 1893, and a 'Private School for Girls' run by Miss Eleanor Faith Goombridge in 1930, all of which were listed in directories. One might therefore speculate that 32 Fore Street remained a private school for over 100 years.

In the early 1980s the plaster coat of arms was being stored outside in the yard, in danger of being lost forever. However, when Mrs Daphne Bryant came across it, she bought and rescued it. At that time no one appeared to know anything about it, so she took photographs and made enquiries through the Records Office. She received a letter identifying and explaining the coat of arms, and kindly gave the plaque and the letter to Lostwithiel Museum.

Centre: *The Lawrance family coat of arms.* (LM)

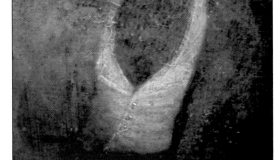

Henry John Daniel, 1818–89. (LM)

Obviously, the Lawrance family was one of standing and it is surprising that so little has been remembered of them locally over the years. Many questions remain unanswered, such as who cared for Margaret Emma in her old age and who had the memorial tablet and tombstone erected? Was Dorothy Bennett an only child or were there younger sisters – in which case are there surviving relatives? Perhaps one day answers might be found to these questions.

In 2002 Mr Tremar Menendez, the curator of Lostwithiel Museum, was offered a small oil paint-ing, by Mrs Ann Tucker of Liskeard. It is a portrait of a long-forgotten Lostwithiel poet, Henry John Daniel, and has brought to light an intriguing story. The painting was found in a junk shop in Stonehouse, Plymouth, by Mr James Laity. It was in poor condi-tion, but he was attracted by 'the intellectual face and thoughtful expression' of the sitter. It eventually came into the possession of Mrs Tucker, and Mr Rapson of Liskeard suggested that she might give it to Lostwithiel Museum, as Henry Daniel was born in the town.

Lostwithiel Museum accepted the portrait readily, and the curator went at once to the Courtney Library at the Royal Institution of Cornwall, Truro, to see what he could discover about the poet. Here he found the book *West Country Poets*, which gives an outline of Daniel's life.

Gillian Parsons has discovered further informa-tion, and a brief history begins to emerge. Henry John Daniel was born in Lostwithiel on 14 February 1818, the son of a wealthy wholesale grocer, Samuel Nanjulian Daniel, who had married Mary Blewett of Illogan in Lanlivery Church in 1817, by special licence. They lived at Windsor Cottage, Lostwithiel. Henry was not an obedient child, he played truant from school, led other boys into mischief and fought with boys from other schools. His headmaster despaired of him and he was sent to a boarding-school in Saltash, where he was again deemed to be hopelessly disobedient and illiterate. He was expelled. He was then sent to study to be a doctor of medicine in Chard, but soon abandoned these studies.

Henry was 16 years old when his father died, leaving him financially independent for the rest of his days. Despite his bad behaviour as a young child, he was deeply affected by his father's death and became a recluse for a time. He changed his way of life and started to study seriously, proving that he was, after all, a very intelligent, talented boy. He studied the Classics and was soon reading Homer in the original Greek. He wrote his first poem when he was aged 20, entitled 'Hours of Solitude', and went on to become a prolific poet, writing thousands of poems in his lifetime, covering a great variety of themes. The Courtney Library has many of these poems collected in Volume II of *West Cornwall Talks*. Many of his poems, written in Cornish dialect, are in a collection called *Cornish Thalia*, also held in the Courtney Library.

Henry married Jane Vascoe of Lanlivery, in Lanlivery Church in 1841, when he was 23 and she was 18. They had four children: Laura, Samuel John, Mary Bertha and Herbert Henry. In 1851 they were all living with Henry's mother, Mary, in Norman Lane, Lostwithiel. Mary died in 1852. It is not known where the family lived after that.

Henry Daniel did not have his collected works published during his lifetime, although he thought of doing so by subscription. His poems were published individually in periodicals and penny broadsheets. This might indicate that his fortune was dwindling. He was a jovial and popular man, possibly led into an intemperate lifestyle by syco-phantic friends, from whom he could never quite escape. He never ceased to write poems.

In 1881 he is recorded as being a lodger in the house of John Sykes of 41 King William Street, Salford. His occupation is described as 'journalist, writer for the press'. Nobody else bearing the name Daniel was at this address. He lived to be 71 years of age and died in Salford in 1889. Henry wrote his own epitaph, which commenced:

> *Here lies a bard, let epitaphs be true,*
> *His vices many, his virtues few...*

and concluded:

> *... who*
> *Laughed at the world, however it may blame,*
> *And died regardless of his fate or fame.*

The eastern extension to the bridge, built in the eighteenth century. Photograph taken in the 1920s. (DB)

The gaol window. (IF)

county MPs in the town. Miss Hext, in *Memorials of Lostwithiel and Restormel* tells an amusing tale of the last county election:

Beneath the Guildhall and the adjoining rooms are two or three small cells... where misdemeanors were imprisoned. The last of these rooms which was lighted by a barred and unglazed window, and which looked out into a narrow lane... was familiarly called 'the cage'. [This is now part of the back room of the museum.] *In 1831 there was a General Election for the County, and four gentlemen offered themselves, Lord Valletort and Sir Richard Vyvyan for the Tory party, and Sir Charles Lemon and Mr Pendarves for the Whigs. The friends of the Whig candidates bribed a wrestler called Polkinghorne, of immense size and great fame... to exhibit himself in this cage. He was supplied with a cask of brandy and another of gin, glasses of which he served out, through the window, to all comers who were of the 'right colour'. At the election there was a five days poll, Mr Pendarves with 1819 votes and Sir Charles Lemon with 1804 headed the poll and were returned for the County. Lord Valletort had 611 votes, and Sir Richard Vyvyan 911. It may be presumed that the Spirit that was shown on this occasion proved irresistible.*

Despite the poor condition of Henry Daniel's portrait, his character shows through, and it is fitting that it has come back to the place of his birth.

During the first decades of the nineteenth century Lostwithiel lost some of its county importance. In 1832 the County Courts were moved to Bodmin and after that year there were no more elections of

Queen Victoria came to the throne as a young girl of 18 in 1837. The following year saw the end of tin coinage. Lostwithiel had long since turned its attention to other things. It was thriving once again, with a booming iron industry and a busy quay. The regular arrival of the mail coach, plus the markets and fairs, kept the hostelries busy and trade brisk.

Chapter 8
POWER, INFLUENCE & SERVICE

Through the centuries there have been families connected with Lostwithiel, who attained power and influence, often by means of their wealth. While some were genuinely concerned for the well-being of the town and county, others were motivated in the first instance by self-interest. The changing relationships between these families and the town reflects the changing pattern of English society.

The Pitts produced Prime Ministers, while the Curteys family and that of the Kendals, Robartes and Edgcumbes produced MPs. Through the centuries a number of professional families have given their services and talents for the benefit of the town and neighbourhood.

INFLUENCIAL FAMILIES

The Curteys Family of Pill

From the very early days and until 1832 Lostwithiel was represented in Parliament by two MPs. According to F.M. Hext (1891) the first to represent the town were Stephen le Rede and Randolph Curteys of Pill, in 1304. Over the next 100 years the Curteys family represented the town in Parliament many more times. Tristram Curteys was MP in 1419, and the oldest monument in the Parish Church is a brass on the north wall dedicated to his memory. Tristram is depicted as an armed knight with spurs and described as an 'armiger' or bearer of arms. He would have been expected to supply infantrymen in time of war. His status was that of a landowner of free but not noble birth; in other words he was a 'franklin'. Some 70 years later, his descendant Richard Curteys became notorious for enclosing the 'town land'.

The last record of the Curteys family was installed in a window in the south aisle of the church, commemorating Caroline Mary Curteys in 1854.

Brass in St Bartholomew's Church in memory of Tristram Curteys of Pill, 1423. (SBC)

The Kendals of Pelyn

The Kendal family of Pelyn have the longest association with Lostwithiel, as they were here for over 600 years. John de Kendale was receiver for the Black Prince in 1351 and warden of the castle, for which he was paid 3d. a day. Finding these duties heavy, John asked the Prince for an assistant. He was allowed to have an assistant who was paid 2d. a day. The Prince paid 1d. of this while the warden was expected to pay the remaining 1d.! Lands at Pelyn were granted to the Kendals, who lived there until Mr Nicholas Kendal died childless in March 1992, leaving the manor-house to the charity, Help the Aged. Kendals represented Lostwithiel in Parliament in 1365 and on at least 20 occasions over 400 years. William, MP in 1570, is remembered as a generous host, although Queen Elizabeth I is said to have suspected his motives! Nicholas, MP in 1640, died fighting for the King's cause.

The market-place in Lostwithiel formed part of the 'town land'. The revenue from this helped towards the upkeep of the church and the bridge. Towards the end of the sixteenth century the trust was not well managed and in 1589 the sole trustee was the Mayor, John Hellyar. On the marriage of his daughter, Catherine Hellyar, to Walter Kendal, this land was illegally leased to the couple. There were also other instances of 'unlawfully making profits for themselves from Corporation property' in which Walter, Richard and Thomas Kendal and Ralph Taprell, were all involved. In 1603 a later Mayor and Corporation filed a complaint in the Chancery Court against Nicholas and Walter Kendal '... who did keep and withhold from the said town the market place... and other trust lands.' The case ended in favour of the town.

Sons of the Kendal family served the town as mayors and recorders, Cornwall as magistrates and sheriffs and the community as lawyers and priests as well as naval and military officers over many centuries. The late Mrs Dorothy de Lancey Nicholls, a much-respected local historian, naturalist and one of the founders of Lostwithiel Museum, was born a Kendal. There are memorials to the family in Lostwithiel and Lanlivery Churches. The house at Pelyn, which dates from the sixteenth or

51

Pelyn House, partially rebuilt after a fire in the nineteenth century. (IF)

Restormel House and Castle. (LM)

seventeenth century, was largely rebuilt after a fire in the 1800s. It has since been sold by the organisation Help the Aged and at the time of writing is occupied by private owners.

Restormel Manor, Leased by the Duchy of Cornwall

The original house, known as Trinity House, was built on the site of the Hermitage of the Holy Trinity that stood beside the quay on the river at Restormel. The date of the first house is not known and, as with many old properties, the building was probably constructed over a period of time, being renovated and enlarged as occasion demanded. It has been leased by the Duchy for many centuries. The Earl of Bedford leased it from Queen Elizabeth I (in the absence of a Duke) in 1559, along with other Duchy lands, after Henry VIII had 'disparked' the land.

Thomas Jones, who gave the Communion Plate to the town and church of Lostwithiel, leased it in 1763, and in 1775 it was occupied by William Masterman, MP for Bodmin and Mayor of Lostwithiel in 1779. He changed the name to Restormel House and possibly extended the building considerably. It was he who developed a 'picturesque' walk to the castle, planting many ornamental trees, including tulip trees. Earl Mount Edgcumbe bought the lease around 1792 and it was occupied by John Hext.

F.M. Hext understood that in the 1860s the Robartes held the lease and the house was again sublet

The County Dairy School at Restormel, 1920s. Mr and Mrs Jennings are on the right. (LM)

to other families. In the early 1900s a family called Jennings lived and farmed there. They ran the County Dairy School at Restormel House and a cheese-making business in Mill Lane, Lostwithiel. Several local girls were in service with them. A Miss Ivy Stuart of 'Gilbury' bicycled to Restormel to give lessons to the children Joy and John Jennings in 1917–20. Later came the Mitchells, who farmed the land for over half a century until, in the 1990s, the National River Authority, forerunner of the Environment Agency, disallowed the keeping of dairy cattle so close to the river (for fear of pollution). The Duchy found the Mitchells another farm. After the handing over of Hong Kong to the Chinese and the last voyage of the Royal Yacht *Britannia* in 1997, Rear Admiral Sir Robert Woodard, Flag Officer of the Royal Yachts, retired. He and Lady Woodard came to live in the house, known at the time of writing as Restormel Manor.

The Families of Boconnoc

Over the centuries Boconnoc has been home to a number of wayward young squires. In the thirteenth century Sir Thomas de Kencia was raiding Bishop Bronsecombe's deer park on behalf of Earl Edmund, and 150 years later Sir Hugh Courtney was indulging in piracy. Sir Hugh was killed at the Battle of Tewkesbury in 1471. A later Courtney, Henry, Marquis of Exeter was executed for treason in 1538 and the ownership passed to John Russell, Earl of Bedford.

In 1579 Francis Lord Russell sold Boconnoc to Sir William Mohun, who rebuilt Boconnoc House. His grandson, John, was created First Lord Mohun of Okehampton and it was he who hosted King Charles I at Boconnoc during the Civil War. It is said that the King arrived by coach, the first coach to attempt to travel over Cornwall's rough tracks. Progress was only possible because he had enough servants attending him to carry the coach!

The Mohun family did not thrive at Boconnoc – both the Third and Fifth Lords Mohun of Okehampton died as a result of duelling. The barony became extinct and the estate was sold in about 1720 to Thomas Pitt.

Thomas (Diamond) Pitt with the diamond in his hat, painted by Sir Godfrey Kneller. (ADGF)

Left: *Obelisk erected in 1771.* (IF)

driveways laid down on the estate. The First Lord Camelford erected the 123-foot high obelisk in memory of Sir Richard Lyttleton. It is inscribed with the words:

In gratitude and affection to the memory of Sir Richard Lyttleton and to perpetuate the remembrance of the peculiar character of benevolence which rendered him the delight of his own age and worthy the veneration of posterity. 1771.

Son of a Brentford parson, Thomas Pitt had worked for the East India Company, traded in diamonds and had become Governor of Madras. In 1701 he bought a magnificent diamond for £20,500. After cutting, it was claimed to be the finest in the world. Pitt offered it to Queen Anne, who did not want it. He sold it in 1717 to the Duke of Orleans for £135,000. Subsequent Kings of France wore it in their hats.

With part of this money Thomas Pitt bought Boconnoc. He died in 1726, his eldest son Robert surviving him by just one year. Boconnoc passed to Robert's son, Thomas, who became a steward of the Duchy, deputy warden of the stannaries and a capital burgess of Lostwithiel. Thomas married Christian, daughter of Sir Richard Lyttleton.

At the time Thomas inherited Boconnoc, his younger brother William (1708–78) was 18 years of age, and probably already up at Oxford. William (Pitt the Elder) was destined for greatness. He was to become Prime Minister and, later, Earl of Chatham, a most respected and revered statesman. Earl William's second son 'William Pitt the Younger' (1759–1806) became Prime Minister at the age of 24, and remained in office with only one short interruption for 23 years.

The son of Thomas Pitt was created Baron Camelford. He made additions to Boconnoc House, including the 65-foot long gallery in 1771. He also had the gardens landscaped and had many miles of

The Baron's son Thomas, born in 1775, was baptised at Boconnoc amidst great rejoicing. This young man's life, which started so well, illustrates the abuse of privilege. He grew up arrogant and with little self-control but, no doubt, owing to his highly placed kinsmen, he was pardoned for almost every misdemeanour. It seems that only George Vancouver attempted to discipline him, and that to his cost. At the age of 16 Thomas Pitt joined Vancouver's ship *Discovery* on a five-year voyage to survey and chart the West Coast of North America. Vancouver was a strict disciplinarian and Midshipman Pitt was insubordinate and contemptuous of discipline. In 1794 he disobeyed orders and was put in irons for 10 days until he could be sent home on another ship. Two years later Vancouver returned to London. Thomas Pitt, now Lord Camelford, had just come of age and had taken his seat in the House of Lords. Camelford assaulted Vancouver in the street, an event he turned to his advantage by paying for biased newspaper reporting and a cartoon by Gillray, 'The Caneing in Conduit Street'. This cartoon, mocking Vancouver, circulated in London and throughout the ports, bringing ridicule and shame upon him.

Camelford's bizarre behaviour continued, he attacked all who crossed him and killed more than once in illegal duals. His final dual was with a friend, Captain Best, in 1804 when Thomas, Second Lord Camelford, was fatally wounded and died three days later, aged 29. The title became extinct and Boconnoc was inherited by his sister Lady Grenville. In 1840 she gave the estate to her husband's nephew, the Hon. George Fortescue and it remains with the Fortescue family in 2003.

'The caneing in Conduit Street'. The cartoon of Lord Camelford's assault upon George Vancouver, by James Gillray, 1796. (BM)

During the Second World War Boconnoc House and the surrounding buildings and land were occupied by American troops. After the war the house was in a very poor state of repair and it became necessary by 1972 for Captain J.D.G. Fortescue to have the south-west wing demolished. The family has not lived in the house for many years.

The church at Boconnoc, the dedication of which is unknown, was built in the fifteenth century and still has its gallery for musicians at the west end. The coat of arms of Charles I is in the church along with a copy of his letter of thanks, written to all the parishes in Cornwall after the Battle of Braddock Down in 1643.

At the time of writing Mr Anthony Fortescue is working to restore Boconnoc House to its former glory. The extensive gardens, deer park and natural woodlands make this one of the most beautiful estates in Cornwall.

Robert Beale

In 1593 Lostwithiel's MP was Robert Beale, who achieved national fame as the Clerk to the Privy Council of Elizabeth I. He was the official who carried to Fotheringhay Castle the warrant for the execution of Mary, Queen of Scots.

The Robartes of Lanhydrock

In the sixteenth century the Robartes were a Truro family, trading mainly in wood and charcoal, the latter being indispensable to tinners. The Robartes bought woodlands in all parts of Cornwall and, after trees were felled, turned the land to agriculture. They lent money to tinners who paid their debts, and the interest on them, in tin.

The family grew wealthy and Richard Robartes was knighted in 1616. In 1620 he bought the Lanhydrock estate, which, before the Dissolution had belonged to the Priory of St Petroc, Bodmin. Four years later, on payment of £12,000 he was created Baron, at the court of King James I. To ease his own financial situation, the King was persuading the newly rich to buy titles. Baron Robartes started to build his mansion, and the work was completed by his son, John, between 1635 and 1642. The family built up a superb library, continued to buy land and married into older titled families, establishing their position as 'landed gentry'.

John was the leader of the Cornish Parliamentarians, described by Samuel Pepys as 'a very sober man' and known to some as a 'sour puritan'. He had a direct and devastating influence on Lostwithiel's history when, misreading the mood in Cornwall, and with the rank of Field Marshal, he persuaded Lord Essex to bring his Parliamentary Army to Cornwall in 1644. Lord Robartes was, nevertheless, appointed recorder of Lostwithiel in 1647. By 1660 he had become a Royalist and greeted Charles II on his restoration to the throne. He was accepted by Charles and later created Earl Radnor. The Robartes family lived at Lanhydrock for over 300 years.

In the second half of the nineteenth century the Robartes (who owned mineral rights in West Cornwall) showed a benevolent attitude to their workers, caring for them during hard times and building the Miners' Infirmary at Redruth, which Lord Robartes maintained at his own expense. He rebuilt farms and cottages on his estate, his wife taking a caring interest in the welfare of their tenants.

In 1881 there was a devastating fire at Lanhydrock that destroyed much of the house. Only the north wing, which included the long gallery, escaped harm.

Boconnoc House. (IF)

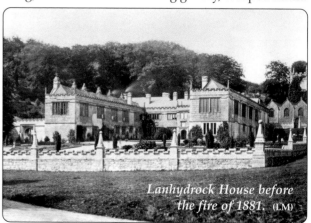

Lanhydrock House before the fire of 1881. (LM)

Lady Robartes was rescued by means of a ladder from an upstairs window, but she died a few days later. Lord Robartes died the following year.

Their son had the house rebuilt as a Victorian family residence, and continued to manage his affairs in the tradition of his father, caring for the welfare of his employees and their families. He lived at Lanhydrock for 48 years, inheriting the title of Sixth Viscount Clifden from a cousin in 1889. He had nine children. His eldest son, Thomas, was killed in action in 1915, and he was succeeded by his second son, Francis, in 1930. Francis remained a bachelor, living at home with his two unmarried sisters, Everilda and Violet.

Francis gave the house and estate to the National Trust in 1953 but continued to live there until his death in 1966. The Hon. Miss Everilda was the last of the family to live at Lanhydrock, living until 1969. The Eighth Viscount Clifden lived away and died without a male heir in 1974, when the title became extinct. Many local people had found employment at Lanhydrock, while others were tenant farmers. Those who remember the Robartes do so with great affection. The beautiful gardens inherited by the National Trust are being developed continually and are a constant source of delight to many thousands of visitors. The visitor numbers for 2002 reached over 200,000, more than in any previous year.

The Taprells

The Taprells came to Lostwithiel early in the seventeenth century from the St Neots area. They were a family of chandlers, and in 1640 John Taprell leased the mansion which became known as Taprell House. William Taprell was Mayor of Lostwithiel in 1644 during the unhappy days of the siege and, over the next 55 years, members of the family held the Mayoralty on seven occasions.

Taprell House was an extensive property, possibly developed into a dwelling from an earlier guildhall at the turn of the century, around the time that Carew was writing of the plundering of the castle. One wonders if the great fireplace and other dressed granite features in the main living quarters might have come from there.

There is a date stone on the corner of the malt-house in North Street, which records that:

Walter Kendal of Lostwithiel was founder of this house in 1658. Hath a lease for three thousand yeares which had Beginning the 29th of September Anno 1652.

This might indicate that the King's Arms Inn, malt-house and cooperage were added to the property at this time. A William Taprell is recorded as being an innkeeper in 1672. The William Taprell who renewed the lease on the house in 1683 was a mercer, dealing in fabrics and fine cloth. Perhaps it was this William

The lease stone on the malt-house. **(IF)**

whose death was recorded in 1709. After this the family is believed to have moved to London, although a Miss Martha Taprell was still living in Lostwithiel in 1717.

Taprell House was later acquired by the Edgcumbe family, who changed the aspect of it, building an imposing new frontage onto Fore Street. This Georgian addition became known as Edgcumbe House, and over the years, after the Edgcumbes had left Lostwithiel, the fabric of the earlier building was neglected. It eventually became the property of the Lostwithiel Borough Council and was used as a builders' store, a morgue, an air-raid shelter, an artist's studio, a Scout meeting-place and a youth club among other things, until in 1992 the Town Council and the Methodist Church pooled their resources and undertook a major restoration of this historic building. The architect, Mr John Carter, was commissioned to design the restoration to include the provision of a small Methodist chapel, with rooms above, and a large separate hall with an upstairs gallery, which the Town Council leases to the County Library Service. The whole project was sensitively and carefully carried out and is a great credit to all concerned. The building has become an invaluable benefit to the people of the town. The dedication of the Methodist chapel took place in February 1993 and the opening of the new Taprell House in May the same year. Taprells from all over the world were invited to be present. There was a civic reception and a party for them in the evening. Taprells from the USA, Canada, Australia, New Zealand and Europe all got together and exchanged genealogies, found long-lost kin and had a great time.

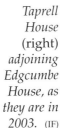

Taprell House (right) adjoining Edgcumbe House, as they are in 2003. (IF)

A video was made over the year 1992–93 to record the restoration work. It is available from Lostwithiel Library.

The Johns Family

During the period 1705–33 a family called Johns monopolised the Mayoralty of Lostwithiel. W.P. Courtney in his *Parliamentary Representation of Cornwall to 1832* says:

The Mayoralty of Lostwithiel might be called the perquisite of the family of Johns for, by means of bribes and threats etc. it remained with one or other of them during at least 20 years. The satellites of the then Prince of Wales knew the value of the family and plied them with blandishments of the most persuasive kind, in the hope of obtaining a footing in the constituency.

At this time the only people allowed to vote in Parliamentary elections were members of the council. The council consisted of seven aldermen and 17 councillors, 24 in total. Each had two votes. In 1705, Russell Robartes and Sir John Molesworth, both Tories, were elected to Parliament. James Kendal petitioned against this return, establishing his right to the place taken by Molesworth. The Mayor, John Johns, had arbitrarily disenfranchised several of the electors before the election!

Again there was malpractice in 1708 by Alexander Johns, Mayor and returning officer. Votes cast in the election were Hon. Francis Robartes (Tory) 20, Hon. Russell Robartes (Tory) 17, Mr James Kendal (Whig) 5, Mr Joseph Addison (Whig) 4. Incredibly, Mr Kendal and Mr Addison were declared duly elected!

It took three petitions and 19 months before the Robartes were declared the rightful MPs for Lostwithiel. Joseph Addison was the well-known essayist who had many eminent patrons, and has been described as 'one of the most illustrious ornaments of his time'.

The Edgcumbes & the 'Pocket Borough'

The Edgcumbes, an influential family of East Cornwall, first came to Lostwithiel and bought property towards the end of the Johns' hold on the Mayoralty. Mr Richard Edgcumbe was made recorder for the town in 1733, the following year he was the MP and in 1738 he was Mayor. According to W.P. Courtney, Mr Edgcumbe was:

The main manager of the little Cornish Boroughs in the interest of Sir Robert Walpole. So great was Mr Edgcumbe's knowledge of the secrets of these constituencies that he was created a peer [in 1742]... in order that the privileges of the Upper House might shield him from

The First Lord Edgcumbe, painted by Jan van Loo. (LTC)

examination by the Select Committee, should one have been appointed.

There is a portrait of the First Lord Edgcumbe in the Guildhall, which had been attributed to Sir Joshua Reynolds. The portrait was painted by Jan van Loo, a French artist who came to England and enjoyed the patronage of Sir Robert Walpole. However, Reynolds had a connection with Lostwithiel. His mother, Theophilia, was the daughter of the Revd Humphrey Potter, who signed himself 'Officiating Minister of St Bartholomew's Church 1684–90'. Theophilia was christened at Lostwithiel Church on 25 June 1688.

The Edgcumbes controlled Lostwithiel for about a century. The position of recorder was handed down from father to son during this time. Taprell House was bought for their own use – it was modernised, in the fashion of the day, to include a splendid granite front onto Fore Street. A substantial dower house was also built next door. The Edgcumbes also constructed the Corn Exchange, with the Guildhall above, on the opposite side of Fore Street, leaving intact the ancient gaol behind it. They built the Market Hall with the assembly rooms above, which for many years was used as the Grammar School. The impressive New Talbot Hotel in North Street was also built by the Edgcumbes. It became known

Engraving of Edgcumbe House, 1890s. (FMH & RIC)

The Market Hall and Grammar School, built 1781.
This photograph was taken in 1890. (FMH & RIC)

as the Royal Talbot Hotel after the visit of Queen Victoria in 1846. This was demolished in 1939 to make way for a new road. All these imposing granite buildings did much to enhance the appearance of Lostwithiel. The Edgcumbes bought up many other properties and land in the town and took over the living of the church.

Mr Courtney, in a footnote, writes that a 'distinguished native of Lostwithiel' (in 1890) informed him that traditionally the Pitts of Boconnoc controlled the borough, giving £6 to each of the 17 councillors at election time to secure their votes. The seven aldermen received no money, but official posts were found for them. At the election following the advent of the Edgcumbes, the Pitts were surprised when their candidates were not elected. It seems the Edgcumbes had given councillors £30 each for their votes and the aldermen had been offered Edgcumbe property at low rents! So it continued until 1832. The Edgcumbes maintained their power over the 24 electors who continued to return their patron's nominees.

However, they achieved no promotion in Parliament once the Pitts took office!

Lostwithiel was no better or worse than most other 'pocket boroughs' and the Reform Act of 1832 was well overdue when it swept all such practices away. Lostwithiel became part of a larger, more democratic constituency.

The Edgcumbes, who no longer had a reason to stay in Lostwithiel, withdrew, giving the Guildhall and the Grammar School to the town. Over a period of 80 years, they sold off the rest of their considerable property. The building now known as Edgcumbe House and Taprell House was sold to Thomas Hoskin in 1911 and was later acquired by the Borough Council. The Corn Exchange has served as a shop and the fire station, and at the time of writing is the Lostwithiel Museum. The Guildhall, which is above the Corn Exchange, has been a school and a magistrates' court and in 2003 is the Town Council chamber. The old Grammar School was used for public meetings after the school closed, then as a soup kitchen around the 1920s, before being occupied by American soldiers during the Second World War. The building fell into disrepair after this. In the 1980s it was replaced with modern flats for the elderly, leaving only the façade of the Georgian structure.

As a postscript to the times before the Parliamentary Reform Act, a Municipal Corporation Commission Report, dated 24 July 1833, stated that during the previous 13 years the Corporation's expenditure had averaged £447 a year and the income about £180. No debt was incurred as the recorder and late patron (Lord Edgcumbe) always made up the deficiency. His Lordship also paid further bills for the council, including, an annual dinner for 24 councillors (£90), two new cloaks for town sergeants (£26.7s.9d.) and newspapers for the Corporators (£25.3s.11d.). No doubt Lord Edgcumbe would be missed by a few inhabitants, but in 1832 a crowd was waiting in Lostwithiel to meet the coach bringing news of the passing of the Reform Act. It arrived at 4a.m., whereupon there was general rejoicing.

The Norway Family

The Globe Inn was the private house of the Norways from the late-seventeenth century. Nevell Norway was born in Lostwithiel in 1717. He made his fortune as a ship's captain, employed by the East India Company, but died and was buried in Lostwithiel at the age of 40, leaving a sum in excess of £5,000. A large part of this was left in trust to his nephew, Nevil Norway.

Nevil, born in Lostwithiel in 1739, was the only son of Joseph and Jane Norway. He set up in business as a merchant, dealing in a variety of commodities including timber. In 1763, Nevil married Sarah Arthur, the daughter of an innkeeper and former Mayor of

Norway House, built 1780s. (BMc)

the town. Some years later Nevil took over the Crown and Septre from his father-in-law and around 1780 he started to build Norway House overlooking the quay. The large house with two wings and large, vaulted cellars was completed before 1790. Nevil Norway set up as a merchant banker, he became a capital burgess of the town and in 1811, at the age of 72, he was Mayor. There is speculation that Nevil had the illegal importing of liquor in mind when he built his splendid house. Indeed, its position and design would certainly lend itself to smuggling. Nevil died in 1815 and is buried in Lostwithiel Church.

Nevil and Sarah had six children. John Arthur Norway, the third child (1771–1813), entered the Royal Navy as a midshipman in 1785. In 1793 he was promoted to second lieutenant. His captain, Edward Pellew, was later knighted and John Arthur Norway served with Pellew in all his actions until 1799. He became first lieutenant in 1797 and while serving on board HMS *Indefatigable*, in January that year, he saw action against the French. He was mentioned in dispatches and was later invalided home. By 6 July 1803 he was commander of HMS *Tromp* in Portsmouth, and was retired on half pay in 1806.

Several years later John Arthur Norway was appointed to the packet ship *Montague* of Falmouth. On 18 October 1813 the *Montague* set sail for

Above: *Captain John A. Norway, 1771–1813.* (BMc)

Right: *William Norway, 1774–1819.* (BMc)

Brazil, reaching Madeira on 1 November. It met the packet ship *Lady Mary Pelham* but was attacked during the night by the American privateer, *Globe*. The following day the *Montague* and *Lady Mary Pelham* spotted the *Globe* again and gave chase, the *Montague* opened fire on the privateer and a close engagement followed. In the ensuing action Captain Norway was injured. Refusing to go below he was hit and killed outright. The crew of the privateer heavily outnumbered the *Montague* who lost 18 out of 32 crew. After being repelled by the *Lady Mary Pelham* and what was left of the *Montague*, the privateer *Globe* escaped.

John Arthur had married in 1795 and had two children born in Lostwithiel. His son Nevil Norway also joined the Royal Navy, rising to the rank of lieutenant. Some years later the original family home in Lostwithiel was sold and became an inn. It was eventually renamed The Globe after the privateer that had attacked and killed Captain John Arthur Norway.

William Norway, a younger brother of John Arthur, traded as a merchant in Egloshayle, Wadebridge, where he married Mary King in 1798. He had a large family and it was his second son, Nevell Norway, born in 1801, who carried on the family business after his father's death in 1819. One dark night in February 1840, Nevell was returning home on horseback from market in Bodmin, when shortly before reaching Sladesbridge he was attacked by two men, robbed of a large sum of money, then brutally murdered. A reward of £200 was offered for the apprehension of the culprits. The murderers, brothers William (aged 36) and James Lightfoot (23) were soon caught and stood trial on 30 March 1840. Each blamed the other for the murder but they were both found guilty and sentenced to be hanged publicly at Bodmin Gaol on Monday 13 April 1840. A large crowd of up to 10,000 people gathered to witness the hanging.

Nevell's grandson, Arthur Hamilton Norway, 1859–1938, was born at Egloshayle. He was a travel writer and the father of Nevil Shute Norway (1899–1960), who emigrated to Australia, and using the pen-name Nevil Shute, became a novelist, best known for his wartime novel, *A Town Like Alice*.

Norway House was sold during the nineteenth century and was the home of John William Colenso, Mayor of Lostwithiel at the time of Queen Victoria's visit in 1846. From 1865–71 it was a boarding-school, and in 1891 it was the home of Colonel Sir Coleman Battie Rashleigh Bt., another Mayor of the town. The house has since been divided up, making three spacious family dwellings.

Bruce McDonald of Polscoe, who grew up at Norway House, is researching the Norway family history and has contributed this information.

The Fosters

The Fosters were tanners of Lostwithiel who, in the eighteenth century, moved to live at 'Castle', the

The Fosters & the Hexts

Right: *Miss F.M. Hext, author of* Memorials of Lostwithiel and Restormel, *published in 1891.* (LM)

Centre: *The Fosters' carriage outside Lanwithan House, c.1880.* (RE-C)

Bottom: *A wedding in the Foster family, 1880s.* (RE-C)

country house at Lantyan. (This house could be on the site of the castle of King Mark, father of Tristan and husband of Isolda, the ill-fated lovers, *see Chapter 1*.) The valley was cold and sunless as its Cornish name implies, and in 1829 the Fosters bought land and built Lanwithan on the east bank of the river, which enjoys the sun all day. They had already become bankers, building Foster's Bank (now Barclays) and marrying into other banking families. During the nineteenth century they served the town as Mayors and helped to finance the building of the Bodmin Hill and St Winnow Schools. They built St Saviours Chapel of Ease and the reading-room for the benefit of those in St Winnow Parish who lived in the Bridgend area. When the tanning business was finally closed down, the Fosters gave their sale rooms in Church Lane to the church.

Although in the nineteenth century 13 children were born to the family in one generation, no male Fosters survive today and the owner of Lanwithan in 2003, Mr Richard Edward-Collins, inherited the property through the female line. The last Foster in Lostwithiel was Miss Loveday, who lived at Oak Cottage and served on the council.

The Hexts

The Hexts were a professional family of lawyers and Army officers, who came to Lostwithiel in the mid-eighteenth century. Different members of the family lived at Restormel House, a town house in North Street (built in the nineteenth century) and Cowbridge, on the hillside overlooking the valley. The Hexts were Mayors on 18 occasions over a period of 135 years.

Miss Francis Hext is remembered for her book *Memorials of Lostwithiel and Restormel*, which she published privately in 1891. It is understood that she had about 50 copies printed, which she gave to friends and institutions. There are very few around today, and these are highly valued. Lostwithiel Library holds a copy on reference and the Town Council owns one, as do a few privileged individuals. More highly valued still are two further copies of the book, in which Miss Hext had extra empty pages inserted. These pages she embellished with her own photographs and sketches, many of them coloured drawings of the coats of arms of prominent local families. One of these precious books is kept in the Courtney Library at the Royal Institution of Cornwall in Truro, the other was given by Miss Hext to the Working Mens' Institute of Lostwithiel. When this organisation became defunct, the book passed, with the building, to the Lostwithiel Social Club, which now has the responsibility for the safe keeping of this treasure.

Miss Hext did other good works, one of which was the restoration and erection of the medieval lantern cross near the south porch of the church. She lived at 1 Queen Street and the land behind her house, between Shute Lane and Tanhouse Lane, was her garden. This is where Lostwithiel's tulip tree flourished for so many years. When the tulip tree was felled in 1999, it was believed to be about 120 years old – so it may well have been planted by Miss Hext. This tree was a source of great pride and joy to the people of the town. It was a spectacular tree and, having reached its full height of 29 metres, was thought to be the tallest of its species in the UK. In 1990 Dr McCurdy bought the house, which had the

Left: *'This Ancient Cross Repaired and Restored to Lostwithiel by Frances Margery Hext AD1882.'*
(IF)

Right: *Lostwithiel's tulip tree in 1993, probably planted c.1880 by Miss Hext.* (IF)

tree in the garden (Miss Hext's garden having been developed into a number of housing plots). Then in 1991 it was found that a taller tulip tree was growing in Stourhead, Wiltshire. This was a disappointment, but Dr McCurdy and Lostwithiel still took pride in the lovely tree.

In 1992–93 Dr McCurdy began to have worries about it. He feared the weight of the main limbs was starting to pull the tree apart so it needed to be braced at the fork. A preservation order had been put on it in 1989, and nothing could be done without special permission. A year or two later 'honey fungus' was suspected and Dr McCurdy called in more experts. He grew fearful that the tree might come down in a gale (having the tree in his garden was no longer a source of pleasure to the doctor). After deliberations at the highest level, with even the Ministry of the Environment being involved, a decision was finally reached. The verdict was that the tree would have to come down. In October 1999 the work was carried out. Mr Paul Brewer arranged that a section through the trunk should be kept. The section was treated and at the time of writing is displayed in the museum. The growth rings have been related to events of local interest over the past 120 years.

We know that Miss Hext took an interest in unusual and ornamental trees, as she made special reference in her book to those planted near to Restormel Castle by William Masterman. His tulip trees would have been about 100 years old when Miss Hext knew them. Perhaps they inspired her to plant the one that Lostwithiel enjoyed for so many years.

THE METHODIST CHURCH IN LOSTWITHIEL

The influence of John Wesley on the town was of a different order. John Wesley first came to Cornwall in 1743 and found amongst the Cornish people a predisposition to receive his message. He came regularly to Cornwall, making 32 visits over 46 years. Surprisingly, his only visit to Lostwithiel was just two years before his death when he was 86 years old. He noted in his journal '11 a.m. Monday August 17th (1789) Lostwithiel, talk'.

It is difficult to account for this apparent neglect of Lostwithiel throughout Wesley's ministry to Cornwall, unless perhaps the domination of the town by the Edgcumbes prevented anyone from inviting him. It certainly was not that the people of the town were indifferent, as within a year of his visit there was a Wesleyan Chapel in Lostwithiel. This was built in King Street and opened in 1790.

Methodism, as it came to be called, attracted people of all social classes. It became a separate, free church, and later there were a number of secessions from the main Wesleyan movement. Although making a late start in Lostwithiel, Methodism became very strong in the town. In 1837 a Methodist United Free Church was opened on the Bank, and in 1859 a Primitive Methodist Chapel was built in Bridgend. Before 1880 a Congregational Chapel had been built on Restormel Road. Many craftsmen and tradespeople in the town joined the Nonconformist movements and were known as dissenters.

As soon as there was a free election for local councillors in 1885, the dissenters began to take an active part in local government. There had been discrimination against Nonconformists for over a century. Not until 1828 were they allowed to hold office in national or local government. All baptisms and marriages had to be registered at the Parish Church until 1838, and it was not until 1880 that Nonconformist ministers were allowed to officiate at burials in consecrated ground.

As the congregations grew in numbers and wealth, early chapels were replaced with bigger

View from Terras Hill before 1880. The first Wesleyan chapel in King Street can be seen on the right. (DB)

Left: *Wesleyan Chapel, built in 1880.* (LM)

Below: *The second Bank Methodist Chapel under construction in 1900. The cattle market in Queen Street can also be seen.* (LM)

Left:
Demolishing the Wesleyan Chapel, 1967. (LM)

Right:
Opening the Methodist Chapel at Taprell House, 1993. Architect, John Carter, is third from the left. (JB)

and better buildings. In 1880 the Wesleyans built a large Victorian Gothic church (where the Royal Talbot Hotel car park is located in 2003), moving out of their original chapel, which was converted into houses. In 1900 the United Methodists built a large granite-fronted chapel on the Bank.

The town would appear to have been fairly evenly divided between Church and Chapel, and for many years regular Sunday worship was part of family life for most people. However, the attendance at church and chapel was to decline, and Lostwithiel's Congregational Church was closed before the 1920s and converted into houses.

When the Methodist Church was reunited in 1932 all the chapels in Lostwithiel were not needed. The Primitive Methodist Chapel was first to close in 1933, and became a dwelling. In the 1960s it became obvious that the Methodist population of the town could not support the two big chapels (the Wesleyan and the Bank Methodist) standing almost side by side, and there was a dilemma as to which should be kept and which should close. Neither congregation was willing to lose its chapel and attend the other. Meanwhile, the two chapels were sharing a young minister and were administered jointly by a group consisting of elders from each chapel. By far the more powerful members of this group were those belonging to the Bank Methodist Chapel – amongst them were businessmen of influence in the town. It was a time of great unhappiness for all concerned.

Meetings were held, prayers offered up and architects consulted, in an effort to reach a decision. The consultants came down in favour of the Wesleyan Chapel. It was more solidly constructed, allowed in more sunlight, had level access, toilets and a car park, so agreement was reached to keep open the Wesleyan Chapel and close the Bank Methodist Chapel. However, the Bank Chapel men did not give up. They decided that some alterations were needed to update the building, and the Wesleyan congregation was persuaded to close its chapel while this work was done. Meanwhile, men were employed to remove the interior wood panelling, ostensibly to investigate the underlying masonry! Then some of the administrators, claiming that the cost of alterations and restoring the panelling would be prohibitive, sought permission from a higher authority to sell off the Wesleyan Chapel. Permission was granted, the chapel was sold and subsequently demolished. All that remains is the Sunday-school room, which has since been converted into a private dwelling.

Very few of the congregation of the Wesleyan Chapel joined the Bank Methodist Chapel – most found other places in which to worship, including St Bartholomew's Church. The congregation at the Bank dwindled and in 1987 it too was sold and converted to flats.

After this, the Methodists used St Saviours as their place of worship, until the opening on 20 February 1993 of a new chapel and meeting-room within the refurbished Taprell House. This small, bright chapel has been a success, and it has given the present generation of the Methodist community a new lease of life.

The miners wear a curious woollen dress, with a cap like

this : and the dress thus : and they generally

have a candle stuck in front of the cap.

Left: *Queen Victoria's sketches of miners in* Leaves from the Journal of Our Life in the Highlands, *following a visit to Restormel in 1846.* (RAW)

Above: *Industrial buildings at the entrance to the mine, c.1908.* (LM)

Right: *Miners emerging from Taylor's Level, c.1908. Mr Oscar H. Jarrett, manager, is second from the right.* (LM)

Chapter 9

THE VICTORIAN ERA

It was a proud day for Lostwithiel when Queen Victoria, aged 27, a young wife and mother, taking a holiday on the royal yacht with her consort, Prince Albert, came ashore to visit Restormel Castle and the Restormel Iron Mine. It was the first visit of a sovereign since Charles I had routed the Parliamentary Army here in 1644. This was 8 September 1846 and the Queen wrote in her diary, 'We drove [from Fowey] through some of the narrowest streets I ever saw in England.'

There is a story that the royal coach took the wrong turning and instead of coming down the hill to the town, went directly along the lanes and down a track to the castle. The people waiting to greet her in Lostwithiel were disappointed and she, no doubt, was terrified! The Queen described Restormel Castle as 'very picturesque' and went on:

We visited here Restormel Mine. It is an iron mine. Albert and I got into one of the trucks and were dragged in by miners. The miners wore a curious woollen dress with a cap... There was something unearthly about this lit up cavern place... The miners seemed so pleased at seeing us and are intelligent good people... It was quite dazzling when we came into daylight again.

The royal party entered the mine at Taylor's Level, opposite the site of the bowling-green. On leaving, the royal visitors paused to greet the dignitaries of the town on Market Street, which has been called Queen Street ever since. The mine became known as the Restormel Royal Iron Mine and the Talbot Hotel as the Royal Talbot.

On 25 September the *Royal Cornwall Gazette* printed a copy of a miner's official report of the visit:

D Sir this is to let you know that I have the Higher Honour of Conducting the Queen Victoria and Prince Albert Und grownd yesterday the 8th of Sept. I can assure you I Laboured hard to Make every Nesary Preparation for her Majesty and the Prince to go und grownd and so Did Cook. We first Waranted perfectly safety we prepared 5 ungrownd Wagons the queen and Prince Albert went in the first Wagon. Mr t... walked in through the level and I by his Side Conducting queen and Prince Albert with 4 pulling Wagon By a Roope... Upwards of 200 fathoms then the queen and Prince

walked 14 fathoms through the level. I put the Pick in Prince Albert's hands Wich He took it And broke a stone of ore. I Hold My Hat cap for him to break it in. He took it out of the Hat and Put It in his pocket. I am happy to let you know That we never Make the least Shade of Blunder Whatever I have I ham thankful I know Not how to express myself to you for your kindness had it not been for you I should never had had the high Honour conducting her Majesty undgrownd, our Mine is working favourably. Wee are well thank God for it.

One side-effect of the iron mine was the pollution of the river with arsenic and other poisons. In 1860 an enquiry was held into the cause of the decrease in the salmon fisheries. Apprentices and servants, who ate salmon at least twice a week (it being a cheap source of protein), had in earlier days petitioned their masters for a change of diet, blaming the salmon for making them feel ill. It turns out that they were quite correct to have their doubts about the fish!

There were various other mining ventures around Lostwithiel, notably the silver lead mine at Boconnoc, called Silver Vein. This never lived up to expectations and was a great disappointment. The tiny St Nectan's Church had been enlarged, in the expectation of increased population. Some years later the aisle that had been added was taken down.

Norman Pound's analysis of census returns for 1841 and 1851 show that although the population was growing overall, there must have been considerable migration of young men away from Lostwithiel. The 1851 census shows a marked drop in the number of men between the ages of 10 and 35 years, when compared with the number of males under the age of 10. However, the number of young women grew. Indeed, the proportion of young women to young men increased to 2:1.

People on the move were mostly from poor families. In the days before compulsory education, ten years was considered a suitable age to start work. Those leaving home would be semi-skilled or unskilled workers. There was plenty of work for women and girls – many were employed as domestic servants living in their masters' houses.

The 1841 census gives the occupations of 473 persons, mostly heads of households. A total of 38 were of independent means, 187 were craftsmen, including those involved in building, carpentry, leather work and clothing, 93 were in agriculture, 51 were merchants, which included retail and hawking, and 54 were miners. There were 27 professional men, including doctors, teachers, lawyers, agents and clerks, 14 bargemen, and 9 unskilled workers, chimney sweeps, laundresses and bargemen. There was pressure on accommodation so people with rooms to spare would take in lodgers. A total of 54 lodgers were registered in 1851 – ten lodged in one house in Fore Street, nine of whom were hawkers, a common occupation at that time. One house on Bodmin Hill held 25 occupants: the owner (a brush maker) and his wife, a female servant, seven more married couples, seven children and an elderly widower.

The overcrowding and squalor must have been prodigious, even for those days. Soon after this the Borough Council introduced a policy of inspection and licensing for lodging-houses.

Lostwithiel is well supplied with inns and taverns but years ago, when it was smaller, there were many more. They catered for the coach passengers, the hauliers, travelling merchants and farmers coming to market, as well as the local populace. The King's Arms, Royal Talbot, Globe, Royal Oak and Earl of Chatham are all still very much alive, but in the mid-nineteenth century Ann's Gallery was the Town Arms, The Dolphin was at Bridgend, and opposite the Post Office was The Golden Eagle. Byways, on Bodmin Hill, was a 'kiddly' (having a six-day licence to serve beer and cider). This was well placed for the miners to quench their thirst as they came down from the iron mines at the top of the hill. There were also hostelries called The Sailor's Arms, The Malt Shovel, The Crown & Sceptre and The London Inn. Where were they?

It was in 1846 that Lostwithiel people celebrated the passing of the Cornwall Railway Bill, but they had to wait another 13 years before trains reached the locality. In 1859 the main-line railway from Plymouth to Truro was opened, and the maintenance workshops were built at Lostwithiel. In the same year the gasworks went into operation. The foundation-stone for 'the much talked of gasworks' had been laid in 1858 with 'some ceremony and wine drinking'. It was sited on the Moors behind the Gooseytown cottages, conveniently placed for supplies of coal barged upriver. It was a time of great excitement except for those people living east of the river. The *Royal Cornwall Gazette* reported:

It was intended to extend the gas into St Winnow [meaning Bridgend] but it appears that the Lord Lieutenant wishes to keep the inhabitants of that parish in the dark and will not allow it to be taken over the old bridge.

The same year the first Fowey lifeboat was launched. It came to Lostwithiel by rail, sailed from here down to Fowey and round to its base in Polkerris. It was a 30-foot six-oared boat called *The Catherine Rashleigh.*

The opening of the Lostwithiel–Fowey railway line a decade later added further to the town's economy, although it damaged the river traffic, in the same way that the main line had damaged the stage-coach business. That said, coaches did not disappear altogether. Indeed, there are elderly people in Lostwithiel, even in 2003, who remember the livery yard of the Royal Talbot Hotel (on the site of the new Royal Talbot Hotel) still busy with horses until well into the twentieth century. River traffic continued on a reduced scale up to the 1930s.

In the mid-nineteenth century there were intermittent outbreaks of cholera, no doubt as a result of densely inhabited and unsanitary housing. In 1833 the stannary gaol was used as an isolation hospital.

Consideration was given in 1862 to the laying of 'a common sewer from end to end through one of the streets.' The estimated cost was about £100. It is recorded that 'upon receiving this report, the vestry passed a resolution to the effect that the construction of the drain was feasible but not expedient.' Steps were taken to find the appropriate authority to be responsible for 'nuisance removal'. It was finally decided that the Mayor and burgesses were to be the authority responsible, and that they had the power to levy a borough rate to deal with sewage disposal. During the nineteenth century the monthly cattle markets were held in Queen Street and added greatly to the 'nuisance'. It was suggested that the market be moved to the Moors (Coulson Park), to which came the sharp response in a letter to the *West Briton* in 1886:

... the removing of the cattle market to the Moors would be doing a great injury to the business property and the tradesmen generally... he must also bear in mind that clean streets done without trade or traffic will not provide [for] doctors' and butchers' bills.

An early print of the railway coming through Lostwithiel. (DB)

Some time later pipes were laid to carry untreated sewage into the river. On animal-slaughtering days the river ran red and it is said that the trout grew fat and flourished.

Towards the end of the nineteenth century, levels were driven into the hills in search of fresh water, which was then piped to convenient places. There were a number of 'shoots' in the town that many people can remember. St Cadock's Shoot was, until the end of the twentieth century, still used by many local people in preference to the tap water supplied in modern times by South West Water Company from the waterworks higher up the river.

Before 1870 education was not compulsory. There were private schools in Lostwithiel for the children of those people who could afford the fees. John T. Stephens, who had taught in educational institutions in Ireland, married Jane Rowse in January 1856 in Bodmin Parish Church. They took up residence at Hellier (Hillyar) House, Lostwithiel and opened it as an 'academy' or boarding-school for male students. Jane was responsible for all the domestic arrangements. Four years later they moved to Kingdon House and opened an academy there, staying for six years. The fees for boarders were £18–£20 per annum. Kingdon House was that part of the Royal Oak Hotel which backs onto King Street. The 1861 census records John and Jane Stephens, their four children, nine male scholars aged 9–17, and two servants living at the academy.

In need of more extensive accommodation, the Stephens moved their school once again, in 1865, to Norway House. The 1871 census shows that they had eight resident students aged 9–13; the numbers of day students would not show on the census. John and Jane and their family emigrated to the USA in 1871. Perhaps the Education Act of 1870, bringing education to one and all for 2d. a week, undermined their business. This information was provided by Mrs Ann Tumser, a descendant of the Stephens, who used the internet in California, USA, for much of her research.

After 1870, when education became compulsory, the Elementary School and Master's House were built on Bodmin Hill. The land was given by Lord Edgcumbe and the Corporation gave £355.19s.2d. towards building costs. It was originally a Church of England foundation, but in 1885 Lostwithiel's Borough Council was reformed, enabling Nonconformists to be elected onto the council. The school was, at this time, given over to a non-denominational School Board. The first five elected members of the School Board were Mr and Mrs Foster (benefactors), John Philp, Richard Reed and Joseph Burt – for the first time three 'dissenters' were elected. This was a great breakthrough for the Nonconformists. Indeed, there must be a story of political and religious struggle hidden in this brief statement of fact.

In the early days many pupils left school well before they were 12 years old but most people grew up able to read and write a little.

St Faith's Diocesan Convent was founded in 1864, on the initiative of the Revd Walter Everest, a canon of Truro Cathedral. It was run by Sisters of Mercy from a community in Wantage, Oxfordshire, as a training home for adolescent girls in need of care and protection. Some of these girls came from beyond the Tamar and were a long way from home. It was known as 'a penitentiary for wayward girls'. The regime was

St Faith's Convent, now known as Peregrine Hall. (LM)

Advert for St Faith's laundry in Bodmin Deanery Magazine, *1939.* (MR)

strict and the girls had no freedom. They were trained in domestic work, particularly as laundresses, and the convent functioned as a laundry for a wide area. The girls usually stayed for two years, but were discharged only at the discretion of the Sister Superior. On leaving, most girls went into domestic service. At the turn of the century St Faith's was one of 238 Anglican penitentiaries for girls across the country.

The building itself was designed by the well-known architect G.E. Street (who also designed Boseglos House on Fore Street). A beautiful chapel was added to St Faith's in 1876 and the vicar of St Winnow acted as chaplain. The late Desmond Trethewey remembered that St Bartholomew's Church Choir went every Christmas to sing carols in the chapel. They were given lemonade and mince pies after the service, but never did they catch sight of any of the girls! When the convent closed in 1950 one or two of the girls stayed, married and spent the rest of their lives in the town. It seems they never spoke of life in St Faith's. The building was later sold and used as a youth hostel. It was sold again, the name was changed to Peregrine Hall and it became a venue for medieval banquets, fashionable in the 1970s. It has since been developed into a number of attractive holiday apartments and bed and breakfast accommodation, with spectacular views over the town and countryside from the extensive grounds.

One wonders if the original inmates ever appreciated its unique position.

Popular social evenings throughout the winter months during 1871 were the 'Penny Readings'. Mrs Tumser came across newspaper accounts of these in old copies of the *Western Morning News*. Members of the public were entertained in the Grammar School by a band, singers, piano soloists and readings. The proceeds from the events were used to provide a tea for 160 'aged poor', after which there was an entertainment, to which all who had taken tea were admitted free. The performers at the events included Richard Foster, Revd George Hext, John Stephens, Miss Probert, the Misses Beckerleg and William Pease, all people with a strong social conscience.

In 1874 the Duchy Palace buildings were in a poor condition and, no longer needed by the Duchy, they were sold off in lots to tradesmen in the town. Four years later the Freemasons bought the Old Exchequer Hall and, having made repairs and alterations to meet their needs, they formally occupied it as a Masonic Hall in 1879.

Alterations being made to the Duchy Palace buildings, 1878–79. Note the tramlines from the iron mines. (DB)

In January 1876 a violent storm damaged St Bartholomew's spire, not for the first time. When it had been repaired in 1757 (after being struck by lightning) it had not been raised to its original height and it had a stunted appearance. As a result, after the

Interior of St Bartholomew's Church, 1822, possibly painted by G.B. Lawrance. (LM)

1876 storm, the decision was taken to lengthen it by five feet, restoring it to its original elegance. Mr G.E. Street described St Bartholomew's Church as 'the pre-eminent glory of Cornwall' at about this time. Other repairs to the church were necessary – damp and wood decay were evident. Church restoration was a fashionable Victorian phenomenon which, in the opinion of many people at the start of the twenty-first century, 'has much to answer for'. St Bartholomew's was closed for a year in 1878 and services were held in the school on Bodmin Hill, which still belonged to the Church. Miss Hext, in *Memorials of Lostwithiel,* tells succinctly what happened:

The whole interior was laid open, the old pews were cleared away, the gallery at the west end was taken down, the flooring was swept away and brought down level to the bases of the pillars... the vaults beneath were hermetically sealed with cement on which were laid brown encaustic tiles... The plastered ceiling was taken down and replaced by a panel roof of pitch pine. The organ which had stood in the gallery was moved to its position north of the chancel.

This organ had been bought by subscribers in 1828. Before that, psalms and hymns (only those printed in the Prayer Book were allowed to be sung in church) were sung by a choir accompanied by a variety of instruments, and all were positioned in the gallery. When the hymn had been announced a red curtain was drawn across the gallery hiding the performers from view. 'Nevertheless' writes Miss Hext, 'those of the congregation whose seats faced the east, always turned round to the gallery when the singing began.' At about this time the right of way through the church tower, which had been in use for 500 years, was closed, and pedestrians were redirected west of the tower.

The tanning industry, so long a staple of the town, was discontinued around this time and Mr Richard Foster, tanner and Mayor, gave his market and sale room to the church to serve as a Sunday school and church rooms. These rooms are still in regular use in 2003.

In 1884 universal parliamentary suffrage for men was finally achieved. Lostwithiel was still an 'unreformed borough', having had in 1835 too small a population to be eligible under the Municipal Reform Act. However, in 1885, following a petition to the Privy Council, signed by nearly 200 local people, the town was granted a New Charter by the Queen. The old Corporation of Mayor, six councillors and 17 assistants was formally abolished. The new Charter provided for a council of 12 persons elected from not less than 21 candidates. The freely elected councillors were to choose a Mayor from amongst their number and elect four aldermen, not of their number.

On 2 November 1885 the election took place. A total of 238 votes were cast by the 280 people on the electoral roll. The candidates stood as 'churchmen' or 'dissenters', and six of each were elected:

Richard Foster, Churchman, 166 votes.
Richard Reed, Dissenter (lime burner), 138 votes.
Thomas Halls Knight, Churchman (coal and timber merchant), 132 votes.
Edward Collins, Churchman (draper), 130 votes.
John Santo, Dissenter (butcher, retired), 127 votes.
Philip Rundle, Dissenter (butcher), 127 votes.
John Bartlett, Dissenter, 118 votes.
Jonathon Hugill, Dissenter, 115 votes.
William Burton, Churchman (butcher), 114 votes.
Colman Battie Rashleigh, Churchman (gent), 109 votes.
Wm Scantlebury, Dissenter (carpenter, retired), 107 votes.
Thos Sherwell, Churchman (farmer, retired), 107 votes.

They elected Mr Foster to be Mayor, and the four aldermen chosen were Mr Pease (solicitor), Richard Rundle (auctioneer), John Philp (builder) and J.H. Dingle (merchant). Miss Hext recorded that on Sunday 15 November 'the whole new Corporation attended by two Sergeants at Mace, came to the Morning Service, according to the ancient and invariable custom.'

It seems that thereafter, some dissenting Mayors did not see fit to attend the church service. There were also disputes concerning the ancient 'town lands', the income from which had hitherto been used for church maintenance. This was finally settled in 1888. However, in more recent times, when the Mayors have been Methodists, the civic services have been held in the chapel they attended regularly (usually the Bank Chapel) and the Methodist minister has been the Mayor's chaplain.

For many years through the nineteenth century there had been an annual burlesque known as 'Mock Mayor Choosing' held in the same week as 'Mayor Choosing', which at that time took place in October. Four men were drawn in a cart escorted by two mock constables. All were masked, wore long noses, and in motley dress were quite unrecognisable. A halt was made at each street corner and mock officials were elected. Every man was given a role: Mayor, recorder, even 'down as low as hangman'. Then 'The Calender' was read out (an account of all the transgressions of people in public life over the past year), which enabled the people of the town to express their dissatisfaction with the way in which the town had been governed. Written in satirical verse, this was an occasion to display wit, express derision and vent spleen. It is said to have degenerated into coarseness, which was the reason often given for the eventual demise of the custom. However, the following address delivered at the Royal Talbot Hotel, at a dinner given to mark the disuse of the ancient ceremony of Mock Mayor Choosing, on 23 November 1886, would indicate other, deeply felt reasons:

Once more my late Mock Burgesses around the board we meet,
Drawn by an unexpected call from our self sought retreat.
And though unlike our older feasts, this is a gift unearned,
We've done it justice; and our thanks are heartily returned.
Since the old Corporation's gone, with all its empty fuss,
And better growth usurps its place, there is no need for us
To keep our yearly carnival in this enfranchised town,
And hold removed abuses up, that we may run them down.
Ye bolder few, who bore the brunt, your occupation's gone:
No more to mount the civic car, your quaint disguise you'll don,
Nor from your torch-illumined height will fling your taunts and jeers
To gratify the broader tastes or shock mock-modest ears.
No more ye men who held the shafts and let the shouting throng
From Bunker's Hill to Royal Oak you'll haul our car along.
Ye Crier, who with loud 'Oyez!' proclaiming went before,
Yours is a most important part, and hardest to give o'er,
For you within the good Mayor's door received the brimming bowl,
And from our subjects willing hands drew their accustomed toll.
(But ah! the toll we levied then and in a supper ate,
Now goes into the hungry bag that holds the Borough rate!)
Our clerk who kept the calendar, that catalogue of crime,
Plays the detective now no more, but has a restful time.
And we who did the unseen part, in secrecy at home
(Of whom just three are with us here, and one's at Ilfracombe)
No more we'll scoff at Council feasts, nor sentence folk to gaol
Nor satire peaceful citizens, nor at our rulers rail;
We'll blacken paper never more for choosing of Mock Mayor;
We ceased when 12 elected men stood round the civic chair.
Now all who kept the custom up, through good and ill renown,
Your old support you have withdrawn and let it totter down.
Its time is past, it's turn is served, in ruin let it lie:
We know not those who saw its birth, we all have seen it die.

Map dated 1888, showing railway developments and tramlines from the iron mines to the jetties. (BF)

So, another century had brought much change. Lostwithiel had seen the county courts moved to Bodmin, the end of tin coinage and the tanning industry, the sale of the Duchy buildings and the loss of jurisdiction over the River Fowey, yet it was enjoying vastly improved communications and public services, as well as increasing employment for its people. The men all had a free vote and felt that, at last, they had a part in the democratic government of their town and country. Women had to wait a while longer for this.

Right: The newly built Lostwithiel Working Men's Institute, seen here c.1891. (LM)

Below: Cottages on Bodmin Hill, c.1900. (LM)

Above: *Drawing of original Peace Memorial, Bridgend, erected in 1902.* (IF)

Above right: *Horse-drawn wagonette driven by Mr Frank Secombe, jobmaster at the Royal Talbot Hotel stables, 1905.* (LM)

Right: *The Duke and Duchess of Cornwall visit Restormel Castle in 1905. Lord Clifden is wearing a bowler hat* (on the right), *with Lady Clifden* (centre) *and the Hon. Tommy, killed in action in 1915* (far right). (LM)

J. A. BESWARICK,

MANURE, CORN AND FORAGE MERCHANT,

LOSTWITHIEL.

Left: *Bodmin Hill corner c.1910.* (DB)

Chapter 10

INTO THE TWENTIETH CENTURY

THE EARLY 1900S

The twentieth century saw greater and faster change in the world than any other previous period in history. The improvements in rail transport, plus the development of motor transport, faster ships, aeroplanes, helicopters, electricity, telephone, radio and television have, in 100 years, completely changed the way we live, as have computers, the internet, and e-mail.

Towards the end of the nineteenth century, trouble was brewing in South Africa between the British and the Boers. This eventually developed into war, starting in October 1899. George Hoskins, who was a rural postman (and was to become Mayor, 1925–27) was one of 15 Lostwithiel men who fought in this war. As a reservist in the Rifle Brigade he was called up in 1899 and was away for three years. George wrote a number of letters to his friends in the Post Office, which his colleague, Cyril Daniell, passed to the *West Briton*. Nine published letters from South Africa form part of a scrapbook of newspaper cuttings, given to Lostwithiel Museum by George's daughter, the late Miss Winifred Hoskins. The letters reveal the confusion, carnage, degradation and suffering that are features of war. George was involved in the rounding up and imprisoning of Boer families in concentration camps, but he wrote that in his opinion they fared better than the British soldiers. He grieved over the death of Audrey, the baby daughter he had never seen:

It is with a sad heart I refer to the death of little Audrey, always having had such good accounts of her. I was looking forward to the time when I should see her. I cannot close this without thanking the many friends who were so kind to and helped my wife in her sad trouble.

He also expressed sadness at the passing of the Queen.

After the British victory in 1902 the soldiers returned home and were presented with medals. Later, a monument funded by parish subscription was erected at Bridgend. It bears the inscription 'Peace Memorial AD1902' but no names. There is no record of local men killed, so we might assume that Lostwithiel was very lucky and lost none of its sons.

The memorial, made by stonemason Mr Nicholls, grandfather of Warren (Mayor 1992–94), incorporated a shoot, a constant supply of piped running water. Some time after the Second World War the monument was hit by a lorry. The pipe was fractured and the obelisk was knocked to the ground where it broke in two. It lay beside the road for some years. In the early 1950s, after lengthy and fruitless negotiations with an insurance company, the council decided not to have it repaired. Miss Loveday Foster of Oak Cottage, herself a member of the council, asked Mr Nicholls, son of the mason who had made the monument, to do the repairs and paid for the work herself. One piece of the obelisk was repaired and reinstated, but the water-supply was never reconnected.

During the first decade of the century, the iron mines were becoming uneconomic and were running down, so it was inevitable that the industry came to an end. Luckily for the working men of Lostwithiel, the railway maintenance works were in need of more men. The miners learned new skills and the town escaped the hardship of unemployment.

In the early days of the twentieth century, the need for a properly organised cattle market became obvious. For possibly a century or more, the livestock markets had been held in Queen Street (called Market Street before 1846). A group of interested men formed a company and in 1906 the market was established on the site of the old iron mines offices. This was of great benefit to the farmers and a relief to many people unconnected with farming. The congestion and filth in the street associated with the market was alleviated at last. There were many butchers and slaughterhouses in Lostwithiel around this time and there was an important trade in meat, which relied on the railway for distribution.

Coulson Park was opened on the common in 1907, with joyful celebrations, thanks to the generosity of Dr Nathaniel Coulson. The common had always been a part of Lostwithiel life (the site of grazing land, sawmills and later the jetties for loading iron ore) but never before a place for leisure, as it has been since. At the turn of the century, otter hunting with hounds was one of the pastimes of Lostwithiel's working men. Boxing was also popular.

Motor cars were beginning to make their appearance on the roads. As far back as anyone could

Waiting for a visit by the Duke and Duchess of Cornwall, 1909. The royal couple stayed for four minutes, and did not alight from their car, but shook hands with the Mayor, drove slowly along the Parade and waved to the assembled children and elderly, who were singing 'God Bless the Prince of Wales'. (DP)

Above: *Limestone beside the town quay, c.1910.* (LM)

Left: *The Celtic cross at Nomansland in Edwardian days.* (DB)

remember there had always been a Skelton's workshop in North Street. The original Mr Skelton had set up his business in 1823 as a wheelwright and manufacturer of agricultural implements. Bill Skelton, a descendant, had been an inventive engineer and had made the original 'butterfly plough', which moved the share laterally. This invention won a gold medal at a Crystal Palace exhibition in the 1880s. Skeltons made their own 'penny farthing' bicycles and pioneered the making of 'safety bicycles', using chains to drive the wheels. The chains were made by hand, link by link. Skelton's firm moved with the times into the motor-car business and in 1911–12 were the sole agents in the area for Ford cars, when the 'Tin-Lizzie' cost about £150. There was a garage here until the mid-1990s, after which time houses were built on the site, now known as Field Close.

YEARS OF SOCIAL CHANGE

The First World War changed life for everyone. Soldiers of the Sherwood Foresters were billeted in the town, recruiting parades were held, many men and boys volunteered and marched away, some of them never to return. Women took on men's work and kept the home fires burning. A soup kitchen was run in the old Grammar School; with the wage-earners away fighting, there was not much money and many families suffered hardship.

Gill Parsons tells of how her grandfather survived the sinking of the *Lusitania* in 1915:

Tom Matthews was born in 1887 in St Winnow Parish, and on leaving school became a slaughterman for a local butcher. His brother-in-law, Arthur Martin, had emigrated to Michigan USA in 1908 and was earning good pay in the copper mines. Arthur came home on a visit in 1912, and Tom decided to go back with him to work in the copper mines for a while. Tom planned to send money home and to save enough to set up a family business on his return.

At the outbreak of war in 1914, Tom and Arthur decided to return to Cornwall, but at the eleventh hour, having got as far as New York docks, Arthur changed his mind. He was, incidentally, a non-swimmer. He said goodbye to Tom and stayed in the USA. Tom boarded the Lusitania *on 1 May 1915, bound for Liverpool and carrying almost 2,000 passengers.*

On Friday 7 May, sailing off the southern coast of Ireland, round the Head of Kinsale, just a few hours out of Liverpool, the liner was torpedoed by a German U-boat. The Lusitania *sank within 20 minutes, with the loss of 1,195 lives. There were 764 survivors.*

Tom found himself in the sea. Being a fit young man of 27, and a strong swimmer, he managed to survive the cold water for four-and-a-half hours, helping to save other lives before being rescued himself. He returned to his wife and son in Lostwithiel, and was subsequently awarded £26

Pupils at St Winnow School, 1914. Left to right, back row: *Billy Sturgess, Jim Turner, Violet Wendon, Dorothy Wendon, Ivy Hoskin, Dorothy Hore, Meg West, Eva May;* centre: *Tommy Scantlebury, Harry Acklank, Leonard Mitchell, Joe Sandy, Billy Coad, Billy Guy, Billy Bennett, Arnold Harvey, Ewart Hoskin, Leslie Hoskin;* front: *Ada Yeo, Eliza Turner, Christopher Hore, Gladys May, Dorothy Chalice, Elsie Chalice and ?.*
No name has been recorded for the boy on the front row (far right) *who moved and lost his head!* (DP)

*Mr Edward John Talling (wearing bowler hat)
with men of the Sherwood Foresters, billeted
in Lostwithiel in 1915.* (PD)

compensation for the loss of all his possessions.

*Tom joined up and served with the Army for the rest
of the war. On his return from active service, he opened
his own butcher's shop at 9 Quay Street, known as T.
Matthews & Son. Tom ran the shop for 39 years, his son
Howard working in the business with him. Tom retired
at the age of 70 and died peacefully at the age of 74.*

Throughout his life Tom was very reluctant to talk
about what he experienced when the *Lusitania* sank.
His family knows only the barest outline of his story.

Thomas Matthews (seated) *photographed in Calumet,
Michigan, before the First World War.* (GP)

By a strange coincidence, it happened that the
father of the girl Tom's son later married (Gill
Parsons' maternal grandfather) was serving with the
Royal Navy off the coast of Ireland and was involved
in the rescue of the survivors from the *Lusitania*. He
was Leonard Bloomfield, and had lived at Lanlivery
in his youth. After leaving the Navy, he farmed at
Lewannick, then on retirement came to Lostwithiel.
Tom's brother-in-law, Arthur Martin, stayed permanently in the USA, and the families still keep in touch
and visit each other.

There was further hardship after the war,
especially for those families who had lost husbands,
fathers, sons. It was difficult for young people in
Lostwithiel to find work and many left the town
in order to try their luck elsewhere. Others turned to
'jobbing'. This meant doing any job for which there
was payment, such as gardening, delivering milk,
moving furniture or farm labouring. By keeping
busy all day, a living could be made.

Women had proved their worth during the war
years and won some voting rights in 1917, but it was
not until 1928 that universal suffrage for those aged
21 was achieved. One young man to recognise the
importance of this development and who seized his
opportunity, was the late Sydney Brewer. He sought
election to the Borough Council, and being a baker he
was up early and his afternoons were free. These he
put to good use canvassing the ladies. He recounted
with a chuckle that he romped home at the election!

During the years between the world wars the
'wireless' began to develop. It became very popular
and widened the interests of the population. The
weekly cinema shows in the church rooms were also
popular in the 1920s. Silent films were shown in the
Grammar School and Miss Treleaven played an
accompaniment on the piano to suit the action on
the screen.

The increasing use of the telephone was changing
the way in which business was conducted. The town's

Advert, Brewer's Corner, Bodmin Hill, 1920s.

Above: *Richard Eyres, licensee, and his son Herbie outside the Royal Oak in 1922.* (LM)

Above left: *Beckerleg saddlers, c.1918.* (LM)

Left: *Flooding in North Street, 1928. Skelton's Garage is on the left.* (LM)

Right: *Mr Offord's woodwork class, c.1926. Left to right, back row: Len Crocker, Jack Toms, Gerald Goodman, Rex Stephens, ? Tucker, Melville Sandercock; centre: Adrian Daniell, Dick Olver, Bert Vincent, Clarence Pope, Henry Stephens, Percy Pope, Stanley Phillips; front: H. Stead, Russell Ball, Enodor Daniell, ?, ?, Reggie Keast, Mr H.J. Offord.* (HJO)

The Post Office before renovation in 1936. (DP)

Staff outside the renovated Post Office, 1936.
Dick Parsons, postman, is fifth from the right. (DP)

learned to drive, decarbonise, fit new tyres and apply skid chains to their new vehicles!

Before the war Lostwithiel's Post Office was a Crown Post Office, employing 14 men and 3 women. The local telephone exchange was housed on the first floor of the building until the 1960s.

Social life was blooming in Lostwithiel during the 1920s. The decade saw the birth of the Women's Institute, the Town Band and the Bowls Club, all of which took off with a flourish, and are still thriving in 2003. The Tennis Club and the Operatic Society have gone, but the Scouts and Guides live on from generation to generation.

After the excitement of the 1920s, however, came the economic depression throughout the western world that has since come to characterise the 1930s. Lostwithiel was lucky: the railway maintenance works continued to employ men and that, together with the new milk depot, proved to be the town's salvation. However, the town did not totally escape the effects of the depression and many young men left home to look elsewhere for work. Some emigrated to Australia, others went to London. Some found work more locally in Plymouth or St Austell. They travelled daily by train, but the fares soaked up much of their income and their days were long and poorly rewarded. Some young, single men were attracted to HM Forces, particularly the RAF, so they signed up, with high hopes of an exciting and financially secure life.

It was a different story for local women. There had never been much variety of employment for them in Lostwithiel and indeed married women generally did not 'go out to work' in the 1930s. Many jobs that women do now were reserved for men in those days.

Duke Street in 1930s. (DB)

exchange was manned at the Post Office, which was also the site of Lostwithiel's first telephone. The Royal Talbot Hotel was Lostwithiel 2 and the Co-op, number 13. The doctors had 'phones, but very few private individuals could afford them. There were one or two public telephones in the town, which were used largely for emergencies. Mrs Gill Parsons has newspaper cuttings from the late Dick Parsons' collection which recall the renovation of the Post Office in 1936 at a cost of £2,000. The manual telephone exchange was brought more up to date and a central-heating system was installed. The new premises were opened in January 1936, just prior to the introduction of electricity. The building was wired up in readiness, but temporary gas lighting had to be fitted.

The Post Office staff worked hard to manage the several collections and deliveries each day. Postmen delivered mail to Lerryn, Sweetshouse, Lanlivery and Luxulyan with only a push-bike for transport until 1935, when motorised mail vans were introduced. Three senior postmen, Dick Parsons, Albert Bagley and Cyril Daniell, were taken off other duties and given one week's tuition, during which they

Until the Second World War took the men away, girls were never seen behind the counter in a bank. Assistants in the grocers shops were all men. Young girls worked 'in service' in the houses of the wealthy, or in hotels. There were jobs as companions to elderly ladies and nursemaids to young children. A few lucky girls were employed in ladies' dress shops and hairdressing was becoming popular. There was a limited amount of office work available but certainly not enough to satisfy the needs of the community. There were a few jobs for married women in nursing, the district nurse and the midwife were greatly respected mature ladies. It had long been common practice for people with spare rooms to take in lodgers, as this provided some extra income for housewives. Apart from this, married women could usually only find work helping others with washing, ironing and housework.

Early in the 1930s a scheme was devised to collect milk from local farms and co-ordinate marketing. This was initially undertaken by the Great Western Railway. Milk was sent up-country by rail. In 1932 Nestlé, the international dairy produce firm, built a depot here and ran a fleet of trucks to bring in the milk, employing about 20 men. This business proved successful and grew throughout the 1930s, providing employment for girls as well as men and improving the lot of the local dairy farmers.

1930s Schooling

The two schools in Lostwithiel, St Winnow and Bodmin Hill, were both smaller than they are at the time of writing, although they catered for pupils up to the age of 14. Most children left school the day before they turned 14. At the age of 11, children took 'the scholarship' and about 20 per cent were selected to attend Grammar School. They could choose to go to Bodmin, Fowey or St Austell. There was transport available to all of these places, but most pupils opted for Fowey (which was quite small with about 120 pupils) and travelled on the train each day. These children generally stayed at school until they were 16 and took the School Certificate Exams (equivalent to the modern GCSE).

Mrs Jean Hick has happy memories of Bodmin Hill School. In the junior classes she learned to write with a pen and ink. This was not easy as the split pen nibs would bend if they were pressed too hard, and the ink would splatter over the page of the exercise book. It was always a challenge to keep the first page of the book tidy. To keep the pupils motivated, the teacher would give a penny to those who kept the tidiest complete book. She also gave a penny to those children who got all their sums correct!

Discipline was strict and there was never much bad behaviour in school. Misdemeanours were punished by 'caning', a stroke of the cane across the palm of the hand. This could sting quite badly, so both boys and girls thought twice before speaking out of turn or breaking the rules.

Every morning the school met for a short assembly, which included a hymn, the Lord's Prayer and a few words from the headmaster, which might be praise or a telling-off. There were no hymn books at the Bodmin Hill School in the 1930s, so the words of the hymns had to be learned by heart. Poetry was also learned in this way, and Mrs Hick will never forget 'The Owl and the Pussy Cat'.

Lunches were not provided at school. Only children who came a long way brought pasties, the rest went home. In most families, dad too was home for his midday meal, so this was usually the main family meal of the day.

Bodmin School had six teachers, one for each class up to the scholarship year. The headmaster taught all the pupils between 11 and 14 years of age.

Lostwithiel's days were punctuated by bells. The school bell rang to summon the children to school, but before that, at 6.50a.m. and 7a.m., the railway-workers' bell had already alerted them that their day was about to start. A church bell rang out to call the volunteer firemen whenever there was a fire.

Lostwithiel in the 1930s

In the early 1930s Lostwithiel was a self-contained little town and nobody needed to travel far for shopping, as reflected in the 1935 *Directory of Shops*. There were tailors, drapers, a china and glass shop, a jeweller, a saddler, cabinet-maker, haulage contractor, ironmonger, wireless shop, gramophone dealer, chemist, agricultural engineer and implement maker, watchmaker, bill poster, photographer, boot and shoe shops, bakers, and several butchers and slaughter-houses. There was a flourishing Co-op, which dealt in many aspects of retailing, from pasties to coal. There were also two garages.

The cost of a visit to the doctor was 5s., which is what a young school-leaver earned in a week, working in Vida Carter's dress shop. Alternatively, there was an insurance scheme called 'the panel' for people who worked for an employer. This cost 6d. (approximately 2p in modern money) a week.

The town had two policemen. One lived at 1 Bodmin Hill, the other on Shoot Hill. These two men kept the town in order.

When electricity was finally brought to the town by overhead cables in 1936, this leap into the modern world was hardly noticed. Much of the residential property in the town was owned by a small group of men, who were also the owners of the gas company. Of course, they did not rush to convert their properties to electricity. The first properties to be connected to electric power were the new Co-op (Londis in 2003), which was being renovated at that time, and the Post Office. Gradually house owners had their homes connected, and their wives were delighted

Five generations of a family at a christening in the 1930s. Great-great-grandma Richards is holding baby Lilian Talling. Lilian's father Fred Talling is standing with great-grandma Honour Keast (left) and grandma Elizabeth Mary Talling (right). (PD)

and airy, and the health and happiness of the people moving into them reflected the improvement in their conditions.

In 1938 there was a fire in one of the cottages in Gooseytown. Kate Walkham, the mother of eight children, had gone out to make a 'phone call from a public telephone box, regarding her eldest child who was in hospital. Her three youngest children, aged three, four and five, were at home. On her return, the cottage was alight and the children upstairs. Kate made her way in and rescued them all, using the bedroom window as a means of escape. Iona (now Mrs Wilton of Bodmin) remembers it all vividly:

The house was gutted and everything in it lost. All I remember seeing afterwards was Father's silver cup, won at boxing, all burnt up. We moved into a house in Philp's Court, off Duke Street, one-up, one-down, husband, wife and six children. Granny Walkham lived in the house next door, she took in two boys. One shared tap in the yard, and one shared wash-house between four houses.

Kate Walkham's children, 1938. Left to right: *Malah Tamara Myra (aged three), Cyril Douglas Ivor (four), Iona Phyllis Laura (five), Edgar Wallace Albert (six), Richard John Percy (seven), Jean Yvonne Ruth (eight), Joyce Frances Kate (nine), Norah Mary Elizabeth (ten).* (IW)

Despite the hardship the family survived and have very many descendants living in 2003.

During the 1930s the use of the motor car increased dramatically and in 1935 the driving test was introduced. Miss Christine Rowe (now Mrs Barnicoat) was the first lady in Lostwithiel to take the test in April 1936 – she passed first time.

Christine Barnicoat (née Rowe) in her Morris motor car, 1936. (CB)

with the difference it made to their lives. It is worth noting that many houses in the town are still supplied by overhead cables.

Early in the 1930s 'washday' (always Monday) meant hard work for the housewives. Starting early in the morning by lighting fires to heat the water, then rubbing, rinsing, mangling, drying and ironing, the exhausting work went on all day. Irons in the early 1930s had to be heated either by filling them with hot coals, or by placing them on the stove or fire to heat. These got too hot, then rapidly cooled down. Gas irons were better, but the temperature could not be easily controlled. Electric irons (in the early days these were plugged into the light sockets), and later electric washing machines, were a great boon to those who could afford them.

Many small houses, built for miners a century earlier, were still occupied, although living conditions for the tenants were far from satisfactory. They had outside taps and lavatories, small windows and no gardens. Council-houses were built in Lostwithiel from the mid-1920s through to the 1950s to replace them. These were built on the hillsides and had spectacular views of the river valley. They were light

Desmond Trethewey, a qualified motor mechanic, was appointed in 1936 to the post of RAC patrolman, covering the area between Lostwithiel and Dobwalls. He was issued with a push-bike, a uniform and a box of tools. His brief was to leave Lostwithiel at 9a.m., cycle to Dobwalls and do point duty on the corner until sunset, unless called away to deal with a breakdown. There were few of these and hardly any accidents. Calls for help were carried by other road users and usually involved broken fan belts. Desmond was never called upon to use his first-aid skills. He helped and advised tourists, who often did not know where they were, and he was expected to salute cars carrying an RAC badge. He enjoyed this work, especially in the summer. Desmond was paid by cheque once a month and found it a big improvement on his previous job! He remained a patrolman until the war started.

The increase in traffic had a great effect on Lostwithiel, it being on the route from Plymouth, via Liskeard and St Austell, to Truro. However, the only way through was the medieval bridge and North Street. There was often congestion at Bridgend and in North Street, especially when trains were passing through. Traffic tried to push through in all directions, there being no one-way system. Market days presented the worst problems as the only entrance to the cattle market was from North Street. Sheep and cattle for market were herded through the town, or carried in lorries, which caused long delays in the narrow streets. After the sales, many animals were herded (often by young boys, hired for a few pence) over the bridge to the railway station yard, to be transported away in cattle trucks. People tell stories of bulls being led along North Street blindfold, and of cattle taking fright as they crossed the bridge and jumping over the parapet into the river.

In 1938 a decision was made to build a bypass road. This plan was not universally popular in Lostwithiel as several properties had to be demolished. Some cottages near Cott Road were lost. Houses just beyond the Post Office at the end of Queen Street came down and, worst of all, so did the Royal Talbot Hotel on the corner of Queen Street and North Street. This last was an integral part of the town's history. It had been built by the Edgcumbes during their period

of influence, and for very many years had been a coaching inn and the place where balls, concerts, glittering parties and political gatherings were held. In 1939 the new Royal Talbot Hotel was built across the road, on the site of the original coach-houses and stables. It never achieved the prestige and status of its predecessor. The building was not as gracious and did not lend itself to glamourous occasions.

Two new bridges were constructed in 1939 to carry the new Liddicoat Road over the railway and river. The river bridge is an attractive piece of civil engineering and is perhaps under appreciated by many of us in the town. The railway bridge was replaced in 1993 by a stronger, uglier construction, to comply with EEC regulations. The bypass made a tremendous difference to the town, which became a safer place – life became noticeably more tranquil. There were still problems, such as the sewage that still went directly into the river. This was particularly offensive on the days when animals were slaughtered close by the railway crossing, and in the hot summer months. The river was prone to fairly frequent flooding when the high tides and heavy storms coincided, but Lostwithiel coped with these adversities.

There was a good community spirit and a good social life for all. The church and chapels were well attended, there were 36 choristers in the church choir, all men and boys. Sunday was a day for everybody to wear their 'best clothes' and most children went to Sunday school. Mothers' Union and Church clubs prospered. There was a Working Men's Institute and numerous public houses. Many clubs, some of which had been founded in the previous decade, flourished. There were Saturday-night dances at the Drill Hall (in town, by the river), where the local dance band played regularly. Carnival and regatta days were highlights of the 1930s summer, as were the annual Quay Street fairs. Here the rides were powered by electricity generated by steam engines. A favourite was a beautiful engine known as 'Gladiator'. The smell of the steam engine and the organ music always brought a thrill of excitement to the town. In 1936 the people of Lostwithiel got their hearts' desire, when Mr Henry Williams came to town and built the Glyn Cinema in the corner of the old Duchy Palace complex.

Throughout the decade the quality of life in the town gradually improved. Housing, availability of work, working conditions, transport, radio and cinema all served to widen the horizons and open up new possibilities, especially for women.

This was a time when a great deal of deference and respect was afforded to professional people. This made the lives of those in authority much easier, they were rarely challenged to account for their actions. Six years of war sparked further change in peoples' lives and attitudes, so that the society we have at the start of the twenty-first century demands that everyone is accountable to someone else, and respect has be earned.

The new Royal Talbot Hotel, built 1939. (CCCB)

Left: *The Royal Talbot Hotel, the scene of many glittering occasions, was demolished in 1939 to make way for the new bypass.* (DB)

The new bridge built in 1939 to carry the bypass over the river. (CCCR)

Left: *Lostwithiel Scouts on a horse-drawn carnival float in 1935, representing 'Jack Payne and his Bonny Boys'. The scouts included:* Ken Ashton, Ken Henwood, Harry Jeffery, Horace Dunkley, Ken Rook, George Ellory, Dennis Parsons, Desmond Talling. Jack Swatton (on far right) *was 'Jack Payne'.* (D&ET)

Below: *Church pageant, 1936. Left to right, back row:* Donald Carne, Victor Tearle, Donald Dunkley; *centre:* Vera Trethewey (née Walkham), Grace Keast (née Harvey), Emily Collings (née Pope), Margaret Carne, Nellie Pope, Charles Wherry, Revd T.A. Webber, Arthur Ashton, ? Bassett, Mary Goodman, Pat Carne (née Willis), Jean Hick (née Wevell), Desmond Trethewey; *front:* Christine Barnicoat (née Rowe), Mark Brewer, ? Secombe. (DD)

Above: *Lostwithiel Army Cadet Force, 1939, with inspecting officers from Bodmin ACF. Left to right, front rank:* Pat Cousins, Jack Cockwill, ?, ? Cousins, Garfield Ashton, Ernest Bayliss; *second rank:* ?, ?, ?, Leslie Stephens. (LS)

Bodmin Hill School group, 1937. Teacher: *Mr Joe E Levers.* Left to right, back row: *Maurice Talling, ?, Ken Guy, May Lander, Pearl Toms, Eileen Speare, Ken Pearce, Victor Tearle, Arthur Philp;* third row: *Albert Stead, ?, Norah Walkham, Molly Ham, ? Coad, Jean Vincent, Elsie Tullet, Charlie Wherry, Ian Jeffcoat;* second row: *Eileen Collins, Pat Carne, Alma Parsons, May Netherton, Joyce Vincent, Jean Speare, Ruth Wenmouth, Vera Tancock, Phyllis Green, ? Nicholls;* front: *Les Searle, Geoffrey Docking, Gordon Pearce, Leslie Stephens, Garfield Ashton, Billy Tearle, Douglas Swiggs, Keith Liddicoat, Colin Brown.* (LS)

Bodmin Hill School group, 1938. Left to right, back row: *Ronnie Philips, Reggie Crocker, Myrtle Redmond, Rosie Pearce (née Brown), Maureen Pearce, Pam Steed, Jean Dawes, Johnnie Walkham, John Parsons;* centre: *Mark Brewer, Brian Honey, Joan Hoskin, Roseday Cox, Jean Coon, Noreen Pearce, Hilary Wilcock (née Philp), Daphne Gibbs, Mervyn Taylor, John Nicholls;* front: *Ivor Turner, Paul Brewer, Margaret Green, ?, Pam Holmes, Pat Pearce, Mollie Marshall, Foy Hendicott, Melville Parsons, Denny Wilton, John Rowe.*

The Civil Defence stood down in 1945. Left to right, back row: *Geraldine Littleton, Thelma Parsons, Enid Cousins, Beryl Santo, Dorothy Penwarden, Iris Pearce, Delphina Ead, Betty Chapman, Mrs Goodhart, Mrs Carne, Bert Thomas, ?, Clarence Harris, Charlie Goodman, Leslie Gardener, Alf Alexander, ?, Dickie Docking;* centre: *Betty Round, Doris Coombe, Muriel Stockman, Nellie Talling, Enid Hamlin, Doris Ball, Rene Yates, Joyce Levers, Roddy Carthew, Gwen Bailey, Reggie Penny, Mavis Goodman, Harold Bartlett, Betty Stephens, Wilfred Coad, ?, Mr Whell, Eileen Collings, Mr Butt, ?, Mary Hicks, ?, ?, ?, Eileen Spear, Harry Alston, Vera Trethewey (née Walkham), Maggie Cavell;* front, seated: *Austin Johns, Winnie Boldero, Miss Lilian May, Fred Stockman, Christine Barnicoat (née Rowe), Mr Goodhart, Clifford Burt, Dr Rudge, Dorothy Wheeler, Mr May, Beryl Harris, Michael Oates, Dorothy Oates, Mr Lean, Robina White.* (CCCR)

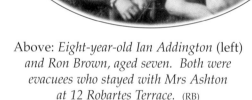

Above: *Eight-year-old Ian Addington* (left) *and Ron Brown, aged seven. Both were evacuees who stayed with Mrs Ashton at 12 Robartes Terrace.* (RB)

Above: *Spencer Brown, Mayor, inspects the Home Guard, 1944.* (LM)

Left: *Victory parade, 1946. Lostwithiel Band was led by Harry Goodman* (left) *and Joe Levers.*
(DP & CCCR E12999)

Chapter 11

THE WAR YEARS

The Second World War brought great changes to Lostwithiel, although the changes happened gradually as the war progressed. Many local men were called up, and into the town came 'troops' from far and wide, British, Javanese, Spanish and American. Lanwithan House, Boconnoc House, the Band Room and Grammar School were taken over. Farm buildings at Pill were requisitioned. The town became very full and busy. Women took over men's jobs, and everybody was involved in 'the war effort'. The older men who were not called up joined the Home Guard and had regular training in defence. Children helped with the collections of 'salvage', old pots, pans, newspapers and books to be recycled.

Mrs Christine Barnicoat (née Rowe), who was born in St Winnow Parish in 1914, provides a first-hand account of living in Lostwithiel during the war years. She worked in the Co-op office during its heyday between 1930–64 and has been involved with the town and the church all her life. She writes:

The Munich Agreement 1938 allowed us 12 months to prepare for what lay ahead and this time was put to good use. I had always had a horror of gas, having heard people talk about it after the First World War, so I decided the best thing to do was to learn how to deal with it. I had always been keen on first aid, too, and when ARP (air-raid precautions) volunteers were called for, I joined. Dr Rudge was in charge of the Ambulance and First Aid section. We learned to deal with the practical side of bandaging and splinting. This was before war was actually declared.

On 1 September 1939 the local Territorials, together with their searchlight, left to take up duty in the Plymouth area. It had been a familiar sight for some time, to see them practising, catching a passing plane in the beam, although this didn't always happen...

On 3 September Mum, Dad and I went to church as usual. Revd Webber delayed the start of the service. Mrs Webber had waited at home to hear Mr Chamberlain's 11a.m. announcement, she came in to tell the vicar, who told the congregation what had been said, 'war has been declared'.

The bells were silenced and evensong was stopped because blackout for the church was impossible. Right from the beginning of the war we had to 'black out' all windows with dark curtains and we were advised to

criss-cross the glass with sticky tape to prevent broken glass from flying, in the event of a blast from an explosion.

That was when I started knitting on a Sunday, a thing I had never done in the past, just one of the traditions the war swept aside (church people had refrained from leisure activities on Sundays). We knitted scarves, socks and balaclava helmets for the Red Cross to pass on to the troops. For ourselves we were busy with 'make do and mend'. As my mum said, 'We'd been doing that for years!'

The Youth Fellowship carried on playing badminton and organising social events to raise money for charities [and] later on to entertain troops billeted in the town. They ran dances in the Church Hall [otherwise known as the church rooms] for 1s.0d. or 1s.6d., in the Drill Hall it was 2s.6d. Music was provided by the Duchy Band. On one occasion the American Army provided a band, we needed earplugs.

At work, various members of the staff were called up and were replaced by girls, older men and part-time married women. When an air-raid alert was sounded, ARP members had to go to the 'report post' in the Municipal offices. Usually this involved just waiting for the 'all clear'. To begin with, all members reported, day and night. This was changed later and we worked on a rota system which was much better. We met regularly for practice and passed our first-aid exams. We also practised rescue work in Taprell House.

Early in 1940 a newspaper advert appeared, asking for people to train as Civil Nursing Reserves. Qualifications were two first-aid certificates, a Home Nursing certificate and 90 hours practical work in a hospital. Dr Rudge arranged Home Nursing classes (which later developed into a St John Ambulance Nursing Division under Miss May). He also arranged for me to work at the Emergency Hospital in Bodmin. This was a section of St Lawrence's taken over 'for the duration' (of the war). I worked there every Sunday 8a.m.–6p.m. as a nursing auxiliary, and later spent my annual holiday as a St John Nurse at the Redruth Miners' and General Hospital. I loved the work.

We had some service personnel at Bodmin, including Dunkirk casualties. Later we had patients from an old peoples' hospital in Epsom. The poor souls were so weary and confused on arrival after such a long journey.

After Dunkirk, troops were billeted in the town. The first were the 43rd Battery Royal Artillery with their vehicles and guns. They were at Pill Farm. Other places were taken over, [such as] Lanwithan House, the Band Room, the Grammar School and the King's Arms long room. The Church Hall was used by Roman Catholic evacuees as a school and place of worship. The Bank Chapel schoolroom was a rest centre (WVS) and the Weslyan schoolroom was a canteen.

The ARP gradually got uniforms, stretchers, blankets and a converted ambulance. Gwen Bailey's car was used for 'sitting cases'. Bert Thomas was the ambulance driver and I was his deputy. There were two First Aid and Rescue teams, led by Les Gardiner and myself. There were weekend schools at Port Eliot and county competitions to keep us on our toes.

The appearance of the countryside was changed by concrete blockhouses (or pill boxes) built along the roads as defence points in case of invasion and 'dragon's teeth' were built into the roads, also as an anti-invasion measure. All signposts were removed from town boundaries, road junctions and railway stations, and large water tanks were built in various parts of the town to hold reserve supplies. There was no street lighting and cars used only one headlamp, fitted with a darkened mask.

No bombs fell on Lostwithiel, but once it was strafed by gunfire from a plane and the church clock was a casualty, a small piece of its stonework was chipped. Old Mr Whetter had a piece of shrapnel hit his trilby hat! I was in the cinema at the time and the clatter as the plane went over was quite alarming. One night a stick of bombs was dropped, the Home Guard searched for them, thinking that they had not exploded. They had exploded in the river at full tide, and at low tide six craters were revealed. Two land-mines fell, one on Trewether Farm and one at Tollgate, again, thankfully, there were no casualties. One night during an alert, I was in Fore Street and saw a burning plane fly over, it looked like a fiery cross. I am not sure, but it could have been the Dornier that crashed at Boconnoc.

Lostwithiel Fire Brigade fought fires in the Plymouth blitz and Mr Tearle was killed in action there. We could clearly see the glow in the sky as Plymouth burned.

Special savings weeks were organised to raise money for the 'war effort'. 'Salute the Soldiers', 'War Weapons Week', 'Warship Week' and 'Wings for Victory Week' were all occasions for parades, when everybody would turn out. Special drives were made to collect scrap metal, garden railings were removed, kettles and aluminium saucepans [collected] to be built into Spitfires. The iron grille from the town gaol window was sawn off and left beneath the window for collection. It was never collected, so after the war it was reinstated.

Mum had a soldier and his wife billeted with her, Cyril and Rene Cave. One day Rene was poorly and the doctor said he would send a nurse to give her an enema. Rene told him there was a nurse in the house who would do it, so I did! Cyril and Rene moved on with the 43rd Battery Artillery. The Plymouth blitz brought lots of people [to Lostwithiel] wanting places to stay. We had

a family, Mr and Mrs O'Brian and their daughter Pat. Mr O'Brian used to work at HMS Raleigh at Torpoint, where he had been recalled as a CPO Naval Reserve. He left on the 5a.m. train every morning.

Fairly early in the war I started horse riding with Bird Truscott (later Mrs Bill Nicholls), Dad's cousin. Bird had two horses, Spinaway and Cinders. Double summertime gave us long evenings, and on my half day we rode all over the place, Fowey, Par, Bodmin Moor, Cardinham and many more places. It was a pleasant relaxation from our normal jobs. Bird joined the Land Army and occasionally I helped too.

At this time I was still running my car, but I laid it up in 1940 before it became compulsory, as I could not bear the thought of lives being lost bringing petrol to this country. I think the ration was 4 or 5 gallons a month. After this I bought my own horse, a bright chestnut called Lassie. Bird and I had endless pleasure with our horses. Lady Howe and Florrie Liddicoat often joined us on our rides.

When the district nurse was very busy, we St John nurses were called upon to help out. I remember one stint I did, which was to go each evening for a week to dress the ulcers on an old gent's leg.

As deputy driver of the Civil Defence ambulance, I was called to take an old lady from Lerryn to Bodmin hospital. It was very sad because her husband was also in bed sick and we felt pretty certain this was the final parting for them.

Various troops came and went, amongst them were Pioneer Corps, Spaniards, white and black Americans. There was also a number of young Javanese men, who had just escaped the Japanese invasion and joined the Dutch Navy, they were stationed at Pill.

Where we lived at 5 Bodmin Hill, our garden ran out to the wall of the Grammar School yard. The black Americans were billeted in the Grammar School and sometimes they would come into the yard and sing. They had good voices and it sounded fine – a choir, not fairies at the bottom of our garden! These Americans had set up a mobile laundry in Coulson Park.

In the early hours of one Sunday morning there was an alert and when we reported for duty at the ARP HQ we found a crowd of soldiers outside. They were delighted that we had to open up, and they all came inside and sat down. Apparently, while they had been dancing at the Drill Hall, someone had stolen their lorry and they had no transport back to camp some miles away. At breakfast time several of us helped to cook a meal for them at the King's Arms. Their lorry was found later in a lane near Pelyn.

Rationing meant a lot of extra work at the Co-op and we had an extra office to deal with coupons, etc. Our office also had to deal with dried milk, orange juice and cod liver oil for mothers and babies. The shop was allowed a certain amount of beef to make pasties, and customers had to queue up at the office window to get tickets in order to buy the pasties, first come, first served.

I kept up a correspondence with three or four local boys

who had joined up and I also had a pen-friend who was a New Zealander. He was a prisoner of war in Italy and later in Germany. When he was released in April 1945, he stayed here for two weeks before returning home to New Zealand. We kept in touch with him and his wife and then with several other members of his family.

Early in 1944, or maybe earlier, the build-up of munitions became evident. Special lay-bys along side roads and especially on Greymare, were made and soon piled high with shells. We got so accustomed to seeing this that it was accepted as part of the scenery. Then, suddenly, it all disappeared, soon to be followed by D-Day. Although there was a lot of hard fighting still to be done, it did seem at last, as though the end was in sight.

After V.E. day on 8 May 1945, the Civil Defence was stood down. We had a photo taken of the group which included Report Post staff, messengers, wardens, St John Ambulance nurses, First Aid and Rescue teams, drivers and attendants. We held a special social evening at the Royal Talbot Hotel and I presented Dr Rudge with a cheque.

Wartime conditions did not stop overnight but it was good to know that the fighting and bombing were over, at least in Europe.

When the Americans became involved in the war their troops took over Boconnoc House and the estate. Lostwithiel became a place for the storing of ammunition ready for the invasion of Europe. The Americans built a railway siding to the east of the station, and throughout the days and nights there was a continual banging and clanking as trucks arrived loaded with shells. These were transferred onto lorries and taken to be stored in great heaps along the surrounding roads and lanes. Gaps were cut into the hedges and more ammunition was stored in the fields.

Soldiers of all nationalities joined in the social life of the town, the dances in the Church Hall and the Drill Hall were always well attended, as the young people took a rest from their work and relaxed. The cinema was a popular rendezvous and queues for seats were longer during this period than they had ever been before. The Lostwithiel Choral Society continued to put on concerts throughout the war, under the direction of Mr Wilfred Jeffery, and these were always a great attraction and an important event in the town's social calendar. The pubs were full and, of course, there were fights from time to time, when military police were soon in evidence. The worst fight people remember was between two Spaniards, when one died following a stab wound. Generally, however, relationships were comfortable and friendly. Local people were hospitable and invited the soldiers into their homes. Evenings were spent enjoying a singsong around the piano or playing table games (monopoly was popular). The soldiers attended the church and chapels, singing the hymns lustily and even taking a service and preaching from time to

time. Some young girls of marriageable age found sweethearts at this time, married and moved away after the war – some sailed away as GI brides. Some of the young men settled here.

Through 1940–41 evacuees arrived regularly from London and Plymouth. Doreen Brown (née Newman) was five years old when she set off from Paddington Station on an eight-hour journey into the unknown. Arriving here tired, hungry and bewildered, the children were taken to the school to be allocated to their billets, where they met their foster parents. Doreen has been part of the Pearce family ever since, she has never left Lostwithiel. Doreen was not the only evacuee to stay in Lostwithiel, several of them are still here, their grandchildren now second-generation Cornish. Most of the children got on well with their new families. Occasionally there was a mismatch, as in the case of the little Jewish boy who refused to eat bacon and sausages, the staple diet of the family he had joined, who knew nothing of Jewish practice!

Country life was totally strange to the young Londoners. Some of them were very homesick. A group of them planned to go home, and decided to walk along the railway line which would take them back to London. They set off, but luckily they were discovered before they had reached the Liddicoat Road bridge!

Some of the children were fascinated by the animals in the market, they could not believe that the cows produced milk! They would sneak their way into the cattle pens where the 'mothers and calves' were waiting to be sold, and try to squeeze milk into matchboxes.

The house called 'Springfields' at Bridgend was run by Mrs Odessa Tomlin as a home for evacuees who were taken ill. Once they had recovered they returned to their foster homes.

Later in the war, German prisoners of war, many still teenagers, were brought here. Warren Nicholls, who lived beside the railway station, remembers them arriving – the train did not belong to GWR! They were lined up and marched to Lanescot, but before long they were sent out to local farms, to live and work with a minimum of supervision. The Italian POWs went first to a camp near St Nectan's Church. Lostwithiel Home Guard dealt with a Dornier aircraft, which had been damaged over Plymouth and had come down at Boconnoc. Many people remember it flying over Lostwithiel in flames. The crew of the plane perished and were buried in St Nectan's churchyard. Some 40 years later three unexploded bombs from the aircraft were discovered and detonated!

As D-Day approached convoys of RAF tankers drove regularly through Lostwithiel to ports further west. One of the drivers, a young Scot, remembers a motherly lady who had a roadside café here and served the drivers a meal of scrambled eggs as they passed through. The RAF boys called her

'Lostwithoutya'. The lady was Val Strout's grannie. Her family knew nothing of the drivers' pet name for her. The Scotsman was Ian Fraser's uncle, who wrote from Australia to tell this story, when Ian and author Barbara Fraser came to live in Lostwithiel.

In the spring of 1944 convoys of trucks, lorries and tanks passed through Lostwithiel, picking up the stocks of ammunition as they went. The soldiers left the town, which was suddenly very quiet and empty. The D-Day landings were about to start. Almost a year later the country was celebrating victory in Europe, and three months after that, victory in the Far East. Peace at last, after six years of a war in which everyone had been involved.

In 1946 the Mayor of Lostwithiel, Mr Wilfred Jeffery, presented a Certificate of Appreciation for service and sacrifices made during the Second World War, to all the Lostwithiel men who had served. This was given on behalf of the people of the town. There were ten siblings in the Ashton family. At the presentation, six brothers went up to receive their certificates, Alfred (Army), Arthur (Royal Navy), Bob (Army and Japanese POW camp), Bert (RAF), Frank (Army) and Ken (Army). Of the other two brothers, Max was in a reserved occupation and Garfield was too young to serve, although he joined the RAF after the war. They had two sisters, Nancy and Doreen. The Mayor said he knew of no other family with as many serving members. Had they lived, their parents would have been proud to share these moments with their children.

Every year the town pays its respects to those of the two wars who gave their lives. The church is always full for the Civic Service of Remembrance.

Appreciation Certificate for Active Service 1939–45. (JA)

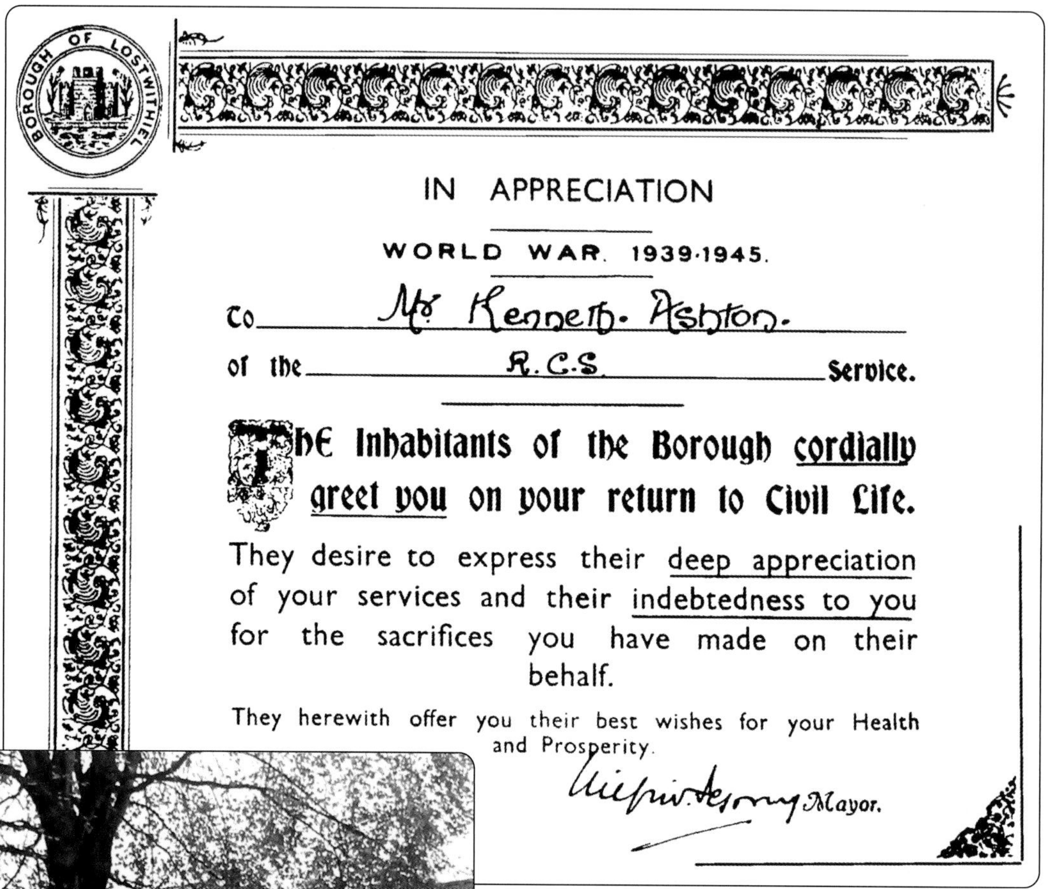

IN APPRECIATION

WORLD WAR. 1939-1945.

To _Mr Kenneth Ashton._

of the ___R.C.S.___ Service.

The Inhabitants of the Borough cordially greet you on your return to Civil Life.

They desire to express their deep appreciation of your services and their indebtedness to you for the sacrifices you have made on their behalf.

They herewith offer you their best wishes for your Health and Prosperity.

Mayor.

The Revd Fred Stevens blessing the new British Legion Memorial Cross, given to the town by Councillor Warren Nicholls. The Mayor, Councillor Chris Jewels, is in attendance, Remembrance Day, 2002. (IF)

Chapter 12

THE POSTWAR YEARS

Together with the rest of Britain, Lostwithiel saw rapid changes in lifestyle after the Second World War. As the men came home, the railway and the 'milk factory' offered plenty of employment. The phenomenon of 'working wives' had been accepted in British society. Women had become used to the benefits of having wages of their own and the added interest of work outside the home, particularly as schools provided midday meals for the children. People had also grown used to the idea of travelling, so there was greater mobility in and out of town and a greater variety of work available.

The social life of the town, which had continued throughout the war years, remained active. The local Amateur Dramatic Society and the Operatic Society, under the direction of Mr Wilfred Jeffery, put on regular performances in the Drill Hall. Smoking concerts were organised in the Wesleyan Sunday schoolroom. These were informal musical evenings, when small orchestral groups, solo singers, pianists and violinists would perform. They were very popular in the 1940s and 1950s. The church choir thrived, under the leadership of Charles Day (a talented musician, who played the classical piano, church organ and in a dance band). The cinema was a popular evening out for most folk, and there was a regular Saturday-night dance in the Drill Hall.

When the Education Act of 1944 was implemented after the war, secondary education was separated from primary, and all Lostwithiel's children over 11 years of age had to travel to Fowey, Bodmin or St Austell to attend school. It was unfortunate for Lostwithiel that secondary education went elsewhere as great opportunities for the development of art, drama, dance, music and sport were lost to the town. Gradually, the local societies began to find it difficult to attract enough younger people to keep them alive, interests had changed, and eventually the Choral and the Dramatic Societies were discontinued.

The building of council-houses, which had started before the war, gathered pace, and those condemned houses that were still inhabited were demolished in the 1950s.

The old custom of 'beating the bounds' was revived in 1946. This still takes place biennially. Townspeople walk the 17 miles around the boundary

Above: *Lostwithiel was busy building houses after the war, 1946.* (LM)

Left: *King George VI and Queen Elizabeth visit the town in 1950.* (LM)

BOROUGH OF LOSTWITHIEL.

PLAYING FIELD

A PUBLIC MEETING

To consider the provisions of a PLAYING FIELD for the Borough, will be held in the

CHURCH ROOM,

ON

THURSDAY, 20th October, 1949,

at 7-30 p.m.

As the subject of the meeting is of vital importance to you, please make an effort to be present.

W. T. ROBINS,

MAYOR.

Above: *Beating the bounds, 1952. Lady Howe is on horseback* (bending) *and Christine Barnicoat is walking* (fifth from left). (CB)

Left: *Announcing a meeting regarding provision of a playing-field.* (DP)

Below right: *The Mayor, Mr Sydney Brewer, proclaims the Accession of HM Queen Elizabeth II, February, 1952.* (CCCR E22165)

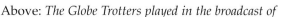

Below: *Queen Elizabeth II and the Duke of Edinburgh in Lostwithiel, 1962. The Mayor, Albert Sykes, was also the vicar.* (LM)

Above: *The Globe Trotters played in the broadcast of 'Have a Go', 1958. Left to right: Ron Brown, Joe Pearce, a visitor from the BBC, Charlie Stephens* (standing), *Cyril Tabb* (seated) *and Bert Vincent.* (DB)

of the town, touching each of the boundary stones as they go, and receiving a thwack with a stick and a new penny from the Mayor at each stone. This is done to ensure that they will not forget where the boundaries of the town lie. In 2003 a boundary stone dating from the nineteenth century was dug out of the ground near Nomansland. It is believed to have been buried at the outbreak of the last war and forgotten (all signposts were removed, in case of a German invasion).

St Faith's Penitentiary for Girls was closed down in 1950 and the building was sold. The memorial brasses are in St Nectan's Chapel.

It was during the 1950s that the King George V playing-field was acquired for the benefit of the town's youngsters. Access was made from the A390, and this new road also gave access to the cattle market, which relieved the pressure on North Street, until then the only entrance to the market.

Meanwhile British Rail had supplanted the GWR and work in the maintenance sheds was drying up, causing distress to some families. However, the milk factory, which was going from strength to strength, was able to accommodate most of the redundant railway workers, in the same way that the railway had provided work for the unemployed miners, half a century earlier. The milk factory also provided regular work for women and girls, and much of the social life of the town was connected with it.

Lostwithiel enjoyed a moment of national fame when Wilfred Pickles brought his BBC Radio Show 'Have a Go' to town in May 1958. The show was broadcast live and there was much fun and hilarity.

The new Elizabethan era saw a boom in the popularity of television, and the Glyn Cinema was forced to close its doors in 1960. More people were buying motor cars and travelling out of town for work, entertainment and shopping. This began to have an effect on business in the town.

In 1962 flats for the elderly were built on the site of the old mill at the bottom of Tanhouse Lane. A happy event of that year was the broadcast on Christmas Day of St Bartholomew's church bells. This was a red-letter day for the ringers, who were widely acclaimed and congratulated, and the occasion is still remembered with pleasure and pride.

Five years later, in 1967, the Wesleyan Chapel was demolished. Then, as a result of local government reorganisation in 1968, Lostwithiel lost its borough status. The borough of Restormel was created, which includes much of mid-Cornwall from Newquay to St Austell. The Town Council was allowed to continue its ancient traditions, and Mayor Choosing and the Annual Civic Service are still very much part of the life of the town, but the important aspects of local government are now the concern of Restormel Borough Council, very little power being left with Lostwithiel Council. However, having greater resources, Restormel was able to bring about some overdue improvement

Charles Day conducting St Bartholomew's choir in the 1960s. Charles was choirmaster and organist for almost 30 years, then served as organist at Boconnoc for a further 20 years. (CD)

Building the flood defences along the western bank of the River Fowey, 1968. (CBu)

Strengthening the foundations of the medieval bridge, 1970s. (CBu)

schemes. In 1968 flood defences along the western bank of the river were started, and in 1974 a sewage-treatment works was built downstream from Coulson Park. By the 1980s the treatment works was deemed to be working to capacity, and there was an embargo on domestic building in the town until 1993, when the works were enlarged. Since then there has been a spate of building and once again in 2003 the disposal plant is reaching full capacity.

The 1970s saw the building of the housing estate at Butts Park, the opening of the museum, the closing down of the cattle market, Queen Elizabeth's silver jubilee, the last serious flooding in the town and the beginning of a highly valued relationship with Pleyber-Christ, our twin town in Brittany. Much of the early bonding had been initiated during the Mayoralty of Ricky Isaacs, Ricky and his Mayoress, Mavis worked hard to see it to fruition. The Twinning Charter was signed by the Mayor, Councillor Jim Jeffery, in 1979, and every year since then there have been cordial exchange visits between the two well-matched, small towns.

Twinning, 1979. The Mayor and Mayoress, Councillor and Mrs Jim Jeffery, with the Mayor and Mayoress of Pleyber-Christ, M. et Mme Coulon. (CBu)

The start of the 1980s was marked by petitions and protests against the demolition of the old wooden railway buildings at Lostwithiel Station. Designed by Brunel, and in use since 1859, these historic buildings were believed not to be in need of replacement, but British Rail decreed otherwise. To everyone's sorrow they were replaced by modern structures. However, elsewhere in town buildings were going up. The foundations of the new community centre were put down in 1982. The town owes a great deal to the late Rex Stephens, Meg Breckon and a host of willing helpers who perceived the need for this building – they believed in this project and saw it through. The Town Council bought the land, and gave the Memorial Fund (set up after the war) to get it started, but the bulk of the funding was raised by the efforts of the community itself. Opened in 1983, the centre is run by the Community Association and caters for the needs of everyone from toddlers to the elderly. It provides facilities for clubs, concerts, drama, dancing, badminton, squash, markets, public meetings, private parties, fairs, the pre-school playgroup and pensioners' lunches and, when needed, it functions as a polling-station! The staff are always extremely busy. The Tourist Information Centre also has its office here. By the 1990s it became necessary

to extend the building to provide more space for youth activities. Funding was found and the young people of Lostwithiel were very much involved in the planning. This additional building is known as 'Oasis'. As well as serving the young people, it provides twice-weekly accommodation for the Cornwall Headway Association (for people suffering the effects of head injuries) and the River Church. The monthly newsletter produced by the association is invaluable, enabling all the organisations in the town to publicise their activities, keeping everyone in touch with what is happening.

In 1983 a new drying tower was constructed at the creamery. This was bigger and taller than planning permission allowed and it was out of scale with the town, causing much controversy. It was ugly, but it seemed to guarantee jobs. However, by 1991 the factory was redundant and the offending tower was dismantled and shipped abroad.

A group of businessmen had taken over the old railway sheds during the 1980s and developed them into the Great Western Industrial Village in an attempt to provide more work. This made a good start, but a fire in 1987 put several units permanently out of action. In 2003 there is a bigger and more accessible industrial estate developing on the site of the creamery, which provides a variety of work.

Fighting the fire at the Great Western Industrial Village, 1987. (LM)

The second lorry to go out of control in recent years. Nobody was hurt in this 1990s accident. (LM)

Also in 1987 there was a horrendous accident, when the driver of a heavy lorry lost control of the vehicle coming down the hill into town and destroyed several buildings. This had happened a number of times before and two similar accidents have occurred since. A German driver who lost his life in 2001 was buried in the cemetery in Lostwithiel. After this last accident, traffic regulations were put into effect to deter heavy vehicles from using this road.

Donald Parsons delivers a telegram from the Queen to Mrs Mary Brewer on her 100th birthday in 1986 (the only one to be delivered in Lostwithiel within living memory). (CBu)

The Queen signs a photograph in the Mayor's Parlour, June 1989. Left to right: An official visitor, Town Clerk Fran Dennison, Deputy Mayor Ida Keast, Mayor Dennis Hutchings, HM Queen Elizabeth, HRH The Duke of Edinburgh, Honoured Burgess of Lostwithiel Paul Brewer. (JB)

The pageant to celebrate Lostwithiel's 800th anniversary in 1989. Lord Cardinham and his Lady ride up to their castle. Left to right: Peter Chew, Jill Reed, Stephanie Chapman, Jo Retallack, John Reed. (JB)

Lostwithiel hosts the Cornish Gorsedd in 1989. (JB)

The Bank Methodist Chapel finally closed after a long struggle to survive, and was developed into flats after 1987.

Meanwhile, the town was starting to plan its celebrations for the 800th anniversary of its first Charter. This took place in 1989 and was marked by a royal visit and a pageant, written by the late Gwen Powell-Jones and performed by a large proportion of the population, in the grounds of Restormel Castle. There was a memorable medieval market in the Parade Gardens, organised by the Chamber of Commerce, numerous concerts, parties, an extra-special carnival week, and Lostwithiel had the honour of hosting the Cornish Gorsedd, the annual assembly of Cornish Bards, that year. Lostwithiel won a Britain in Bloom trophy, the town took real pleasure in its appearance, and there was a great feeling of civic

Members of the Lostwithiel in Bloom committee with their awards in 1989. Left to right: an official visitor, Paul Brewer, Mr Gaffney, Mayoress Dawn Hutchings, Mr Stan Parkyn, Mrs Margaret Parkyn, Mr Mason, Mayor Dennis Hutchings, Councillor Robert Peareth; seated at front: Kitty Chanter, Doreen Brown and Pam Hutchings. (CBu)

pride and an excellent community spirit. The last event of 1989 was the annual Christmas pageant. It poured with rain but, undeterred, everyone trooped into the community centre and, fortified by hot soup and mulled wine, enjoyed the indoor programme. It had been a year to remember.

By the 1980s large stores on the outskirts of St Austell and Bodmin were opening up and attracting shoppers away from smaller, town-centre stores. Shops in Lostwithiel were finding it hard to compete, and the number of empty shops began to rise. The hardware store, women's outfitter, health-food shop, greengrocer, and one or two butchers and grocers closed. Other occupants took over, not always enjoying great success. The businesses that succeeded best were antique shops and cafés. These were helped by the already established antique businesses and by the regular sales and auctions held in Lostwithiel by Jeffery's, which attract dealers from far and wide.

Opening the new surgery, 1992. Left to right: *Mrs Maggie Wombwell, Mr John Wombwell, Mrs Sheila Hanson, Mrs Rosemary Kerr, Mrs Dawn Hutchings, Mayor John Reed, Mrs Michie, Dr Alistair Michie, Mrs Liz Allardice, Mr Dennis Hutchings* (in shadow), *Dr Bowen, Dr Mrs Bowen, Mayoress Mrs Jill Reed.* (CBu)

Inaugurating the recycling bank, 1992. Left to right: *Richard Bower, Lesley Bright-Roberts, Wendy Costello, Adam Richardson, Ian Chanter, Maggie Wombwell, Mayor John Reed, George Bright-Roberts, John Pegg, Meg Breckon, Jenna Pegg, Town Clerk Fran Dennison, Lesley Bower, Jade Bower, Rosina Bower.* (JB)

There has been further development of the antiques trade in the last two decades of the twentieth century. It is still growing, and attracting attention nationally.

The 1990s brought further changes, a new medical centre and a new fire station, both important to the life of the town. The Golf and Country Club, developed from farm land on the edge of Lostwithiel, has been a great success. Attracting members from a wide area, and catering for holiday visitors, conferences and private functions, it provides work for local people and increased trade in the town, as well as being a welcome amenity for many local golfers, swimmers, tennis players and keep-fit enthusiasts.

In 1990 the local Conservative Club finally allowed women to be members and was one of the last four in the country to do so!

On the other hand, Lostwithiel was one of the first towns in Cornwall to take recycling seriously, a group of enthusiasts organised local recycling banks well before the idea was taken up more widely by the borough.

Since 1993 many new houses have been built. Some of these have been small 'infill' developments, blending comfortably into the old town. However, there are also new estates on the surrounding hills which are thought, by some, to be architecturally out of character with the town. For many years it has been laid down that Lostwithiel must have more houses, and it is a fact of life that housing estates will be built in the modern idiom. What is most important is that the people who live in the new houses feel comfortable and happy here and enjoy the rich and many faceted community life Lostwithiel has to offer. There are over 40 different clubs and organisations in the town, something to suit almost every taste and talent, and they all extend a warm welcome to new members.

Lostwithiel is generally a peaceful town but towards the end of the twentieth century it was deeply disturbed. This was after the Town Council rented a piece of land from the Duchy of Cornwall, a few acres of low-lying meadow beside the river, to the north of the A390. The idea was for residents to use it as a park. The council organised a competition to find a name for it, won by Mrs Elsie Vague with the title 'Second Island Park'. This referred to an island in the river where those of her generation had played as children. In order to gain access to the park, one had to cross the main road, so a plan was developed to build a walkway beside the river, under Liddicoat Bridge. American servicemen stationed at St Morgan volunteered to do the work. Funding was made available for materials and the hire of equipment, and a contractor was signed up to provide these. Then things began to go wrong. The original price agreed with the contractor was £12,326, but this was increased to over £28,000 because the National River Authority insisted on the clearing of a sandbank after the initial figure had been agreed.

The contractor was paid in full, but he abandoned the project, having done work valued at less than £6,000. New contractors were found, but the final costs escalated to £57,000, and the council had to take a loan to pay the bills. The American servicemen stuck with the project throughout and it could not have been completed without them.

There were detailed investigations into the affair by both the district auditor and the police. Before the investigations were completed the original contractor had died and the council was in disarray. The Town Clerk, Mayor and two councillors resigned and two ex-Mayors declined to stand for re-election. There were recriminations, and although the auditor's report was made public, only those intimately involved know how mistakes were allowed to happen. No police charges were made and, on legal advice, the council did not seek any compensation. In his report the auditor made a number of recommendations for future procedures by the council. The Mayor of Lostwithiel, who had resigned, was later elected to represent the town on the Restormel Borough Council.

People of the town, who had hitherto taken very little interest in the affairs of the council, woke up to the fact that there were problems. They started to attend council meetings, as there were many questions to be asked. However, questions were not allowed at these meetings. Confidence in the council was badly shaken and when, in 2000, two more councillors resigned, there were an unprecedented six candidates and a turnout of 30 per cent of possible voters at the by-election.

The council agreed to allow written questions from the public, submitted a week in advance, to be read out and answered immediately prior to council meetings. For some time people in the public gallery outnumbered councillors at these meetings, letters were submitted and many complaints and grievances were aired. This has been a good thing, as relationships between the town and its council have improved. As a result of 'prudent housekeeping' the chairman of the Finance Committee was able to recommend that the council pay back the loan in 2003. In 2003 public interest has waned again. At local election time, seven councillors resigned and only three stood to take their place, so there was no election. The council is now left to co-opt four members, 25 per cent of its membership. However, there was a reasonable turnout for the election of two councillors to the Restormel Borough Council.

Despite all this, the year 2000 proved to be a time when the town came together once more in glorious celebration. As the town clock in the church tower struck the midnight hour, signalling the new millennium, the now-traditional New Year Parade of Giants made its way through the town, accompanied by hundreds of people. Then the bells of St Bartholomew's Church rang out to welcome the New Year and there was merrymaking, music and fireworks until well into the early hours of 1 January 2000. There was music, dancing, art and drama throughout the year, which took place in the streets, the playing-field and the parks. The small millennium committee, John Pegg, Meg Breckon, Maryse Jeffery, Brendon Moore, Sue Grigg and Rowan Metcalfe, had worked very hard and prepared a programme of events that was a joy to everyone.

An interesting exhibition called 'Found in Lostwithiel' illustrated and celebrated the variety and number of businesses and enterprises to be found in the town, and there were many more than most people had thought. Although not all were represented in the exhibition, there are approaching 100 small businesses in Lostwithiel in 2003.

'Lostwithiel in Bloom' was a new venture, inaugurated in 2000. A voluntary non-competitive organisation was set up to raise money and do the work, to provide floral displays for the town's streets and approach roads. This was initiated by Peter and Diane Best who, together with a willing army of volunteers, dug, planted and watered. Shopkeepers and householders responded to the spirit of the venture, and colourful flowers brightened up the approaches to the town and the grey stones of Lostwithiel's ancient buildings. This enterprise continues from year to year and is supported and appreciated by many people in the town.

Many others worked hard to make every undertaking a success. The Rotary Club's carnival week was packed with exciting and enjoyable events. Although 2000 was one of the wettest of recent years, only one event was spoiled by rain. At the opening of the permanent sculpture exhibition in Second Island Park the rain was so heavy that the park became a quagmire and the small, assembled gathering retired to the Mayor's Parlour! The year ended with the Christmas pageant and finally the New Year Parade of Giants, in a spirit of goodwill and optimism for the future.

One of the giants in the
New Year parade, 2000. (IF)

Left: *Golden jubilee party at Byways, June 2002. The group includes: Geraldine Hoare, Ann Brewer, Mrs Dunn, Jean Hick, Joe Biggins, Joyce and Ken Hatton, David Robson, Keith Hatton, Pauline and Clive Dustow, Mayor Chris Jewels and Mayoress Ann Jewels.* (IF)

Right: *New buildings on the Brunel Quay housing development nearing completion, June 2003.* (IF).

Left: *In 2002 the Car Centre on Quay Street was demolished.* (IF)

Right: *For two weeks in May 2002 there was a unique opportunity to see the Duchy Palace opened up to the river. During this short time excavations were carried out by the Cornwall Archaeological Unit.* (IF)

For years the future of the old GWR engine sheds and the railway yard has been discussed. Some people dreamed of a community arts centre, with theatre, museum, art gallery, studios and workshops, but it did not happen. Eventually the site was bought for housing and office development, and at the time of writing work is going ahead to convert the old Brunel buildings along the river, and to build further flats. Planning authorities are instructed to link new housing developments with the rest of the community. The Restormel planners therefore proposed a footbridge over the river from the Brunel site to the Parade. This caused a major uproar and another site further downstream, near to the railway bridge, has been proposed, although at the time of going to press nothing has been resolved. Perhaps nothing will be done until the building is completed, the new residents have moved into their flats, and their views are heard.

A wonderful opportunity to open up the river front opposite the Duchy Palace, was lost when the old garage on the site of the medieval quay was sold to the Co-op. Many people who were in favour of having a Co-op backing onto the river (where older residents remember there was a Co-op in years gone by) are now having second thoughts. Since its opening in 2002, the heavy delivery vehicles have caused problems along Fore Street, mounting the footpath and driving within inches of the shop fronts.

The Eden Project, which has achieved international fame and acclaim since it opened in 2001, is only six miles from Lostwithiel. It has already had an impact on this small town, in that many more people are visiting and staying here, and discovering its charms.

Lostwithiel's heritage and unique place in Cornish history is appreciated more widely year by year. Those who have not visited before are surprised and delighted by the lovely countryside surrounding the town. The antique shops are attracting new people from far afield, catering and accommodation is of a high standard, and providing for the holiday visitors is becoming increasingly important to the town's economy. As this develops it is important for everyone that Lostwithiel maintains a fine balance – it must be sure to keep intact the very character that makes it an attractive place to visit and a compelling place in which to live.

Left: *By October 2002 the Co-op had replaced the Car Centre.* (IF)

Right: *The Drill Hall, occupying an historic riverside site, was once the venue for many social activites. In 2003 it is used only by the Army Cadets and its fabric is sadly neglected* (IF)

=== *Church Bells* ===

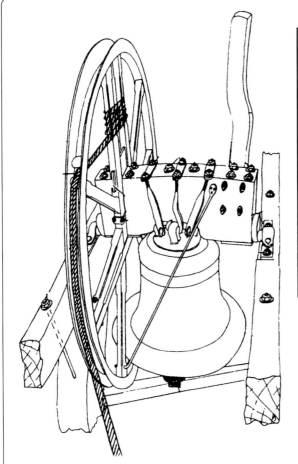

Old Ringing Tower Rules, c.1700

We ring the quick to church, the dead to grave
Good is our use, such usage let us have
Now up on end, at stay, come let us see
What laws are best to keep. Sobriety,
To swear or curse or, in a choleric mood
To strike or quarrel, though he draw no blood
Or by unskilful handling mar a peal
Such shall pay sixpence for each single crime
T'will make him cautious against another time.
What forfeitures are due in here expressed
Here is a box to take the same when ye
have transgrest
And we, the whole society of ringers do agree
To use the same in love and unity.

Left: *Drawing showing the mechanism of a church bell.* (SBC)

Ringers of the Christmas Day broadcast, 1962. Left to right: Donald Dunkley, George Stephens (captain of the tower), Arthur Pope, Ernest Clook, Howard West, Jack Riddle. (SBC)

Chapter 13

THE CHANGING PATTERNS OF COMMUNITY LIFE

It is evident that there are many varied activities taking place throughout the year in Lostwithiel. Organisations have to compete for space to pin their posters on the notice-boards around the town, and the telegraph poles are frequently put to this good use.

Over the years many institutions and organisations have come and gone, meeting the needs and interests of the people, although many have stood the test of time, changing and developing as occasion demanded. The old employers, the railway, cattle market and creamery are no longer part of the life of the town, but many long-established, voluntary organisations go from strength to strength. These, together with many more recently established groups, make up the life of the community. The bell-ringers company of Saint Bartholomew's Church is perhaps the oldest.

THE BELLS & RINGERS OF ST BARTHOLOMEW'S

For at least five centuries the people of Lostwithiel have heard the church bells ringing out across the valley, calling the faithful to worship, proclaiming a wedding or lamenting a death, celebrating a victory or a national event. For almost three centuries, until 1939, the fourth bell was the 'fire bell' to summon help to fight a fire.

As midnight approached on 31 December 1999 the lantern tower and steeple of St Bartholomew's Church were bathed in light and a small crowd gathered to watch the hands of the town clock, as the twentieth century slipped away and the third millennium took its place. The master of the bells rang the midnight hour on the tenor bell, before the six bells in the tower rang out a joyous peal of welcome to the new century. The ringers on this historic occasion were Simon Brewer (master), David Dunkley, Marc Dunkley, Geoff Brewer, Graham Hoskins, Liz Chudleigh and Malcolm Hicks. At midday on Saturday, 1 January 2000 the bells pealed once more, together with the bells of every other church in the land.

In 2003 there are six bells in the tower. Numbers one, two, three and six provide the clock chimes, and number six (tenor) strikes the hour. There is a lever in the ringers' chamber attached to the wall, which detaches the hammers, used for the clock, away from

the bells while they are being rung manually. If these hammers were not detached, severe damage would result. The exceptions are the fourth and fifth bells, which are not used for the clock. This is why the fourth bell was always used as the fire bell. It is because the striking hammers were detached, ready for the ringers, that the midnight hour at the millennium was rung manually.

Bell-ringing can be a lifelong interest. Ringers enjoy the close companionship and loyalty of the team. To illustrate this, there have been just four captains of St Bartholomew's tower throughout the twentieth century. In the year 2000 there were 15 ringers at Lostwithiel. Simon Brewer, the captain in 2003, says 'The best age to start is between 12 and 13'.

Mr Donald Dunkley, who first learned the art of bell-ringing at St Bartholomew's as a boy, was a regular ringer here for 30 years, before moving to Truro, where he has been a member of the Truro Cathedral company of ringers for many years. Donald has collected a great deal of information about the Lostwithiel bells, and much of the information that follows is from his research and personal memories.

Between the years 1547–53 a Mr E.H.W. Dunkin made an inventory of church bells in Cornwall. In it he recorded 'Lostwythiel Item iii bellys'. The fourth bell was probably added when a clock was installed some time after 1641.

In the year 1757 there was a great storm in Lostwithiel. Lightning struck the spire, 20 feet of which was 'entirely thrown down', crashing through the roof, damaging pews, windows and much besides. The spire was so badly cracked and damaged that it had to be taken down. The falling masonry, and possibly the lightning strike itself, played havoc with the clock, bells and all their intricate mechanisms, smashing wheels, iron straps and supporting beams. Mr Smeaton, who was at that time engaged in building his lighthouse off Plymouth, came to Lostwithiel and wrote a detailed account of the damage. Seven years later, the bells were recast and a fifth one added. The work was done by the Penningtons, a family of bell founders who had come from Devon and set up a business in Stoke Climsland, which operated for well over 100 years. The lettering on the bells was in capital letters. The first bell was inscribed, "I CALL YOU ALL TO FOLLOW ME'

PENNINGTON FECIT 1764*.' The diameter at the mouth, 26½ inches. On the second bell was the inscription 'PENNINGTON FECIT 1764'. The diameter at the mouth, 27 inches. The third bell was marked '*JOHN WESTLAKE JUN. AND JOHN JOHNS, CW+ PENNINGTON FECIT 1764.' The diameter at the mouth, 29½ inches. The fourth bell was inscribed, 'THE REV. JONATHAN BARON, VICAR AND MAYOR+ PENNINGTON FECIT 1764.' The diameter at the mouth, 31½ inches. Finally, the fifth had the inscription, 'THE GIFT OF THE RT. HONBLE. LORD EDGCUMBE, RECORDER: PENNINGTON FECIT 1764.' The diameter at the mouth, 34½ inches.

In 1876 the church suffered another violent storm, and yet again the spire was damaged. It was decided that a major restoration of the church should be undertaken, as there were other alterations the Parish Council wished to make. When the spire had been rebuilt in 1764 it had not been raised to its original height, so in 1878 it was given an extra five feet, raising it to 110 feet in total. The bells were rehung at this time.

In 1924 the bells were all recast by Gillet & Johnston and a treble bell was added, thereafter called 'Number One' (thus moving the titles of the existing bells up by one number), giving Lostwithiel a peal of six.

Lostwithiel belfry is unusual in that, owing to the restricted space, the bells are hung at various levels. Musical expertise and great engineering skills were required to ensure the balance and harmony of the peal.

The ringers of Lostwithiel have a long and distinguished record, having won many awards over the years. *The West Briton* on 26 July 1839 reported that a ringing match in Bodmin, contested by 11 sets of ringers, had been won by Lostwithiel, with a first prize of eight sovereigns (a very large sum of money in those days). For many years there were cash prizes for bell-ringing contests. This practice was eventually discontinued throughout the Diocese of Truro by Bishop Key (1960–73). It did nothing to dampen the enthusiasm of the ringers, who were perfectly happy to compete against other towers in friendly rivalry and receive nothing more than certificates as proof of their successes.

In November 1958 *The Cornish Times* wrote that the senior members of Lostwithiel ringers had formed a team, the combined age of which was 444 years. They challenged other towers to produce a team to match their ages. The peal they rang was described as 'a first-class touch' proving they had lost none of their skills. Their challenge was never taken up.

Willie Burrows wrote the following piece in *The Cornish Guardian* on 29 November 1962:

Honour for a Cornish Tower.
A feature of the Christmas broadcast will be 'Bells around the World' in which a team of Cornish bell-ringers will play a prominent part. *The BBC, having consulted the Central Council of Bellringers, have chosen a Cornish tower to represent the three western counties of Somerset, Devon and Cornwall. The demand was for a six bell peal of Call Changes, and the BBC has selected the bells of the Parish Church of St Bartholomew, Lostwithiel.*

A recording was made on Tuesday 14 December, a bitterly cold night. The ringers were: George Stephens (captain), Arthur Pope, Ernest Clook, Howard West, John Riddle and Donald Dunkley (tenor). The peal was conducted by George Stephens, who also called the 120 changes. It was broadcast on Christmas morning in 1962. The ringing was of the highest standard and was hailed by critics and experts from all parts of the UK as an outstanding example of call-change ringing. Both the tower and the BBC received complimentary letters from all over the world.

Donald Dunkley writes:

In June 1971 the Truro Diocesan Guild of Bellringers paid a special tribute to Mr George Stephens, to commemorate his 87th birthday, and his 45 years as Captain of the Tower and Ringers of St Bartholomew's. The peal chosen was the beautiful but complicated 'Stedman Doubles'. The peal consisted of 5,040 changes, with 15 callings, and took 2 hours 32 minutes to complete. Throughout the peal, not a single change

St Bartholomew's bell-ringers, June 2003. Left to right, back row: *Brenda Gilbert, David Dunkley, John Woolley, Jim Pearn, Graham Hoskin, Geoff Brewer, Malcolm Hicks, Liz Lutey;* centre: *Mike Fitzpatrick, Margaret Burgess, Simon Brewer (captain of the tower), Sonia Pearce;* front row: *Shirley Hooper, Scott Carthew, Marc Dunkley.* (IF)

is repeated and at the end the bells must ring 1:2:3:4:5:6. George stayed with us for a long time, before going for tea. On his return we were just finishing the peal, and as we finished he came over to us with tears in his eyes saying 'I take my hat off to you, I take my hat off to you, a perfect peal if ever there was one.'

George Stephens died in 1974 at the age of 90. He had been born in St Veep and had first learned to ring as a youngster on the famous Pennington virgin ring. As a last tribute to George, five of the band who rang for the 1962 broadcast, plus the new captain, Simon Brewer, rang the bells of St Bartholomew's half muffled. Donald goes on to write:

I feel very proud that St Bartholomew's is my Mother Church, and that I was taught to ring there under the guidance of George Stephens. I am so pleased to find... that the tradition and good practice of ringing is maintained. Great credit is due to Simon Brewer, who has been the captain of the tower for almost 30 years. Simon too was a trainee under George Stephens. It is good to see that all the members of Simon's family are ringers, and closely associated with the tower.

I am proud too that my son David, also a pupil of George Stephens, and grandson Marc are regular ringers at St Bartholomew's.

LOSTWITHIEL FIRE SERVICE

Lostwithiel's need for a fire service was probably at its greatest in the Middle Ages, when the houses were small, huddled together, built largely of timber and thatched with straw. It is likely that when fires occurred everyone would turn out as quickly as possible, carrying buckets of water from the river, but there are no records of this.

During the seige of Lostwithiel in the Civil War, fires were recorded at Bridgend. Cottages were set alight by fire from a Royalist gun on Beacon Hill. In the same month, August 1644, the Duchy Palace was destroyed by fire. This was an act of vandalism by the occupying Parliamentary Army, whose soldiers outnumbered the population by about ten to one and who would have been sure to prevent any attempt at fire-fighting.

As the people rebuilt their town they developed the beginnings of a fire-fighting service, one of the

Lostwithiel's first fire-engine from 1761. (LM)

The steam fire-engine, 1904, called 'Loveday'. (LM)

Contemporary magazine illustration of the fire at Lanhydrock in 1881. Lostwithiel Fire Brigade was one of many to attend this fire. (DB)

first in Cornwall. The new bell (the fourth), installed in the church tower after the Civil War, was used as a fire bell to summon all able-bodied men to man the fire buckets. The practice of using the church bell as a fire bell continued for almost 300 years, until the outbreak of war in 1939. During this war the ringing of church bells was used only as a warning of invasion and a siren was used instead to signal a fire.

Lostwithiel's first 'fire engine' was the gift of Lord Edgcumbe in 1761. This is now exhibited in the museum. The appliance (basically a portable water trough) was hauled to the fire by several men and the troughs filled with water from buckets. The water was hand pumped, using a pump handle at each end of the appliance. The hose could direct the water a distance of about 25 feet. It was replaced in 1804 by a more efficient, horse-drawn pump, operated manually by a pump handle on each side. This engine, or one like it, together with others from neighbouring towns, attended the major fire at Lanhydrock in 1881, when much of the building was destroyed.

The first steam-powered fire-engine was a horse-drawn 'Merryweather' of the Cam type, purchased in 1904. The Mayoress, Mrs Hext, officially started the engine, which was named 'Loveday' in honour of her daughter. The Mayor, George Hext, was the captain of Lostwithiel's Volunteer Fire Brigade at the time.

Firemen in 1920s.
Left to right,
back row:
A. Brown,
F. Phillips,
A. Alexander,
W. Tearle;
front: *P. Eade,*
W.H. Talling,
C. Jeffery,
H. Nicholls,
F. Jones,
R. Walkham,
C. Vine,
E. Carne. (LM)

The fire station was for many years in Church Lane, but by 1914 it had been moved to the old Corn Exchange, the museum in 2003. This is where the 'Loveday' was housed. One of the more notable fires attended by a 'steamer' was a farm fire at Bosmaugan, where there was more cider than water available for fire fighting and the cider was used very successfully!

The 'Loveday' gave good service for many years. It was eventually restored in about 1950 and sold to a Mr Parsons of St Columb for £20. Soon after this 'Loveday' was hired out to help pump out a quarry, earning four times the purchase price in fees!

In September 1939 the National Fire Service was formed and the Lostwithiel Unit was commanded by Section Leader Bill Tearle. It had a trailer pump, which was kept in the Fore Street station, and was drawn by a lorry kept at Skelton's Garage, Bridgend. Motorised vehicles had taken the place of horses to draw the engines some time earlier. The Lostwithiel NFS was frequently called out for duty in Plymouth, Devonport and Torpoint during the blitz of 1940–41. In April 1941 24,000 incendiary bombs were dropped on Plymouth. Three quarters of the total damage done to the city was caused by fire. During one of these raids Section Leader Tearle, commanding the Lostwithiel Unit, lost his life. He was one of Lostwithiel's earliest casualties of the war. Section Leader Wilfred Jeffery took over command of the unit. In his team were, amongst others, Percy, Frank and Joe Pearce, Sid Abbiss, Harry Nicholls, Owen Huddy, Ned Talling, Jim Jeffery and Alwyn Ball.

During the war, young women volunteered for duty in the NFS. There were two full-time members and 12 part-timers. They were paid a retainer, issued with a uniform and attended training sessions once a week. They were: Leading Firewoman Lorna Hawken (Mrs Turpie), Jean and Betty Wevell (Mrs Hick and Mrs Semmens) Mavis Bennett, Iris Nicholls, May Guswell, Edie Nancollas, Alice Jolliffe, Pat Sherwell

(Mrs Jeffery), Pat Broom, Betty Wikinson (Mrs Rawlings) and Rita May. Hilda Chilwell (Mrs Yeo) and Myrtle Tearle were the full-time firewomen.

The part-timers did one evening a week on duty, between 7p.m. and 9p.m. They staffed the fire station and were in telephone communication with the station at Bodmin and the local Chief Fire Officer. Betty Rawlings remembers that the first job they did when they came on duty, after checking in with Bodmin, was to light the fire in the old gaol! This must have been very much appreciated by the firemen who took over the duty from them. Every night throughout the war, four firemen spent the night in bunks in the old gaol (unless they were called out). One of their extra duties was to sound the air-raid siren when necessary. The message came by telephone: 'air-raid warning yellow' or 'air-raid warning red'. If it was a red warning the siren (kept in Edgcumbe House) was sounded.

In 1948 the County Fire Brigade was formed and Lostwithiel was one of 29 fully operational stations with a trailer pump. It was based at Skelton's Garage, Bridgend.

Reorganisation of the County Fire Brigade in 1950 threatened the Lostwithiel station with closure. There was fierce opposition to this, led by alderman Wilfred Jeffery, who took the case for Lostwithiel to the Home Office. This earned a reprieve, but in 1952 the unit was disbanded.

However, all was not lost as a volunteer unit (Auxiliary Fire Service) was soon in place, led by Chief Fire Officer Phillips. The engine, the Green Goddess, was kept at Skelton's Garage. Roger Pascal, who had always had a passion for the fire service, came to Lostwithiel in the 1960s. He settled here, married and was immediately involved with the Lostwithiel Volunteer Unit. It was not long before he was leading it.

The Green Goddess with its orange flashing lights

was only called out in cases of dire emergency. Bodmin and Wadebridge had kept their retained status and dealt with most big fires. Roger campaigned constantly for 'retained' status for Lostwithiel and kept his volunteer crew in regular training at Bodmin Barn Park Fire Station. For this they were paid a bounty of £10 a year.

Eventually, in 1969 his dream came true and Lostwithiel Retained Station B17 was opened on Bodmin Hill, 'under the leadership of Sub Officer R. Pascal, a man of determination and very high standards, who was promoted to Station Officer in 1972.' The Green Goddess was painted red and the orange lights changed for blue. Lostwithiel Brigade won numerous efficiency competitions under Roger's leadership. All the firemen were paid a retainer and an additional fee for attending a fire. Tuesday nights were, and still are, training nights when firemen gather to practise their skills and routines.

Lostwithiel station was at a disadvantage until it received a radio. Until 1990 the siren was used to summon the firemen between 7a.m. and 11p.m. At night a bell was sounded in the houses of the men on duty. Since 1990 firemen on call have carried bleepers.

One night in June 1983 there was a call from Boconnoc to attend a fire in the pheasant hatchery. Lostwithiel Brigade turned out at once. Sadly, Station Officer Pascal was not to return, he suffered a heart attack whilst on duty at the fire and died in the ambulance on the way to hospital. This was a great blow to the brigade and to the whole of Lostwithiel. Roger's great contribution to both the volunteer unit and the County Fire Service will always be remembered and appreciated. David Abbiss took over the leadership of Retained Station B17 until 1991, when he passed on the baton to Victor May.

In 1992 a new fire station was opened, providing more space for the two appliances, a Dodge-Renault water tender with extending ladder and an L4T Land Rover, a smaller vehicle. The new station also includes improved training facilities with a training ground and tower. The approach road was named Pleyber-Christ Way in honour of Lostwithiel's twin town in Brittany. There are 12 retained firemen altogether and a team of six is always on call. In a small town like Lostwithiel, there is always the problem of having enough men available during the day. They need to work locally and be able to take time out immediately they are summoned. As the compulsory retiring age is 55, retired men cannot volunteer for service.

On 5 March 2001, a new fire-engine was delivered to Lostwithiel station, a Mercedes Benz water tender with a three-tiered ladder, capable of climbing the hill out of Lostwithiel at 32mph, a splendid replacement for the Dodge-Renault, which had given excellent service for 15 years. In 2003 the Station Officer is Francis Doney. Ever mindful of its great heritage and proud tradition, the Lostwithiel Fire Service goes forward into the twenty-first century.

Lostwithiel Fire Brigade, 2003. Left to right: *fire-fighters P. Rowe and H. Lewis, Sub Officer J. Doney, fire-fighters B. Ashwin, N. Newby, C. Massy, L. Collins, leading fire-fighter A. Grose, fire-fighter D. Webster, leading fire-fighter J. Peareth and Station Officer F. Doney.* (IF)

THE CIVIC REGALIA

From 1189 until 1968 Lostwithiel enjoyed borough status. It must always have been one of the smallest boroughs in the country. The town cherishes its regalia with great pride. The silver mace and oar were given to the town in 1670 by Silas Titus, MP for Lostwithiel. The oar symbolised the jurisdiction the town held over the river. Both symbols are carried by the Sergeant at Arms and the Sergeant at Mace (mace bearer) on all civic occasions. The mace (originally a weapon) is carried upside down in the presence of the monarch. As long as people could remember, these two positions were held by older men, until Mrs Gwen Powell-Jones became Mayor in the 1980s. She invited Andrew Daniell, then 17 years old, to take the post of mace bearer, and he became the youngest person in the country to occupy this position. A few years later, his friend and relative, Jonathan Abbiss took the post of Sergeant at Arms. (They are both descendants of Nathaniel Daniell, 1789–1879, Lostwithiel's first letter carrier.) It is Jonathan's responsibility to ring the bell and call the people to attention at the Mayor Choosing ceremony. This is, in fact, a misnomer, as the Mayor is chosen in advance and is sworn in at the ceremony.

The Silver Seal of Lostwithiel and Penknight dates from 1732 and bears the 'Lostwithiel Emblem'. It was presented by Mr Edgcumbe (before he was raised to the peerage). George Hoskins, Mayor in 1925–27, looked into the mystery of the design on the seal, which had been described as 'the Borough Arms'. However, it seems there are no arms registered to Lostwithiel, so the design is more correctly described as an 'emblem'. The design on the seal dates back to 1401. The original was a single tower with a tree on each side and a fish in the water. It is not known why or when the trees were replaced by thistles.

Civic Regalia

Left: *Sergeant at Arms Jonathan Abbiss carrying the Silver Oar and Sergeant at Mace Andrew Daniell.* (WL)

Above: *Councillor John Pegg, Mayor in 2000, wearing the robe and chain of office.*

(IF)

Right: *The original design of the Lostwithiel Emblem, 1401.* (LTC)

Right below: *The Silver Seal of Lostwithiel, 1732.* (LTC)

Left: *The Communion Plate, a gift of Thomas Jones Esq., 1775.* (LTC & SBC)

The Silver Hammer, presented by Dr Barclay-Allerdyce, Mayor 1899–1900, is in the shape of the hammers used by Cornish tinners. The Mayoral chain was founded by Dr Barclay-Allerdyce, and more links have been added by Mr R. Foster, other Mayors, Dr Nathaniel Coulson and subscribers. There is also a set of weights and measures (ranging from 56 pounds to 2 drams) and liquid measures (from half a bushel to half a gill) which are dated 1741.

The Mayoral robe was given by Mr William Pease in 1887 and the Deputy Mayor's robe was presented by Mr Wilfred Jeffery in 1938.

The Communion Plate was the gift of Thomas Jones Esq. in 1775 to the Mayor, Minister and Inhabitants of Lostwithiel. The pieces are inscribed:

Presented to the Mayor, his Brothers of the Bench, the Minister, Assistants and other inhabitants of the Borough of Lostwithiel, pursuant to the Will of Thomas Jones Esq. deceased, which he thereby desires they will accept as a Token of the great Respect he has always borne them. He died 7 July 1775.

This plate was used regularly at Communion Service for very many years. In 2003 it is kept locked away for safety reasons and, sadly, is rarely brought out to be used or seen.

THE RAILWAY, A WAY OF LIFE...

For almost 100 years the lives of many people in Lostwithiel were influenced by the railway. At the turn of the twentieth century there were about 100 men employed locally by GWR.

In July 1846 Lostwithiel enjoyed a day of festivity, with bell-ringing, music and dancing in the streets at the news of the passing of the Cornwall Railway Bill. However, it was another 13 years before a railway

Milltown Viaduct before 1896, a wooden structure on stone pillars. (LM)

came to Lostwithiel. Negotiations concerning the sale of land to the Cornwall Railway Company took a long time. When construction finally started, it brought more employment to an already busy town. The iron mines were flourishing and the gasworks were under construction. On 12 November 1858 the *Royal Cornwall Gazette* reported of Lostwithiel:

... a great number of men are employed by the Cornwall Railway preparing the timber for the permanent way and... in erecting the station buildings... so that lodgings for mechanics etc. are very badly to be obtained, and this once dull town is now almost as busy as a beehive.

The main-line railway from Plymouth–Truro opened in May 1859, bringing new opportunities for work, trade and travel. People's lives were changed for ever.

The *West Briton* reported that at 10p.m. one night in April 1861, a truck containing four tons of hay caught fire in a tunnel near Lostwithiel:

Cutting the line to Lostwithiel from Fowey (the docks are in the background) before 1869. (D&ET)

GWR employees at Lostwithiel, c.1900. (LM)

Left: *Lostwithiel Station, Brunel buildings, 1950s.* (RM)

The maintenance sheds became the GW Industrial Village, seen here after the fire in 1987. (IF)

Lostwithiel signal-box, 1980. (RM)

The long goods train entered the station... and the fire lit up the countryside for miles around. The wooden buildings were in danger but disaster was averted by the presence of mind of Mr Bush the company engineer, who detached the truck and passed it under the water tank.

In October 1874, early one morning, a loaded truck became detached at Doublebois station and 'rushed down the line at rapid speed... until it reached Lostwithiel, a distance of nearly ten miles. The line was fortunately clear of traffic.'

The opening of the Lostwithiel–Fowey line a decade later added further to the town's economic prospects, although there was a decline in the stage-coach business and in river traffic over these years.

Not only did Lostwithiel have a station, but the maintenance workshops were located here, between the station and the river. These were fine stone buildings and included lifting sheds, paint shops, smiths and carpenter's shops, machine shops, stores and offices, all designed by I.K. Brunel.

By the beginning of the twentieth century the iron mines were closing down, which coincided with the growing need for railway maintenance workers – a livelihood was therefore provided for many redundant miners. The railway remained a regular source of employment, developing and extending well into the twentieth century, but from 1950s, under British Rail management, maintenance work declined, then dried up completely. The creamery then became the main employer of the redundant railway workers.

In 1976, despite vigorous opposition, British Rail modernised Lostwithiel Station, demolishing Brunel's wooden buildings on the down line, and in 1981 the same fate befell the building on the up line. This was seen as an act of unnecessary vandalism and caused an uproar in the town. Luckily the stone maintenance sheds were not demolished, although for many years this site has been falling into decay. Brave efforts were made to develop an industrial village here in the 1980s and 1990s.

Time rolls on and nothing remains the same. In the twenty-first century things are set to change again. The original buildings are being preserved and converted into houses, flats and business premises and once again there will be life and purposeful activity on the east bank of the river.

The passenger service to Fowey was used daily for almost 100 years. Several generations of school-children remember it well. Closed to passengers in 1965, the line, along one of the loveliest routes in the country, is now used solely to transport china clay to Fowey docks.

Mr George Mewton of Barn Park, who started work on the railway in 1937, remembers the days when working on the railway was a way of life, full of interest, comradeship, loyalty and pride. George was a Bodmin boy, who decided at the age of 22 to work for the Great Western Railway. It seemed to him that the railway offered an interesting and secure livelihood. George had already met Miss Loveday Parsons, a Lostwithiel girl, while visiting here with a friend. Soon their thoughts were set on marriage and the young couple started to save from their modest earnings for their future together.

George started as a porter in Devon, then he was appointed as a shunter and moved back to Cornwall, then to Plymouth. Soon after this the war started and the workload for railway workers was vastly increased. The men worked 12-hour shifts, seven days a week. In 1940 George was very much involved with receiving soldiers as they arrived back in Britain from Dunkirk and getting them onto trains to take them to their various destinations. He has many horrific memories of the plight of those men.

Work on the railways was of great importance during the war and was a reserved occupation. George was given a job in the Onslow signal-box near Bodmin. He was also given the opportunity to rent a vacant cottage beside Bodmin Road (Parkway) Station. George was earning £2.4s.6d. (£2.23 in modern money) a week, which included pay for two hours overtime, a decent wage in those days. He and Loveday married in November 1940 and moved into the cottage. Almost at once they had two young evacuees billeted with them, boys aged 11 and 13. Loveday was delighted with her home and the garden, where they grew vegetables to supplement wartime rations. Wounded soldiers, on their way to the Headland Hotel in Newquay (used as an emergency hospital during the war), were often shunted into a siding beside the cottage, and Loveday would talk to them and bring them tea. They also met many American soldiers who were en route for Bodmin Barracks. Life was never dull.

Signalmen worked 8-hour shifts during the week and 12-hour shifts on Sundays. They had one Sunday off in three. These were long hours of responsibility, but George enjoyed his work. There were six classes of signal-box, depending on the responsibility carried by the operator, the number of trains, plus the number of points and signals to be controlled. George was promoted through a number of boxes eventually being transferred to the Class 3 box at Bodmin Road. This was a busy box with lots of responsibility and hard work, there was rarely a minute during the shift to relax, but living close to his job was a real bonus. He had travelled many miles by push-bike over the years!

George and Loveday had a son, Trevor, who attended the Church of England Primary School at Respryn. In the 1950s there was also a small church and a Methodist Chapel at Respryn. Lord Clifden allowed Trevor to cycle to school through the grounds of Lanhydrock. When Trevor won a Grammar School scholarship, he chose to go to St Austell Grammar School and travelled daily by train. As he grew older, the family attended St Bartholomew's Church in Lostwithiel and Trevor sang in the choir. The Mewtons had family and many friends in Lostwithiel and it seemed inevitable that they would come to live here one day. So in 1958 they moved to Lostwithiel, and once again George was travelling to work on his bike!

In 1961 George was appointed to the Class 2 signal-box in Lostwithiel. In the 1960s Lostwithiel was a very busy box. There were clay trains and milk trains, and in addition to the main-line trains from Paddington–Penzance there were hourly passenger trains to and from Fowey.

George was never involved in any railway disasters, but he does recall witnessing several horrifying near misses. He remembers with pleasure the many colleagues he worked with, and the goodwill, comradeship and laughter they all shared, the shunters, the booking clerks, the porters, as well as the many maintenance engineers, masons, carpenters and smiths who worked across the line in the railway yard. George experienced the decline in work during his 20 years in the Lostwithiel signal-box. As road transport developed, work was lost from the railway and men were laid off. The Fowey passenger service closed down as more and more people travelled in cars. The number of signal-boxes between Plymouth and Penzance was gradually reduced from 38 to just eight in 2003.

Even in the heyday of the railway, there was only one Class 1 signal-box between Plymouth and Penzance, which was at North Road, Plymouth. Whilst working at Lostwithiel, George was offered this box. This was a tribute to George and demonstrated the trust British Rail had in him, but although he was delighted at the recognition, he declined. His family was happy in Lostwithiel and the increase in salary did not justify the move.

He retired in 1981, since which time he has led an active life in the Church and the community. George and Loveday have celebrated 62 years of marriage and are enjoying retirement together.

Ralph Motton's experience of work on the railway was quite different, although he overlapped with George by over 30 years. He started work with the Great Western Railway immediately after his 14th birthday in 1944 as lad-porter. He remembers that one of the requirements for the job was that he was 5 feet 10 inches tall. Ralph retired after 45 years' service, in 1989. He had a variety of jobs during this time, including signalman, guard and chargeman, but he is especially well known in Lostwithiel for his spectacular floral displays at the station during the 1980s. These brought gasps of delight from passengers alighting from the trains, and streams of people from the neighbourhood came to the station just to see, admire and enjoy the flowers. Thinking back over 45 years, Ralph has many memories of his working life on the railway.

He could not have seen more changes.

His first job as a lad-porter was carrying coal and lighting fires in the various offices and the waiting-room (coal was supplied for employees' offices but not for the waiting-room, so this was taken unofficially from the engines). He was also responsible for cleaning windows and lighting the gas lamps. One of his jobs was to deliver parcels, and he particularly remembers the different smells of these. On six days a week there was a 14-pound (approximately 6 kilograms) box of yeast for Brewer's bakery. Fresh fish arrived from Grimsby for Mr Frank Burt, a dealer from Boconnoc. 'Toe rags' were large packs of salted fish in hessian bags, which had a completely different smell. The most pungent of his parcels were biscuit boxes containing dog meat – offal from Grampound, which had to be delivered regularly to various dog owners. Entrails were sent up-country from the slaughterhouse at Bridgend and Ralph had to collect these, but they were fresh and not too offensive! He had a push-bike with a large carrier in front of the handlebars, on which he zoomed around the town and countryside. His most awkward parcels were cabin trunks. These were picked up and went in advance of passengers, and there were always a few at the beginning and end of boarding-school holidays. Ralph could manage as many as three cabin trunks on his carrier at one time, although this meant he could not see where he was going! He remembers coming to grief swinging out of Quay Street into the Archway.

Taking on water at Lostwithiel. (LM)

All manner of goods were labelled 'parcels', new-born calves, boxes of one-day-old chicks, young lambs. Ralph recalls a cartoon which exactly caught the feel of the time, it was a picture of a dog running across the station yard and captioned 'Catch that dog, it's a parcel'. He enjoyed dealing with the baskets of pigeons which arrived from Redruth. The pigeons had to be labelled with the time and set free from the bridge over the line.

Household coal and coke arrived by rail for the Co-op. It was offloaded by Mr Edgar Rickard with only a shovel, each coal truck holding about 16 tons. Mr Rickard would weigh the coal and put it in bags for a lorry to pick up and deliver around the town and neighbourhood. Most of the provisions for the Co-op and Brewer's shop came in by rail.

For many years the milk factory sent milk to London, 10 to 15 tanks a day were dispatched, each tank containing 3,000 gallons of milk. There were two trains a day. It was even known for tanks to be put on the 10.36p.m. passenger train to London, if the factory was late in loading. Milk was also sent west to Truro and Falmouth, and this would be carried in churns on the passenger train.

China clay from a number of small 'dries' would go to Fowey via Lostwithiel. Clay from these dries was also sent to Scotland. A 'dry' is a place to which clay from the pits is sent to be dried out, before being transported in powder form. Ball clay from Devon was sent to Fowey. At one time the railway had over 500 wagons to carry clay. In 2003 the tanks carry 30 tons and a train load may consist of 14 or more tanks.

During the Second World War, the station was very busy with trains carrying ammunition. The trucks ran onto specially built sidings and were unloaded by soldiers and the shells were taken away into the countryside in lorries. After the war, passengers would arrive at Lostwithiel from London with a lot of luggage. They were en route to Fowey, from where they would board cargo boats (usually carrying clay) and travel as passengers.

The goods shed was rented out and used by a firm for the storing and sale of basic slag, fertiliser containing phosphates, formed as a by-product during steel manufacture. There used to be an old railway coach in the goods yard, and an old wooden building, which contained animal feed, corn and pellets from Silcocks, a well-known poultry food supplier. These came in railway trucks and two of the station staff on 'early turn' would unload the trucks together with Mr Wilfred Welsh.

Old broad-gauge coach in the goods yard, photographed in 1922. (CB)

After two years of National Service in the Army, Ralph returned to the railway and worked as a signalman. He used to cycle to work along the track. Later he became a guard, and this was perhaps his favourite job. He was a guard for over 11 years. He travelled between Exeter and Penzance, on the main line and on branch lines, ferrying passengers or freight, cement, diesel, petrol and liquid gas. The hours were irregular and he often worked through the night. These were long days and nights, and he was left behind in Exeter on one occasion, but there was always something of interest, something different going on. Ralph remembers how he used to travel to Wadebridge from St Blazey on a train pulled by a small engine with a maximum speed 14mph. At Wenford Bridge the train would slow to walking pace, and there they would find food and drink beside the line, left by friends of the crew. These were happy days and it was a good life.

During the 1950s the steam engines gave way to diesel, British Rail had taken over from GWR, and from then on there was constant change.

Ralph remembers a royal visit to Lostwithiel in the 1960s. On this occasion he delivered the early morning newspapers to the royal train for the Queen, who had spent the night on the Fowey line, across the river from St Winnow.

Stationmaster William Clemence and Ralph Motton tend Lostwithiel Station garden in 1960. (RM)

Ralph's last five years were back in Lostwithiel as a chargeman. By then the old wooden station buildings and the bridge over the lines had gone, the station staff had been drastically reduced, and there were no longer craftsmen working in the engine sheds – the yard was deserted. Changing times and conditions helped Ralph to make his decision to take early retirement. During his last few years at Lostwithiel Station he worked hard on developing the floral displays. The results of this work gave pleasure to everyone in Lostwithiel and was very much appreciated. The year of his retirement was memorable. It was the 800th anniversary of Lostwithiel's Charter, an important landmark in the town's history, marked by a royal visit, the Queen arriving by train. Ralph was awarded a Duke of Cornwall cut-glass decanter for his floral display at the station.

Elsie Jones amidst Ralph Motton's award-winning floral display in 1989. (RM)

Some of the staff that Ralph remembers from his early days at Lostwithiel Station are: Joe Keast, Harry Penwarden, Stanley Courtney, Jack Roberts, Ronald Eddy, Reg Parker, George Mewton, Jack Daniel, Peter Lobb, Douglas Snowdon (signalmen); Leslie Gardener, Jack Barnicoat, Harry Pope (shunters); Arthur Wilkinson, Albert Tamlin, Oliver Driver, George Poole, Woody Hoskin, Jack Bellringer, Ken Rowley, Jack Cockwill, Brian Chapman, Miss Pat

Flook, Mrs Peggy Goyne, Jimmy Rule, M. Penhaligan, A. Douglas, Frank Goyne (station staff after the war); Leslie Dawes, Michael Willis, Dennis Jane, Ernest Vincent, Miss Betty Wilkinson, Miss Ruth Roberts (booking clerks); Jack Dawson (lampman); Bill Talling (lorry driver); Wilfred Welsh, P. Frampton, Miss I. West (goods shed); Harry Jane, William Clemence, Barry Strong (stationmasters); Mr Evans, Mr Rusty Eplett, Mr A.P. Johnson (area managers).

In 2003 the signal-box is manned and there is still a shunter, but nobody else works on the station. Clay trains come through daily, and some passenger trains stop here, but most of them rush through.

WOMEN'S INSTITUTE

Lostwithiel Women's Institute was founded in 1924 and has flourished ever since. When the ladies celebrated their 25th anniversary, there were 70–80 members.

In 1974, European Architectural Heritage Year, ladies of the Lostwithiel WI researched the history of Trevego and mounted an exhibition for the Royal Cornwall Show. Trevego is a gracious Elizabethan stone house belonging to the Boconnoc estate. Since 1967 it has been the home of John and Joy Foot, who

A WI party at the Royal Talbot Hotel, 1951. Left to right, seated extreme left: Mrs Stick , ?; standing at back: Mrs Jeffery, Miss Diane Brewer; seated left of table: Mrs Eckardt, Mrs Watkins, ?, Mrs Souter, Mrs Soady, Mrs Robson, Mrs Coad, Mrs Huddy, Mrs Mason, Mrs Ball, ?; seated right of table: Mrs Howes, Mrs Green, Mrs Jewels, Mrs Hick, ?, Mrs Watkins, Mrs Littleton, Mrs Cullum, Mrs Francis, Mrs Pope, Miss Lewis, Mrs Tom Redmond; seated at back: visitor Mrs Whiteways, Mrs Doris Liddicoat, Mrs Allport, Mrs Clarke, Mrs Newbury, Miss Loveday Foster, Mrs Phillips, Mrs Robins, Mrs Spencer Brown, Mrs Eastlick, Mrs Harris, Mrs Wilkinson, Mrs Trenerry. (LM)

farm the land. The exhibition included photographs, drawings, a model of the house, and a book containing all the details of the research. Copies of the book have been made, although the precious original copy is in the safe keeping of Mrs Foot. It recounts the history of the various families who have lived at Trevego and traces the developments and embellishments made to the house over the centuries.

There has been a farmstead at Trevego since before the Norman Conquest, probably for over 1,000 years. It was recorded in the Domesday Book in 1086 as Trevocarwinnic (Trevego in St Winnow). The present farmhouse was built as a dower house for Isobel, the widow of Sir William Mohun.

Trevego House, the subject of a research project undertaken by the WI in 1974. (IF)

In 2003 the WI has about 35 members. They are again following up local history and have been researching Cornish inventors, amongst them the Lostwithiel man, Bill Skelton. This project won the Baker Cup, an award made by the Federation of WIs in Cornwall.

THE BOWLS CLUB

The Bowls Club opened in 1926, after much hard work preparing the ground. The Tennis Club opened on the same day on an adjacent site. In its 77th year in 2003, the Bowls Club is still flourishing. For some years there has also been a thriving Ladies' Bowls Club. The Tennis Club did not survive so long.

Lostwithiel Bowling Club, county champions, 1972.
Left to right, back row: *Arnold Liddicoat, Charles Vellacott, Harold Hawken, David Pearce, Alf Fenton, Arthur Cavell, Bob Bennett;* front: *Desmond Medland, Arthur Pope, Doug Townsend (captain), Patrick Chudleigh (chairman) and Ernie Clook.* (PC)

Lostwithiel Tennis Club, 1926. This may have been the official opening as the band played on this occasion. (LM)

THE MUSIC OF LOSTWITHIEL

The Town Band

Lostwithiel's Town Band has a long history and has featured in the life of the town through many generations. There was a band of musicians in Lostwithiel in 1832. It is reported that there was 'music and dancing in the streets' at the news of the passing of the Parliamentary Reform Act, and again in 1846, at the news of an impending railway. In 1885 the Lostwithiel Band, under the command of Nathaniel Prideaux, played for the Flora Dance at the Royal Talbot Hotel assembly room. At this time it was called 'Lostwithiel Detachment of the East Company Rifle Volunteers Band'. This band continued until the outbreak of war in 1914, when the instruments were stored away. It was not revived until 1922, when a small group of young men, led by Norman Chapman, Herbert Eyres and Dick Parsons (then aged 15), took the initiative and sought permission from the council to use the old instruments. With the help of Mr E.A. Russell (organist at St Bartholomew's Church) and Mr Wevell, they learned to play and formed a band. They gave their first concert six months later. An important engagement in the early days was at the opening of the Bowls Club and the Tennis Club on Restormel Lane in 1926. The founder members of all three clubs had been involved in a great deal of work and commitment to get them up and running, and this day was very special for them all.

There were fund-raising efforts over the first few years to buy uniforms. The band entered its first competition in 1946 and became known as Lostwithiel Silver Band in 1947. It played on three royal occasions and was inspected by the royal visitors at the visit of King George VI and Queen Elizabeth to Lostwithiel in 1950, the opening of the Tamar Bridge by Queen Elizabeth, the Queen Mother, in 1962, and the opening of the County Hall in Truro by Queen Elizabeth II in 1966.

Left: *Lostwithiel Band in 1931.* Left to right, back row: *Mr Harris, Eric Blake, Frank Ashton, Herbert Eyres;* second row: *Mr Houghton, Syd Abbiss, Mr Warboys, Mr Wentworth, Vernon Prideaux, Douglas Eade, Arthur Tamlin, Roy Oliver;* seated: *Joe Pearce, Dick Parsons, Alfred Francis, Alfred Alexander, Reg Francis, Reg Vine;* front: *Master Tyrell, Gerald Lean.* (LM)

Right: *Lostwithiel Duke of Cornwall Light Infantry (DCLI) Band play at the official opening of the Tamar Bridge, 1962.* (DP)

The band has had its ups and downs. In 1956 it joined the Territorials and became known as the 4/5th Duke of Cornwall Light Infantry Band until 1967 when it again became the Lostwithiel Silver Band. In 1988 a rival band, Lostwithiel 88, was established and took away some of the original band's players. This was very successful for a while, but eventually disbanded and players rejoined the Silver Band, since when it has thrived as the Lostwithiel Town Band.

Throughout the years it has, in essence, remained the same band, with the same traditions of enthusiasm, hard work and good practice, making music for the entertainment and enjoyment of everybody.

Mervyn Collins

Mervyn Collins has his own recollections of 70 years with the Town Band and adds a personal perspective. Born at Couch's Mill in the 1920s Mervyn grew up in Lerryn until the age of seven, when the family moved to West Lodge, Boconnoc, where Mervyn's father worked in the sawmill. This was his civilian job and he spent many years in the Navy, serving in both world wars.

From the age of seven Mervyn played the piano, practised hard every day and enjoyed every minute of it. He won prizes and competitions from the start. One Saturday evening, returning home from shopping at the Co-op, he paused to listen to the

Right: *Mervyn Collins has played with the band for 70 years. Edna, his wife, has been an active supporter for 50 years.* (JB)

band playing Christmas carols outside St Saviour's Church. One of the players recognised him and called 'you should come and join us' and gave him a cornet to take home and try out. Mervyn was hooked, so he joined the band when he was ten years old. That was in 1933 and at the time of writing he is the longest-serving, still-very-active member of the Town Band. There were other youngsters in the band, all very keen, practising regularly and attending band practices in the old Grammar School twice a week. Mervyn's mother insisted that he continue to practise the piano for one hour, then the cornet for an hour, every day after school. When he started work as an errand boy for the Co-op at the age of 14, the hours were so long there was not enough time to practise both instruments, so he gave up the piano and kept up with the cornet and the band. One of the occasions Mervyn remembers from the early days was the official opening of the Glyn Cinema in 1936.

At the age of 17 Mervyn became a van driver for Brewer's bakery. Then, at 18, he joined the GWR as an engine cleaner at St Blazey. A year after that he was transferred to Westbury in Wiltshire and promoted to fireman (stoker). It was now wartime. He was in Westbury for seven and a half years. During this time Mervyn married and had two sons, but the marriage ended in divorce. During the war, the members of the band were scattered, although they got together and played whenever they could. They also played with different musicians and Mervyn played with other bands in Wiltshire.

Mervyn came back to Cornwall and was a fireman for a total of 19 years. This was very hard work, one man with a shovel kept a steam train pulling up to 15 carriages, rolling from Paddington to Reading in 38 minutes! Mervyn loved it. He later spent two years driving steam engines, before the introduction of diesel, then for the rest of his career he drove diesel engines – a total of 41 years with the railways.

Throughout all this time Mervyn played regularly with Lostwithiel's band – he has played the cornet, flugal, tenor and baritone horn, euphonium, and in 2003 he plays the trombone. He took over as secretary when Dick Parsons, a founder member, retired and Mervyn did this job for 24 years. At the time of writing he is the treasurer.

Mervyn married Edna in 1956 and they are a strong team, supporting each other at every step. Edna grew up in Cardinham. Her father was a carpenter for the Skynners, a family involved in the clay industry, who lived at 'Gilbury' on Summer Street. She left school at the age of 14 in 1946 and came to work as a live-in maid for the Skynners. She believes she was the last person in the area to 'go into service'. Her father volunteered her for the job, when the family was looking for someone! Edna enjoyed it, she stayed for ten years and was in many ways like one of the family. She still keeps in touch with her own generation of Skynners and sees them when they visit Lostwithiel.

Mervyn's sons and their families have always regarded Edna as a second mother and grandmother. Mervyn and Edna have six grandchildren and one great-grandchild. Edna has always been a keen supporter of the band and remembers the days when there was a very active Ladies' Committee, organising sewing parties, sales of work and sponsored events to raise funds. This fell into abeyance when most of the ladies involved grew too old to continue. Mervyn and Edna still raise money regularly, they always have a football lottery game on the go, and they organise regular monthly dances at the Village

Hall in Lanreath. These are 'Old Time' dances and music is played on an electric organ. Edna and her willing helpers provide refreshments and there is a bar. The dances attract a regular clientele and are enjoyed and appreciated by one and all.

The band practises in the GWR buildings twice a week and members are hoping that they will continue to have use of this, or a similar venue, into the future. The costs of running the band are heavy. In addition to keeping instruments and uniforms in good repair, other expenditures include: rents, cost of music, fees for performing rights, a gaming licence, conductor's salary and the hire of a coach, when necessary. The band is in good financial health, thanks to its supporters. It has 25 playing members, several of them young enthusiastic beginners. In 2003 it entered a national competition in Torquay.

After Mervyn retired from the railway he took a job as a driver for the Trewoon Bakery, Holmbush, delivering pasties to Looe, Polperro and Plymouth, and once a month he took frozen pasties to Cheddar Gorge! He only gave up this work when the business closed down in 2001. In his 80th year at the time of writing, he puts all his energies into the band, both playing and fund-raising, and into learning to use the new 'toy' he shares with Edna, a computer. On behalf of the Town Band, Mervyn has recently given an old trombone to the museum. It dates from about 1860 and perhaps is a survivor from the original 'Lostwithiel Detachment of East Company Rifle Volunteers Band'. It is a splendid addition to the museum's collection.

In addition to 50 years devoted to the band, Edna has another passion dating from her early childhood, which is for crocheting. She has silver cups, and several plaques and awards for this work, won over many years. The Railway Workers' Association holds an arts and crafts exhibition at Swindon each year, and Edna won the silver cup in 1981–83, as well as a Special Honours Award on one occasion, for a beautifully crocheted wedding dress and accessories, which involved over 800 hours' work. Edna is probably the only person alive today who is familiar with the Cornish Cockleshell Lace edging pattern. In 1978 a Mrs K. Jolliffe of Polperro was the only person to have it. She passed it to Mrs Retallick of Bodmin, who passed the pattern to Edna, who is seeking anyone interested in crochet that would be prepared to keep this traditional pattern alive. Edna is also making good use of her computer, and has been in touch by e-mail with a lady in Canada, whose granny used to crochet Cornish Cockleshell Lace!

Restormel Youth Brass & Woodwind

This band of young musicians was formed in 2000. They are all very enthusiastic and play at a number of functions and events throughout the year. They enter competitions around Cornwall and proudly bring home many awards.

The Gumbo Flyers

*Restormel Youth Brass Ensemble, 2003.
Left to right, back row: Ben Knight, Sam Shelley,
Joe Shelley, Carla Rogers, Richard Coad, Rebecca Hoskin,
Andrew Coad; front: Sophie Knight, Rebekah Knight,
Isaac Shelley, Megan Vokes.* (SK)

Based in Lostwithiel, the Gumbo Flyers have been described in London's *Time Out* magazine as 'the best Zydeco Band in Europe'. The band formed in 1991 and has played over 1,000 gigs. They have played in Europe and USA, but most of their work has been in the South West of England where they are in great demand. The musicians all love making their music, and aim to get every member of the audience 'rockin' and ravin'' along with them. Every year they draw the crowds onto the quay at Fowey during the du Maurier Festival.

The Blues Bandits

Lostwithiel has other well-supported, talented groups bringing live music to the town. The Blues Bandits have been around since 1987. Their first gig was at the Royal Talbot Hotel, where they played rock and roll and 1950s and 1960s music. They are in demand for private parties, public functions and play in the inns around the region.

Margaret Parkyn

Margaret Parkyn, 1988. (CBu)

Mrs Margaret Parkyn brought music to Lostwithiel in the 1940s, when she played with the all-girl band from Blisland for dances at the Drill Hall. Here she met and married Stan, and has been keeping the town entertained ever since. Church organ, piano, accordion, Margaret enjoys them all and so do her audiences.

LOSTWITHIEL CARNIVAL & REGATTA

The annual gala day (forerunner of the carnival) was originally organised by the British Legion, until it was taken over by the Town Band, and for a while during the 1950s, by the Young Conservatives.

Gala day in the 1940s and 1950s was celebrated with the Flora dance, decorated boats on the river, the crowning of the queen, a carnival procession and a dance in the evening. By the 1970s this had developed into a week of events, and was known as the Band Carnival. It reverted again to a one-day event during the 1980s. The regatta dates back to at least 1875. In the 1940s and 1950s it was a major one-day

Poster announcing the carnival that was cancelled in 1939. (DP)

Lostwithiel Carnival

Below: *Carnival group on the steps of the Bank Chapel, 1947. Left to right, back row: ?, Mr Willis, Dr Rudge, Mr Jeffery, ?; centre: Mr Charles Billing, Nancy Ashton, ?, Jill Marshall, Mrs Marshall, Mr Douglas Marshall MP, Mr Charles Vincent; front: Barbara Keast, Queen Daphne Daniell (now Stephens), Enid Parsons.* (LM)

Above: *The first gala queen after the war was Nancy Ashton in 1946. Her attendants were Iris Daniell (left) and Joyce Toms (right).* (JA & CCCR D1826)

Cornish wrestling at a carnival in the 1980s. (CBu)

Carnival procession 2000. Debbie Duguid is holding Deneka. (IF)

event of competitions, sports and fun on the river, run by the regatta committee. One of the events in those days was the 'greasy-pole' competition, in which boys, armed with sacks of flour or soot, aimed to knock each other off a greasy pole, protruding out over the river.

This languished until it was revived by the newly formed Rotary Club in 1979. Eventually in 1993 the band and Rotary Club combined the two events and in 1995 the Rotary Club took over the organisation of the whole enterprise, which became carnival week as we know it in 2003. The regatta has become 'charity fair day' heralding a week packed with a variety of events. There is something for everyone, theatre-in-the-park, donkey racing, pram racing, duck racing, wrestling and various other competitions, a band concert, a choir concert, a fair on the playing-field, a street party, culminating in the carnival procession, music, dancing and fireworks. Many people and organisations in the town make their contribution to the success of carnival week, it is a major enterprise and raises a lot of money for charity. Although Lostwithiel no longer chooses a queen, everyone looks forward to that special week in July with eager anticipation.

LOSTWITHIEL CATTLE MARKET, 1906–76

The first lot given for the auction in aid of the Red Cross, 1940. Left to right: *auctioneer Wilfred Jeffery, Mayor Spencer Brown, farmer James Stephens, Viscount Clifden, the Hon. Misses Robartes, farmer Dunstan Mitchell* (behind), *Bill Burrows postman;* child in the ring: *David Williams.* (JJ)

The cattle market played an important part in Lostwithiel's life for 70 years. The following is an extract from a talk given to Lostwithiel Old Cornwall Society on 27 October 1988 by Jim Jeffery, then its chairman. Jim was the last secretary of the Cattle Market Company before it went into voluntary liquidation in 1976. He retired as senior partner of 'Jefferys of Lostwithiel', the cattle market auctioneers, in 1988. A chartered surveyor and a national past

president of the Central Association of Agricultural Valuers, he was Mayor of Lostwithiel, 1978–81:

Lostwithiel's first Charter granted a market to the town, but the market, as we knew it, was something that came about in 1906. We do not know when the first public cattle auction was held in Lostwithiel, but we do know that cattle and possibly other livestock, were sold in Queen Street [Market Street before the visit of Queen Victoria in 1846]. *Early in the twentieth century there was an obvious need for a properly organised cattle market, having its own premises and full facilities for dealing with, and auctioneering livestock. Provision was later required for washing down cattle lorries, which were non-existent in 1906. A group of interested people got together and Lostwithiel Cattle Market Ltd was the result. This is an extract from my report as secretary at the last Annual General Meeting of the company in 1976:*

In 1906 it was decided to form the Company and the Certificate of Incorporation was issued by the Registration of Joint Stock Companies on 23rd June 1906.
The following are extracts from the Memorandum of Association:
1. The name of the Company is 'The Lostwithiel Cattle Market Ltd'.
2. The Registered Office of the Company will be situated in England.
3. The objects of the Company are:
a) To acquire, take over and purchase the Talbot Yard, otherwise the Iron Mine Yard and the buildings thereon situated in the Borough of Lostwithiel and numbered 73 on the Tithe Map of Lostwithiel.
b) To lay out land as a cattle market and properly equip same and to hold markets and fairs for the sale of cattle and to levy and charge tolls in connection therewith.

The names and addresses of subscribers who 'are desirous of being formed into a company' were: George Hext of Cowbridge, Lostwithiel, JP for Cornwall; James Thomas of Tregays, St Winnow, Farmer; William Wevell of Hazelmere, Lostwithiel, Farmer; Fred Wallace Rowe of Trevego, St Winnow, Farmer; Clarence Tuckett of Killigarth, Polperro, Farmer; William Henry Copplestone of Polscoe, Lostwithiel, Farmer; Arthur Santo Liddicoat of Glenview, Lostwithiel, Farmer; John Littleton of Sweethouse, Auctioneer; John Jennings of Restormel, Lostwithiel, Farmer.
The earliest minutes I can find are dated 17 February 1929. Mr Fred Rowe was re-elected chairman. Other directors at the meeting were: James Nicholas Sherwill (my father-in-law) of Ethy Barton, St Winnow (the Sherwills were originally from South Devon but had farmed Ethy Barton for several generations); H.J. Ede of Tregenna, St Veep, Farmer; James Stephens of St Winnow Barton, Farmer; Harry Copplestone and John

Jennings (previously mentioned); George Venning of Langunnet Farm, Boconnoc, Farmer; James Henry Jeffery (my grandfather), businessman, town councillor and later Lostwithiel's first Freeman; James Venning, who was then the auctioneer and founder of my firm.

My father, Wilfred (seven times Mayor and one of the last Freemen of the borough)... bought the business in 1935 when it became Venning & Jeffery (there are still a few old farmers who refer to it by that name). Some years later, in the 1950s, we amalgamated with Herbert Rowse & Son of St Austell when we became Rowse, Jeffery & Watkins. The last change of name in 1987 shortened it to 'Jefferys'.

Among the things discussed at a 1929 meeting was the need to acquire more land for the market. This became possible in 1934, when my family moved into Woodclose, which had a very large garden. Part of this was sold to the company, and was converted into a penning and sale area for store-cattle. The fire station now occupies this land.

During the Second World War the cattle market became a collecting centre for the Ministry of Food. Fat stock was brought to market to be graded and dispersed to slaughterhouses by the Ministry. Stock, other than fat, was still auctioned, but the auction of fat stock did not return until after the Ministry ceased their operations. During the war, old farm-type buildings in the market were commandeered by the Army and used for billeting the troops. These were pulled down after the war.

The market continued to operate successfully for many years, but owing to a change in the pattern of sales, the mode of farming, the increase in road transport and events generally, the auctioneers had no option but to cease trading in 1973.

Pre-1945 most of the stock was walked to market, thus clogging the roads on market days, but with the advent of cattle lorries, producers were able to travel greater distances, to where, perhaps, better facilities and more competition prevailed.

Lostwithiel Cattle Market Ltd had a share capital of £1,000, and in its entire life this was never increased. In retrospect perhaps this was a mistake, increased capital might have enabled better facilities, but who can tell? The sale of shares to local farmers was encouraged, in an attempt to give them a direct interest and use its facilities more. In practice this had little effect.

It is probably fair to say that the cattle market might be seen to reflect the general trend of mercantile business in the town. Those who, like me, were born here, saw the general decline of town business, as larger towns attracted it away. When the company was in its heyday, perhaps in the 1930s, so was Lostwithiel. It was a thriving shopping centre, and was able to supply almost everything the consumer wanted.

Until well after the Second World War, the only access to the market was from North Street. It is difficult to imagine how large cattle lorries got in, but they did! Even so, something had to be done to get better access, so the Cattle Market Co. and the Town Council, who wanted access to what is now the playing-field, jointly entered into negotiation with the owner of the land, which is now Pleyber-Christ Way. This resulted in the council acquiring the land and making a new road, giving us a new entrance. The old North Street entrance was restricted to a pedestrian way.

By 1973 the market, which was by then heavily subsidised by the auctioneers, had to be closed to business, as it was no longer viable. The company applied for planning permission for residential purposes, but was turned down. Negotiations were entered into with Restormel Borough Council and the County Council. The old, original part of the cattle market was sold to Restormel Council to be used as a car park, and the land where the new fire station stands was sold to the County Council, specifically for that purpose.

During its 70 years in existence, the cattle market made a significant contribution to the town and its people. However, nothing stands still and while the loss of the market is regretted, those of us who were involved in the 1976 AGM look back on the days of the market with considerable affection.

THE MILK FACTORY

The Lostwithiel creamery, 1932–91 (more commonly known as the milk factory), provided work for local people during the crucial period when railway workers were being made redundant and women were looking for employment. It became the main employer locally and was central to the life of the town. Mrs Gill Parsons worked in the creamery for many years and contributed this account of its history, while Mr William Martin, factory manager from 1959 to 1986, provided the facts and figures:

The milk depot was originally set up by GWR to help local farmers in the depressed days of the early 1930s. It was soon taken over by Messrs Nestlé (a subsidiary of the Anglo-Swiss company). Until that time there had been no co-ordinated marketing of ex-farm milk, and as a result, prices were low. Local farmers responded well to the introduction of a collection depot, and from the early days in October 1932, 500 farms sent in milk, averaging 14 gallons (64 litres) a day per farm, giving a daily total into the depot of 7,000 gallons (31,990 litres).

The depot employed about 20 men, all of whom were local, except for senior management. It was sited adjoining the railway, where raw milk was transferred to rail tankers and sent daily to many areas of London, for pasteurisation, bottling and doorstep delivery. The only entrance to the depot was into the factory gate at Bridgend, immediately east of the medieval bridge. The churn lorries had to approach along North Street and over the old bridge, or down the hill at Bridgend (the same routes taken by the cattle lorries on market days!).

117

Left: *The creamery vans, ready for action, 1933.* (LM)

Below: *Creamery staff, c.1944.* (CCCR E9154)

In April 1937 Nestlé sold to Cow & Gate Ltd, with a change of name to 'Dried Milk Products'. By the 1950s to early 1960s 1,600 farmers were involved and 25,000 gallons, (114,250 litres) a day were being dealt with at the depot. The continued increase in farm production encouraged Cow & Gate to expand the depot in 1958 into a manufacturing creamery. Machinery was installed for the production of whole milk and skimmed milk powder. New offices, laboratories, water treatment and sewage treatment plants were built. There were some problems at this time, with an unpleasant smell from the sewage plant, and although things improved after the first 'teething troubles', this was never wholly eradicated. Three months after production started, Cow & Gate merged with United Dairies under the Company name of Unigate.

A familiar figure in the 1950s was Mr Nicholls with his pony and trap, bringing his milk churns to the depot from Pill and Lanwithan Farms. Although mechanisation was rapidly taking over, there were still some people who preferred the older, simpler methods of conducting their business.

Further expansion took place in June 1960, when a bottling line for pasteurised milk was installed, enabling Thomas' Dairy in Quay Street and North Street Dairy to buy their bottled milk locally. This was followed by a clotted cream and liquid cream department being established in 1969, when the Coulson creamery at St Blazey was transferred to Lostwithiel. The girls from the St Blazey creamery came to work in Lostwithiel alongside the Lostwithiel girls. Cream was sent every Christmas to Buckingham Palace for the royal family and their guests to enjoy.

There were major changes in the creamery in August 1979, when Unigate sold 14 of their creameries, including Lostwithiel, to the Milk Marketing Board. Under its constitution the MMB was bound to buy every gallon of ex-farm milk produced, and thus brought stability in prices.

The nature of farming was continually changing so that by 1982 the number of farms had decreased to 440, but the daily production of milk per farm had increased to 132 gallons (603 litres) and the daily total into the creamery was 58,000 gallons (265,000 litres). This was the time when the factory was at the height of its success, employing over 300 people, and as many of them lived locally, this probably represented about 25 per cent of the working population of Lostwithiel.

There were very few families in Lostwithiel who did not have someone working in the factory. A wide diversity of skills was required, office staff to deal with every aspect of the operation, laboratory technicians, maintenance engineers, electricians, boiler-house staff, tanker drivers, motor mechanics, operatives to deal with the pasteurisation of the milk, the drying and the making of cream, canteen staff, cleaning staff, all these people felt a loyalty to the factory and worked hard to ensure its success.

Because for many years, nearly every home in the town was involved with the milk factory, the social life was bound up with it too. Every alternate Tuesday evening there was bingo in the canteen, there were regular supper dances at St Blazey football club and coach trips were arranged to see the theatre shows in Torquay and Plymouth. Boat trips down the River Fal and 'mystery tours' by coach were eagerly anticipated and enjoyed by many families in the summer.

To cope with the extra milk, the MMB was forced to increase its manufacturing capacity and Lostwithiel was chosen for expansion yet again. A major development occurred between September 1983 and February 1985, costing £15 million. This included the infamous tower.

During the redevelopment scheme, the EEC was forced to limit the ever-increasing ex-farm supply of milk, and under the Common Agricultural Policy, all dairy surpluses had to be bought by the EEC through a scheme called Intervention. This led to the 'butter and milk powder mountains'. As a consequence, on 1 April 1984, a Quota Scheme was introduced, limiting milk production to the level of the previous year, putting an end to the ever-increasing production. The MMB now found itself with more manufacturing capacity than it required, which in turn led to factory closures.

Lostwithiel's factory survived until the spring of 1991, when work was stopped, workers were made redundant and the tower was sold and dismantled.

For over half a century the milk factory provided work for Lostwithiel people, growing from a modest liquid milk depot to become a fine example of dairy technology, by the time it closed.

Many of the buildings on the site are now being used as industrial units, and there is a wide range of activities going on. There is still a milk factory 'presence'. The garaging and maintenance of the tankers is still carried out on the site, about 50 people are employed. The milk collected from the local farms is taken to a number of centres, including Highbridge in Somerset and Cullompton in Devon and more locally, to Trewithan, where it is prepared to be sold as fresh milk and cream, Davidstow to make cheese, Lifton to be used in the making of rice pudding and custard, and to Rodda's of Redruth for cream.

It is hoped that the maintenance depot will survive and continue to provide employment in this area.

THE GLYN CINEMA, 1936–60

Mr Henry Maitland Williams must have been one of the most welcome of 'incomers' to Lostwithiel when, in 1936, he came here with the express purpose of opening a cinema. A Scotsman, he had left Ayr Academy at the age of 20 and spent four years learning every aspect of the cinema business including projection, engineering, maintenance and management.

He chose the corner of South Street and Church Lane as the site for his cinema. This was originally the site of the medieval smelting house in the Duchy Palace complex. Mr Williams designed the cinema himself and supervised the building of it. He

Left: *Dismantling the drying tower, 1992.* (JB)

The Glyn Cinema, 1936. (D&ET)

organised a competition to choose a name for his cinema, offering as a prize a free ticket for one show, every week for a year. The joint winners were Harry Olford of Par Moor and Billy Tearle of Lostwithiel. The Glyn Cinema was opened in 1936.

There was great excitement at the official opening by the Mayor, Mr W.T. Bassett, the Lostwithiel Band played before the show started, then the instrumentalists took their free seats for the first performance, Gracie Fields in *Queen of Hearts*.

The Glyn was a great success from the start. 'Going to the pictures' quickly became a very popular night out. The programme was changed mid-week and there was always a Pathé News film. There were two showings every evening and a matinée on Saturdays. The cinema had 495 seats and the colour scheme was pale blue, grey and yellow. Prices were 6d., 9d., 1s. and 1s.6d. The auditorium was usually full and the air was always thick with tobacco smoke.

Mr Williams married in 1938. He was 'the Boss' and Mrs Williams ran the ticket office and cash desk. The projectionists were Jack Swatton, Claud Jones, Peter Whells and Des Talling. With a break for active service during the war, Des kept this post from his 14th birthday until the cinema closed. Part-time projectionists were Ron Marshall, David Webster, Paddy Murphy, Charlie Sleep and John Daniell. The doormen were Albert Ward and Ted Tanlock. Over the years the usherettes were Dorothy Phillips, Joyce Pearce, Mary Beale, Pam Stead, Marion Hicks, Mavis Goodman, Beatrice Hicks, Doreen Pearce and Minnie Roose. Minnie and B. Tullet were cleaners and the former was well known for the click of her knitting needles throughout the show and for shining her torch into the faces of children who talked!

The cinema only closed twice. At the outbreak of war all cinemas closed for a week, while staff learned to deal with incendiary bombs. On 26 November 1954 there was no show – the cinema had flooded following a heavy storm. It was the eve of Des Talling's marriage to Eileen Redmond and she remembers she was busy that night carrying her wedding presents upstairs. Eileen lived in North Street, which was also flooded.

During the war there were always long queues of people who wanted to see the shows, but in the 1950s fashions changed. Television caused a big reduction in audience numbers and by 1960 the cinema was no longer viable as a business. Mr Williams was forced to close it down and was unable to sell the property.

He had always had an interest in engineering and inventing and was a member of the Institute of British Engineers and of the Institute of Patentees, regularly submitting his designs for patenting. After 1960 he took a post as Senior Scientific Assistant with the UK Atomic Energy Authority at Doonreay. During the 1970s he designed and had built a flat within the cinema. He and his wife returned to live in the flat in 1977. Mr William's private and unassailable office

was built into the roof space of the building above the auditorium, approached by ladders on an outside wall and a catwalk above the ceiling. There was also an inside ladder behind the cinema screen. One would have needed courage and a head for heights to attempt a break-in! Mr Williams, a true eccentric, died in 1994 having outlived his wife by a short time. In 1995 the property was sold and six small town houses have been built on the site.

THE YOUNG FARMERS' CLUB

In 2003 Chris Terry is the chairman of the Young Farmers' Club. He is proud to tell us that the club, formed in the 1930s as 'Lostwithiel and Lanreath YFC' under the chairmanship of Lawson Turpie, a well-known farmer from St Veep, is still as strong as ever, drawing its membership from both town and country. Originally, the children of farmers joined to learn the skills of stock judging, public speaking, ploughing and animal care – it was a sort of local, part-time agricultural college. There were regular dances and it gained a reputation as a marriage bureau! Even now, many a newly-wed couple emerge from church to be greeted with an arch of pitchforks, the traditional guard of honour of the YFC.

Although the principles at the heart of YFC remain the same, its activities have diversified and now include concerts, drama, pantomimes, sports and other events to raise money for charity. The Young Farmers have fun and are always in evidence on regatta and carnival days.

The Young Farmers at their Christmas ball, 2002. (JB)

LOSTWITHIEL GARDEN SOCIETY

Mr Les Stephens, Hon. Secretary of the Lostwithiel Garden Society, knows more about its history than anyone else in Lostwithiel, having been a founder committee member and in 2003, the year of the organisation's 60th anniversary, having served for 60 years.

Les recalls that the society was founded by Mr Harold Hawken, the headmaster of Bodmin Hill

Above: *The Garden Society Committee, September 2002. Left to right: Mrs Joy Foot (treasurer), Mrs Hilda Sharpe, John Pegg (assistant secretary), Ms Cherrie Lang, Frank Ashton (cup secretary), Mrs A. Richards, Les Stephens (secretary), Miss Valerie Strout (chairman).* (IF)

Left: *Les Stephens tends his chrysanthemums in readiness for the show, c.1960.* (CBu)

School, in 1943. He arranged for the older boys, then 13 years of age, to develop a garden plot to grow vegetables on the field above the school. This 'war effort' helped everyone concerned, providing fresh vegetables and salad crops for the families, earning extra money for school funds (to be spent on football equipment) and establishing a long-lasting interest and love of gardening in some of the boys.

From this beginning the Garden Society grew. Adults in the town became interested and a committee was formed under the presidency of Mrs Sydney Brewer and chairmanship of Mr Hawken. Les Stephens, then one of the older schoolboys, was also elected onto the founding committee.

The society developed and continued to flourish. Many members were particularly interested in growing chrysanthemums, and until 1983 there were two shows a year, in July and November. Mr Hawken's own greatest love in the garden was growing chrysanthemums – indeed, he died while caring for his blooms. The number of classes for competitions increased yearly and cups and awards for prizes were given to the society by many generous enthusiasts.

For 40 years there were changes in the management committee and in the way things were done, and the fortunes of the society fluctuated year by year, as one might expect.

In 1984 a committee was elected which has hardly changed since. It includes: Miss Valerie Strout, chairman; Mrs Joy Foot, treasurer; Mr Les Stephens, secretary; Mr Frank Ashton, cup secretary; Mr John Pegg, assistant secretary; Mrs H. Sharpe, assistant treasurer; Mr L. Richards; Mrs M. Burgess; Mrs A. Richards; Ms Marshall; and Ms Lang. At the time of writing there are in the region of 70 members who are happy with the way in which the society is managed.

The Garden Society's annual show is held in September in the community centre. It is a highlight of the autumn season in the town and attracts a large number of entries and many visitors.

Over the years several well-known local personalities have opened the shows, including Robert Hicks MP, Lady Mary Holborow, Lord Lieutenant of Cornwall, Marian Chanter (a local girl who won the TV competition 'The Krypton Factor') and Beryl Davis of Probus Gardens. In 1990 the show was filmed for ITV's 'Gardens for All' and was opened by Terry Underhill. The film actor Eric Portman 'popped in' to visit the show on one occasion, attracting quite a bit of attention. He was on holiday at his cottage at Penpoll (and is now buried in St Veep churchyard).

Les Stephens recalls a number of excellent gardeners, past and present, including W.H. Coad, Colin Brown, Mr Yeo, Clifford Toms, W.H. Pearce, John Brown, McLellan Sim, C.F. Parsons, J. Keast, K. Eckardt, Eric Baker, Clifford Collings, Norman Vague, Roy Knight, Jack Toms, Ray Coles, Mike Coles, Stephen Peareth, John Pegg and many more – he has many amusing tales to tell about some of them!

The society enjoys a varied programme of events during the year; outdoor meetings and visits in the summer and speakers in the winter. There is always something interesting arranged for members. Mr Harold Hawken will long be remembered – he really started something.

St John Ambulance, Lostwithiel Division

During the Second World War local ladies, under the guidance of Dr Rudge, took classes in practical nursing and first aid. These included Miss May, Mrs Maggie Cavell and Miss Christine Rowe (Mrs

Myrtle Redmond at her Investiture as a Nursing Sister of the Venerable Order of the Hospital of St John of Jerusalem, 1983.
(MR)

Lostwithiel St John Ambulance Nursing Cadets, 1959. Officers, left to right: Mrs Joyce Dunkley (nursing officer), Princess Chula Chakrabongse (county president), Mrs Doris Liddicoat (Mayor), Mrs Mary Brewer (divisional president). Cadets, back row: Gwyneth Cottrell, Rosalie Murphy, Brenda Swatton, Angela Gardiner, Diane Dixon, Carol Parsons; centre: Christine Jeffery, Christine Murphy, Shirley Murch, Edwina Talling, Heather Wilton, Theresa Parker, Lesley Cottrell; front: Joanne Williams, Carol Swatton, Pat Jewels. (MR)

Barnicoat) and the seeds were sown for the formation of a St John Ambulance Division.

Mr Claud Jones set up the Boys' Cadets in 1957 and at about the same time the Lostwithiel Division of Nursing Cadets (girls) was formed with Mrs Joyce Dunkley as leader. There were 16 cadets, but numbers increased rapidly and the following year the division was highly praised by Princess Chula Chakrabongse of Siam, the county president (who lived in Cornwall), for the excellence of its standards. In the 1960s an adult division was formed with Mrs Phyllis Furse as leader and Mrs June Stephens as the nursing officer. Mrs Swift became divisional superintendent and Mrs Dunkley nursing officer for the cadets.

In 1967 Miss Myrtle Redmond joined the Nursing Cadets and became the divisional officer when Mrs Swift retired. At her retirement, a version of 'This is Your Life' was arranged for Mrs Swift. All the county officers of the brigade were present, and every organisation in Lostwithiel paid tribute to her work. She was honoured nationally when she was made a nursing sister of The Venerable Order of the Hospital of St John of Jerusalem, an award which was also made to Myrtle Redmond in 1983. Myrtle was made divisional superintendent in 1973 and brought many imaginative ideas to further the progress and work of the division. By 1980 it had raised enough money to buy a good second-hand ambulance. With this the division was able to carry the sick and elderly and

provide emergency accommodation at functions. At this time Mrs de Lancey Nicholls was president and Mrs Vera Howes the treasurer. Myrtle worked as a first aider, instructor, examiner and speaker at meetings. She organised events and outings both locally and further afield, to educate and maintain the enthusiasm of her cadets. In 1977 she took 37 cadets to London for the silver jubilee celebrations. The 'badgers', a group of six-to-ten-year-old beginners, were keen to learn and fun teaching methods held their interest.

Myrtle retired in 1990 after 23 years of service. Daphne Rollings carried on her good work as divisional superintendent until she had to give it up. Linda Austin is the president at the time of writing. Unfortunately, there is very little support for the local division and Dawn Byrnes is the only nursing adult in Lostwithiel. The cadets and badgers have had to be discontinued as no recruits are coming forward. The ambulance has gone into a 'pool' and is being put to good use elsewhere. The two officers, Sally Larsen and Dawn Byrnes, are serving in other towns. In 2003 Lostwithiel Division is being suspended for a while. The hope is that it will start up again before too long.

LOSTWITHIEL MUSEUM

Lostwithiel's museum is the smallest fully registered museum in Cornwall, possibly even in the country. It is housed in the eighteenth-century Corn Exchange with the much older town gaol behind. It displays, nevertheless, a wide variety of artefacts, domestic articles, craft tools, agricultural implements, ceramics, medals, minerals and costumes. The largest item on display is Lostwithiel's eighteenth-century hand-pumped fire-engine. The impressive photographic collection illustrates the social history of the town since the early days of photography. The museum publishes a local history journal three times a year. There is a small office above the old gaol, which houses the archives and a computer. Arrangements can be made with university departments for students to work with the curator.

The aim of the museum is to record and preserve the history of Lostwithiel, and to stimulate interest in the town's heritage.

The Lostwithiel Museum was founded in 1971 by a few members of the Old Cornwall Society, spearheaded by Mrs Dorothy de Lancey Nicholls, Mr Eric Furse and Miss Esme Santo. The basis of the collection was generously donated at this time by people of the town, in response to an appeal by the founders. The premises were offered by the Town Council at a peppercorn rent.

As a result of a great deal of hard work and commitment by Mrs Sally Whiffing, it achieved registered status with the Museums and Galleries Commission in 1993, and was also registered with the Charities Commission. In the same year the Lostwithiel Museum Association was formed.

There is a constant interchange of information between museum staff and visitors, many of whom come to ask or tell us about their forbears, and offer items of interest from Lostwithiel's past. In co-operation with the Lostwithiel Area Forum, the trustees conduct guided Heritage Walks during the summer season. They welcome new residents and visitors who are interested to learn more about the town.

The museum is a fully independent association, it is managed and staffed by volunteers and makes no charge for entry. Its income is generated by subscriptions, donations, sale of the journal and other items, and the small charge made for the guided walks. It receives occasional grants to buy necessary items of equipment. The volunteers work hard and are grateful to the people of Lostwithiel for their encouragement and support.

Lostwithiel Museum was opened in 1971 by Lord Edgcumbe. Left to right: *Mayoress Phyllis Furse, Mayor Eric Furse, Lady Edgcumbe, Lord Edgcumbe, Mrs Dorothy de Lancy Nicholls.* (LM)

Photograph taken in 1890 of the Corn Exchange (now the museum) and Guildhall above.
(FMH & RIC)

THE MONDAY CLUB

The Monday Club is a highly successful ladies' club of about 30 members which started in the early 1980s.

The Monday Club presents a nebuliser to Dr Michie, 1991. Left to right: *Nancy Deal (secretary), Lilian Rowe, Eileen Talling, ?, Dr Michie, Tony ?, ?, June Rule, ?, ?, Ann Brewer (chairman), Barbara Crago, Lilian Harris, ?, Joan Swiggs, Georgina Bray.* (CBu)

The ladies enjoy regular monthly meetings and combine convivial social activities with the serious business of fund-raising for charity. Over the years they have provided the local surgery with a nebuliser and a bladder scanner, and they have helped the SW Children's Hospice and Derriford Hospital, Plymouth. At the time of writing they are raising funds for FLEET (Front Line Emergency Equipment Trust) which buys equipment for Cornwall's ambulances, rescue helicopters, coastguard units and paramedics.

THE PRODUCE MARKET

Once a fortnight local people and many from farther afield come early in the day to the community centre to buy fresh food directly from the producers. More and more people are responding to this opportunity. Cornish craftsmen also sell their work directly to the public. The market has certainly grown in popularity over the years. It is obviously meeting a need and providing a service. From another point of view, it brings people into the town on a regular basis and boosts trade for local businesses.

THE LIBRARY, TAPRELL HOUSE

The Lostwithiel branch of the County Library is always busy, the atmosphere happy and relaxed. The librarians are welcoming and it is always a pleasure to push open the door and go inside. Taprell House is a place with a great deal of character, and a place where many interesting things happen. The library downstairs makes good use of the space available. It has a bright and attractive children's area, with books for children of all ages. Here groups of toddlers and infants meet regularly for 'story time' to listen and enjoy.

There is a section for 'talking books', videos and DVDs. The three librarians make sure that their clients get all the help and attention they need. Once a month two volunteers take books to housebound members of the library. Every care is taken by the librarians and the volunteers to ensure that they have a selection of books from which to choose, that will be to the members' taste. The public have access to computers and the internet whenever the library is open.

The attractive gallery above serves as a reference area and there is space and furniture here for private study. However, much more goes on in the building – there is a readers' group, an art group and a rug-hookers' group. The gallery is often in demand by societies for meetings, lectures and parties, as well as being a venue for artists, photographers and craftsmen to exhibit their work. The librarians also use this gallery for the children's activities they organise during school holidays. Book sales take place here; cards and booklets of local interest are also sold.

Story time for toddlers at Lostwithiel Library with Debbie Coombe, library manager, 2003. (IF)

Librarian Jan Simons greets Mrs Jean Gadd, 2003. (IF)

The Readers' Group. Left to right, standing: *Pauline Baker, Ann Henderson, Jeanne Jones, Jenny March;* seated: *Gina Crook, Lynne Wilson, Penny White (librarian), Frank Little, Nicky Hendry, 2003.* (IF)

The Rug Hookers, 2003. Left to right: *Judith Newell, Diane Best, Sue Bennett, Pat Howe, John Goodchild.* (IF)

Volunteer 'mobile librarians' Rita Durrant and Peter Best, 2003. (BF)

1st Lostwithiel Brownies, 1981. (PW)

*1 Shirley Ashton, 2 Pat Wilton, 3 Janet Sandercock,
4 Jean Wilson, 5 Rebecca Fishburn, 6 Claire Pearce,
7 Sandra Dungey, 8 Emma Shand, 9 Katrina Phillips,
10 Sharon Crago, 11 Jo Bonney, 12 Katie Young,
13 Jo Carslake, 14 Marie Ashton, 15 Anna Pollard,
16 Margaret Sim, 17 Kay Saundry, 18 Lisa Sandercock,
19 Genevieve Hexter, 20 Victoria Harris, 21 Isobel Vellero,
22 Naomi Dennison, 23 Tara Peareth, 24 Kate Carslake.*

The librarians welcome visitors to this historic building. Since the library moved into Taprell House in 1993, the number of services it offers has grown in a remarkable way, enriching the lives of many people.

GUIDES, BROWNIES & RAINBOWS

The Girl Guides have been active in Lostwithiel since the early 1920s and have a distinguished record – indeed, a number of local girls have become 'Queen's Guides' over the years. There have been many keen and happy Brownies too, working for badges and enjoying their expeditions and camping holidays. The Rainbows group, inaugurated in 1994, is well supported by the five and six year olds, who cannot wait to get started on this exciting adventure of 'belonging'.

The first Promise ceremony of the newly formed Lostwithiel Rainbows, November 1994. Left to right, back row: Guider Claire Mitson, Mayor George Stuchbery, Mayoress Wendy Stuchbery, Assistant Guider Rosemary Robson, young leader Hayley Lambden; centre: Hayley Byrnes, Stephanie Newton, Talisa Powell, Jennifer Whiffing, Gemma Parsons; front: Rhiannon Symons-Brown, Laura Narbett, Ashleigh Charles, Victoria Crago, Jessica Ryder. (CM)

Queen's Guides and Guiders, 1985. Left to right: Pat Wilton, Annamarie Wilton, Shelley Gaffney, Thelma Crocker (captain), Catherine Harris, Barbara Gaffney. (PW)

125

SCOUTS, CUBS & BEAVERS

Many generations of Lostwithiel boys have enjoyed belonging to the Cubs and Scouts. The strength of the local groups has varied from time to time. In pre-war days it was strong, but then lapsed for a while. During the 1950s there was a company of Sea Scouts. Mrs Jill Reed started a new Cub pack in 1973, and soon after this Mr Bert Lane and his son Graham started up the Scouts again. Mrs Sheila Tyack started a group of Venture Scouts for young people aged between 16 and 22. Lostwithiel Beavers, for children aged between six and eight, was one of the first in Cornwall. Over the years there have been many willing adults taking on the responsibility for these groups, Mrs Brenda Hamley ran the Cubs for many years. The Bonney family has been very much involved with the movement, and at the time of writing Simon Bonney is an assistant County Commissioner.

Cub Scout diamond jubilee celebrations, 1976. Lostwithiel Cubs enjoy their share of the 37.7-metre sausage, zigzagged and cooked over an open fire at Tredithick Farm. Left to right: *Jeremy Bonney, Mark Treleaven, Richard Rawlings, Stephen Pearce, Anthony Rawlings.* (ST)

Left: *Lostwithiel Scouts with their raft, ready for the race during the regatta, 1979.* Left to right: *Mark Treleaven, Simon Wills, Richard Gibbons, Christopher Bonney.* (ST)

THIRD FRIDAY FOOD

One very successful and popular enterprise, set up at the start of the 1990s, is Third Friday Food, organised by a committee of ladies working on behalf of the Church. Once a month there is, as though by magic (in fact, it is by means of much forethought and hard work), a restaurant in the church hall, serving a variety of delicious home-made dishes. The tables are beautifully set, decorated with fresh flowers from their gardens and the service is second to none. The clientele, on average about 60–70 people, represents a cross-section of the people of the town. Newcomers are quickly made welcome and the atmosphere is one of great warmth and comradeship. This is a very valuable service to the community.

Above: *The Third Friday Food committee.* Left to right, standing: *Betty Tomlinson, Marlene Cooper, Eileen Lowman, Joy Foot;* seated: *Maggie Cavell, Vera Howes (chairman), Betty Jeffery.* (BF)

There are a number of fund-raising organisations in Lostwithiel, in aid of Cancer Research, Mount Edgcumbe Hospice, SW Children's Hospice, RNLI, Red Cross, Friends of St Bartholomew's Church and many others. The various committees work hard for their causes, numerous enterprises are undertaken, a lot of enjoyment ensues and a great deal of money is raised each year. Lostwithiel people are compassionate and generous with their time and talents.

THE ADVENT WINDOW TRAIL

In 1999, Gina O'Keeffe, Jenni Greenhalgh, Debenie Morse and Ruth Edward-Collins organised an activity for advent, that originated in Switzerland. On 1 December and on each day thereafter until Christmas Eve, a window in the town was decorated, using a seasonal theme, and was lit up in the evening.

The Advent Trail proved to be very popular and each year since 1999 it has led us up and down the shopping streets and into residential areas. Children and parents enjoy finding each new display throughout the days of December, then walking the complete trail on Christmas Eve. This charming approach to Christmas is becoming a tradition.

Chapter 14

PEOPLE OF LOSTWITHIEL

Throughout the centuries the town has influenced the lives of those who have dwelt here, and the people have all in their turn contributed to the character of the town. This interaction is still happening and can be seen in the experiences of a number of people over the past century and to 2003. In some cases these experiences have been local, while others have linked Lostwithiel to distant places and momentous events.

NATHANIEL THOMAS COULSON

Nathaniel Thomas Coulson lived here for only four years, but his memories of Lostwithiel had a profound effect on him and illustrate this interaction. His is a tale of 'rags to riches', and remarkable generosity. Born in 1853, the son of Mary Bradley Coulson of Penzance, Nathaniel Thomas was baptised into the Roman Catholic Church. His mother died in Bodmin Asylum in 1854, leaving a husband and three children aged four years, three years and ten months. His father had been disowned by his family and, on losing his wife, he took his children to Plymouth. Five years later he deserted them, so they were taken into Plymouth workhouse before being transferred to Bodmin workhouse the following year.

At the age of ten Nathaniel was apprenticed to Mr Hoare, farmer of Penquite Farm, where he stayed for four years. During this time he attended Lostwithiel Methodist Church and the Sunday school. Here he was shown sympathy and kindness by Sunday-school teacher, Abigail Santo, who befriended him when some of the children in the class were unkind to him. When he was aged 14 he was given a Bible and 10s. by Mr Hoare, he left the farm and set out to seek his fortune. He joined the Royal Navy and trained on HMS *Impregnable*. During the years 1869–74 he served on seven different ships, and at the age of 21 he became a Freemason and bought his discharge from the Navy at Devonport.

The common before Coulson Park was developed. (LM)

Later that year he emigrated to the USA and took a post as clerk in a granary business in Pennsylvania. His brother and sister had by then married and settled down. Nathaniel was a man with a conscience, he spent several years travelling, looking for his father and eventually caught up with him. When his father died, Nathaniel settled his estate, sent his brother and sister their share, and was left with only £20.

Returning almost penniless to the USA in 1877, he worked for three years and attended night school until in 1880, now 27 years of age, he registered with the University of California and five years later graduated as a doctor of dental surgery.

For 15 years Dr Nathaniel Coulson ran a very lucrative dental practice, investing his money in property in San Francisco, where he had settled, and in 1900 he set off on a trip around the world, including Lostwithiel in his itinerary. While he was here he contributed nine gold links to be added to the Mayoral chain. He gave £100 to establish a park along the river, on the common land where the sawmills had been, and a further sum to provide a footbridge over the river to Madderley Moor (however, owing to disputes over land ownership, the bridge was never built). Believing that emigration should be encouraged, Nathaniel gave money to start an emigration fund for young men in the Bodmin and Lostwithiel area.

As a result of the San Francisco earthquake of April 1906 he lost his entire fortune. Despite this setback Dr Coulson re-established himself and in 1907 the park in Lostwithiel was officially opened with much celebration, and given the name Coulson Park. Two years later the doctor was well on his way to making another fortune.

In 1915, during the First World War, he set up the Coulson War Fund from which people in Lostwithiel benefited. He retired in 1925, once again a very rich man. San Francisco also benefited from his generosity,

Coulson Park, Empire Day, 24 May 1908. (LM)

particularly the multi-denominational Grace Cathedral at the top of Nob Hill. One of his gifts to the cathedral was the bell tower and the carillon of 44 bells, first rung in 1940. One of these is named 'The Sympathy Bell', and is dedicated in honour of Abigail Santo of Lostwithiel, whose kindness Nathaniel never forgot.

He did not visit Lostwithiel again after 1900. He died in 1945 at the age of 92. His name and his generous spirit live on in the riverside park, which has been enjoyed daily by so many people for almost a century.

A biography of Dr Coulson, *The Bells Shall Ring*, by Rosa Lee Bauldwin was published in 1940 in USA. Several people have exchanged visits with representatives of the Grace Cathedral over the years and Lostwithiel Museum has been presented with a copy of this book. The latest visitor to Lostwithiel, re-establishing the link with our mutual benefactor, was Mr Michael Lampton, archivist at the cathedral, who spent a happy day here in the year 2000, entertained by the Mayoress, Glenda Langsford and members of the museum committee.

ODESSA TOMLIN

Odessa Tomlin lived all her long life in Lostwithiel, from 1892 into the 1980s. In her old age she was able to recall many stories of her past as well as stories her mother had told her, going back 150 years. Her maternal grandfather, George Burton, had been born in Gooseytown in 1828, when the cottages beside the river (built for the bargees and sawyers who worked in the mills) were new. (The neighbourhood was so called because geese were kept on the common. It is now known as Park Road and Coulson Park.) George Burton was a sawyer whose wife died having their 13th child. Odessa's mother, Emma, born in 1868, was their 11th child.

An article written in 1871 described Gooseytown as:

... a poor, miserable, wretched looking hamlet. The houses... are approaching collapse... within they are dirty, comfortless and dank... sometimes there is an

Samuel Short with his wife Emma (née Burton) and children, Ernest, Mary and baby Odessa in 1894. (LM)

unseemly mixture of the sexes, all huddled together in the same sleeping room... no wonder we have so much immorality among us... the drains are all open... reeking refuse is thrown upon the dunghill or into the cesspool hard by.

When Leslie Mayell (Mayor in 1975) was interviewing Odessa and mentioned this article, she was indignant, responding 'that's wrong, it makes it out worse than a slum and it wasn't.' Her grandfather had a garden and kept a pig. Like most families they had a barrel of salted pilchards for the winter, and their rubbish was thrown into the river.

As the children grew up they went into service, as Odessa explained:

They had to make room for others coming along... they didn't bother about schooling, but my grandmother had all her children christened, so there must have been a sense of what was right and proper.

Emma married Samuel Short of Duloe, in St Bartholomew's Church, Lostwithiel, when she was 20. Samuel had come to the town to be a porter and gardener at the Royal Talbot Hotel, a position he held for 40 years. The family lived at 6 Duke Street and Emma gave birth to four children there.

Odessa told stories she had heard of her father's involvement with the Mock Mayor Choosing

The Short family and soldiers billeted with them, outside 6 Duke Street, 1915. Left to right: *Soldier, Mary Short, Emma, Samuel, soldier, Odessa (later Tomlin), soldier.* (LM)

Vivian Hony's christening at Trewithan in 1939. Outlined, back row, left to right: *Miss Maud, Miss Ellen, Miss Ada;* front row: *Miss Emily.* (VH)

William Henry Hony of 13 Summer Lane, 1850s. (VH)

Mary Hony, William Hony's wife in the 1850s. (VH)

ceremonies, when he was lampooned and given the title of 'Champion Tripe Consumer'. She remembered the Boer War and marching with her sister up the St Austell Road, with others from the town, to see off the reservist, volunteer soldiers. She also recalled the tea parties on the Parade to celebrate the relief of Ladysmith and Mafeking. The children at that time enjoyed sweeties called Kruger's Whiskers, chocolate-covered coconut strips.

Odessa's two brothers served in the First World War and as part of her war service she worked for the Post Office, pushing the handcart loaded with the midday mail, down to the railway station. During the Second World War Odessa and her husband took charge of the hostel for evacuees at Springfield House. Both her parents died during this time. Odessa lived for many years in North Street, she was always happy to talk about the past, and she and the stories she told are remembered by many people in the town .

THE HONY FAMILY

For almost 20 years from 1939, four elderly, unmarried sisters, the Misses Hony, lived together at 9 Clifden Terrace. Emily lived to be 96, Ellen 94, Ada 100 and Maud 88. They and their brothers, William and Charles, had all been born in Lostwithiel between 1859 and 1870. Maud, the youngest of the sisters, probably had the most exciting life. She travelled across the world and was governess to a child who grew up to become internationally famous for his daring and courage.

The family's connection with Lostwithiel dates from the mid-1850s, when William Henry Hony, whose father farmed at Sibleyback, married Mary Thomas, daughter of a noted mining family of Camborne. Mary's maternal ancestry, through the Vivians of Trelowarren, could be traced back to the Plantagenets. They came to Lostwithiel, where William was the accountant to the East Cornwall Bank (originally the Foster and Bolitho Bank, now Barclays) and took up residence at 13 Summer Street

Maud Hony in 1903. (VH)

(then called Summer Lane). They had nine children, three of whom died in infancy. William Henry became the bank manager and by 1871 they had moved to a larger house, 2 Rose Villas (probably on the west side of Rose Hill). William Henry died of tuberculosis at the age of 42, leaving Mary to bring up their six surviving children alone. The children's ages at this time ranged from two to thirteen years.

The family moved to Bodmin and both sons eventually went into banking. Charles married and made his career in Bodmin. The widowed Mary lived there until her death in 1930 at the age of 98. She was a strong character of amazing vitality, she had a remarkable memory until the end of her life and was adored by her six ageing children. William, after a career in America, retired to Lostwithiel and bought 9 Clifden Terrace in about 1935. After his death, just before the outbreak of war, the four elderly sisters moved into his house.

Ada had been a teacher and Maud a governess. The latter had worked with families abroad and had travelled to Europe, North Africa and South America during Victorian and Edwardian times, having many adventures and unusual experiences, and writing fascinating letters home. Perhaps one of her most interesting posts, to us today, was her appointment in 1910 as governess to Count von Stauffenberg. She lived with the family in the castle at Stuttgart. Her pupil was to become internationally famous in 1944 for his part in the plot, and failed attempt, to assassinate Hitler. The conspirators were discovered and shot.

Many people in the town remember the Misses Hony. Mr Vivian Hony of Oundle is the grandson of Charles, he has inherited many papers, letters and photographs relating to his family's history. In 2003 he called on Myrtle Redmond at 13 Summer Street, and was delighted to be made so welcome and to discover the house where his great-grandparents had lived in the early days of their marriage, in the mid-1800s.

RICHARD WALKHAM

Richard Walkham (1850–1927) was known and loved by everybody in Lostwithiel. When he died, it is said, the whole town attended his funeral. The following is taken from an obituary which appeared in the local paper. Mrs Iona Wilton and others of his great-grandchildren have original copies.

An appreciation by J.H.T.
'Do the duty which lies before thee' (Carlyle)
'Duty is a path which all may tread.' (Lewis Morris)

The subject of my appreciation, the late Dick Walkham, did the one and trod the path of the other. This is my only apology, even if one is needed, in writing these few disjointed paragraphs on Dick Walkham.

Lostwithiel has within the last few days lost one of its oldest inhabitants, none better known and few more respected or entitled to it than Dick, a well-known figure in its streets. The ancient borough is the poorer by his tragically sudden death.

Richard Walkham, 1850–1927, the oldest fireman in England. (MRu)

It is not my intention to write his life... but to give a few of the impressions he made upon my mind and the idea I formed therefrom of his life and character.

My acquaintance with him has been of a few recent years only... He was in many ways a man with a strong personality. I always found in his talk a source of pleasure and profit.

Born sometime during the year 1850, he has had a long and varied career, possessing a most retentive memory... Several of his stories, especially those relating to the 'Mock Mayor Choosing', deserve a better fate than relegation to the list of forgotten events. Others, perhaps, are better forgotten; in any case the majority of the crowd that gathered yearly at this function was amused, though occasionally the fun was not seen or the amusement felt, when the speeches became a bit too personal. Dick took a part in this ceremony which has died a natural death and today there is no desire to see a 'Mock Mayor Choosing' revived.

Dick was a good sportsman. His eyes would glisten with pleasure, even his pipe would be neglected, as he related stories of the many runs he had taken part in with the otter hounds. He kept this pleasure up until his death. It was his intention to have a 'day out' on Friday last, but death came to him before the hounds met. To those familiar with the task of following otter hounds, it shows how virile he must have felt at the age of nearly 77 years.

In his earlier days he was a boxer of no mean repute... After a hard day's work in the yard (GWR) he would hurry home to tea, walk to Bodmin and enjoy taking part in a boxing match, walking back to his home after the bout. Known as the 'Boxing Blacksmith', he was a man of fine physique and of great strength, of even temper, never known to lose it, which, no doubt, helped him considerably to down his man when boxing. Not quarrelsome in any way, he never allowed anyone to bully a weaker chum or mate. He was employed for many years in the GWR shops at Lostwithiel Station...

He always kept his promise either to blow an organ or to have a grave ready. He was organ blower in the church and grave digger in the churchyard. He could be depended upon... For over 50 years he was a member of the borough fire brigade. It has been stated he was the oldest fireman in England, proud of his uniform, very proud of his medals and exceedingly proud of the long service he had rendered, most excusable pride in this case.

He shouldered the responsibilities of life in no small degree and he did it too without a complaint. A numerous family, born when a quiver-full was looked upon as riches (and happiness came thereby) but wages did not increase in the same proportion... Many grandchildren too, I do not know the number, but there was room in Dick's heart for all. Today both children and grandchildren have heavy hearts and bowed heads, heavy and bowed with grief and sorrow. His was a nature that gave and inspired love...

Steele said in the Spectator *many years ago, 'the man who does all he can in a low station is a hero.'*

Since writing the above I have attended the funeral and as I anticipated it was largely attended. Practically the whole of the inhabitants of Lostwithiel attended to pay a tribute of respect to the memory of one who won it by his life and actions.

Dick died in the 'doing of an act of grace' for a fellow townsman, and this his last act was not the only deed of kindness, but one of very many that he had performed, and which was a true index of his life and character.

ARTHUR WILKINSON

The first radio ever to receive signals over the airwaves in Lostwithiel was made and used by the young enthusiast, Arthur Wilkinson, at 11 King Street in the 1920s. In later years, when it became fashionable to own a wireless, Arthur became the maker, retailer and maintainer of wireless sets for the population of the town.

Arthur Wilkinson was born in 1897 in Charlestown. Soon after the First World War broke out he joined up and served with the RAMC. After the war he took a job with the GWR as a porter on Princetown Station.

Arthur and Lilian Wilkinson outside 11 King Street in the 1920s. (BR)

In 1920 he married Lilian Liddicoat and transferred to Lostwithiel Station. They came to live at 11 King Street, tucked away to the left at the end of the cul-de-sac. Son Jack (Arthur John) was born in 1921 and daughter Betty, now Rawlings, in 1923. Arthur spent much of his spare time indulging his passion for his hobby, the wireless. Amongst Betty's earliest memories are those of her father working for long hours on his wireless, and taking his sets to the open window of their house to 'tune in' and pick up signals. Imagine his excitement and joy at first hearing broadcast sound on a set that he had made himself, and his delight and pride on being the first person in the town to do so! The neighbours caught the excitement too and would come over to the open window of No. 11 to 'listen-in' with Arthur.

In the very early days, broadcasting was carried on by the research departments of industrial companies and by scientific amateurs. Then in 1922 the British Broadcasting Company was set up in

London to broadcast programmes of news, music, talks and plays, and the craze for wireless soon gripped the nation. Relay stations were set up in 1924 to carry the BBC broadcasts to further parts of Britain, and by 1926 when the British Broadcasting Corporation took over from the Company, 2,000,000 families had acquired sets and were tuning in to programmes.

Arthur responded to the demand and developed a business from home, making and selling radios. Each was fitted into a hand-made wooden box with a lid. The boxes were made for him by local carpenter, Harry Bassett. Arthur regularly worked late into the night, his workbench lit by an oil lamp. He kept pace with the rapid developments in radio, and his business flourished. Radios were powered by wet batteries (accumulators) which needed to be charged regularly, and customers would bring these back to Arthur for charging. The workshop in the garden housed the generator that supplied the electricity for this (there was no mains electricity supplied to Lostwithiel). There must have been a regular stream of people making their way up and down King Street carrying their heavy accumulators.

In the early 1930s there was an opportunity for the Wilkinson family to move to shop premises at 3 Fore Street. The property offered good family accommodation, plus a workshop and garden. As young Jack was growing up sharing his father's interest in wireless, and learning the skills involved, Arthur and Lilian decided to take the plunge. They bought the property and moved the family and the business.

It was an excellent move. The family settled in well and two more children were born, Molly in 1932 and George Venner in 1937. Having a shop in the centre of town was a great bonus. There were numerous sidelines to sell and they began to carry a greater stock of radios. Arthur set up his generator in the workshop and there was always a row of accumulators on charge, each with its owner's name on it. Betty enjoyed helping, connecting and disconnecting the wires between the generator and the wet batteries, and testing the voltage. She liked to be the one to respond to the shop bell, always hoping that it would be a customer wanting a high-tension battery. These cost 19s.6d. each and brought in a fair bit of profit and a smile to her dad's face.

Wilkinson's shop was the hub of Lostwithiel's radio contact with the rest of the world. Once established, 'listening-in' became essential, life without a wireless would be flavourless and dull and no one let their batteries run down if they could avoid it. Everyone shared the excitement of national events as they happened.

Arthur kept his job with the railway and Lillian ran the shop, together with Jack after he left school. Arthur worked in the shop in the evenings fitting up and repairing radios, there was always plenty of work on hand. Betty left school just as George Venner was born, so she spent a year at home helping wherever she was needed. The following year she started work at the railway station as a clerk in the ticket office.

Electricity was first brought to Lostwithiel in 1936. The town was slow to convert from gas, but as it did, radios which plugged into the mains were added to the stocks in the shop. Things were going well with the Wilkinson family business when the Second World War started.

Jack volunteered and joined up in 1940, as his father had done 25 years earlier. Jack joined the RAF as a wireless operator and gunner. Lillian and Arthur kept the shop going for Jack's homecoming after the war. Tragically Jack was killed in Sicily in 1943. He was posted missing, and exactly a year to the day later it was confirmed that he had lost his life. Jack is buried in the military cemetery in Catania, Sicily. Betty and her husband Phil have visited the grave and are satisfied that he is at peace.

Betty met Phil Rawlings on VE Day (8 May 1945) at the railway station in Lostwithiel as he was coming home on leave. Phil's mother had moved to the town during the war. They were introduced to each other by Phil's mother and were married in 1947.

After the war the radio shop developed further. The range of radios available was increasing all the time and very few homes were without one. TV, which had been developed in 1936 and shelved during the war, was beginning to gather momentum in the early 1950s. As soon as there was a transmission mast in this area Lostwithiel people started to be interested, and TV became an important part of the business.

Two more shops dealing in radios and electrical goods had opened up in the town – Crago's, later Pearce's, and McLean's. Business during the 1950s must have been booming, while at the same time, owing to the growing popularity of TV, the local cinema was suffering from lack of support. On reaching the age of 65, Arthur Wilkinson retired from the railway. During 42 years he and Lostwithiel Station had become very much part of each other. He and Lilian gave up the shop the following year, 1963. They went to live with Betty and Phil, who had a house big enough to provide a flat for them. Here they enjoyed independence, together with the comfort of having their family around them. Lilian lived until 1967 Arthur until 1970.

One of Arthur's radios, made in the early 1930s. (BR)

Two years later, a local man called Claud Jones, saw an old radio in an auction sale. Under the lid of its wooden box was the label 'Arthur Wilkinson, 11 King Street'. It was a model made in the early 1930s. Claud Jones bought the radio and gave it to Keith, Arthur's grandson, who has inherited the interest. Keith treasures this family heirloom and keeps it in good working order.

SIR ROBERT HOWE

Sir Robert Howe GBE KCMG, Governor General of the Sudan 1947–55, has a place in the hearts of many older residents of the town. They remember Sir Robert and Lady Howe with affection. Theirs was a romantic love story.

Robert was born in Derby on 19 September 1893. His father worked in the railway yard, maintaining railway engines, and the family lived in a two-up, two-down terraced cottage near the station. Robert was a clever boy and won a scholarship to Derby Grammar School. Here he carried off all the prizes in all subjects, standing back from time to time, to give the other boys a chance.

In 1912 he won a scholarship to Cambridge University, where he proved to be an excellent scholar. When war broke out in 1914 he volunteered for the Army and was commissioned in the Sixth Royal Dublin Fusiliers. He was posted, along with men of the Sherwood Foresters to Lostwithiel. He was 21. Being an officer, he was given a superior billet and found himself at Cowbridge with the well-respected Hext family. Miss Loveday Hext, the daughter of the family, was a lively and attractive young lady, and she and Robert fell in love. This was viewed with dismay and some hostility by her parents and the friendship was discouraged. Soon the regiment moved on and Robert was taken prisoner in the Dardanelles in 1915. He spent the rest of the war in prison camps, using the time at his disposal to learn languages.

After the war, his ambition was to join the Foreign Office. There is a story that his tailor in Cambridge

Recruiting parade in Monmouth Square, 1915.
Captain Robert Howe is front right. (LM)

made him the formal dress that was necessary in those days for his Foreign Office interview, in full confidence that he would be successful and soon able to pay the bill! His first post was as a Third Secretary. He and Loveday had not forgotten each other during their long separation, nor had their feelings changed, and after his appointment they were married, the Hext family having come to accept him.

Robert's rise in the Foreign Office was spectacular. He served in Belgrade, Rio de Janeiro, Bucharest, Peking and Addis Ababa. He was fearless and in China, 1937, when the Japanese ordered all British residents to leave Nanking, he replied 'I propose to remain in Nanking with my staff. The Japanese Government will be held responsible if Britons are injured or British property is damaged.' He was later lucky to escape when a train on which he was travelling was attacked by Japanese planes.

He was appointed Governor General of the Sudan in 1947, under the Joint Rule Agreement between Britain and Egypt, whereby the Governor General was appointed by Egyptian rulers on the recommendation of the British Government Department. The Governor General had always been British. It was a time of great sensitivity, the Sudanese were pressing for self-rule, the British policy was to work towards this end, but the Egyptians were set against it. They abrogated the treaty with Britain in 1951 and refused to recognise the British Governor General any longer. Nevertheless Sir Robert stayed on and continued his work, educating and developing the neglected and backward southern region of the Sudan and working towards the independence of the country.

Sir Robert was tough, a man of strong principles and deep religious conviction. He had powers of diplomacy and strength of character. Knowing that Khartoum was a dangerous place and that two of his predecessors had been assassinated while in office, he said 'We have a great cause in the Sudan and I shall fight for it.' He and the Sudanese had grown to like, trust and respect each other. In January 1954 the first all-Sudanese Government assumed office, beginning a transitional programme which was completed in 1955. Not until then did Sir Robert retire. On 1 January 1956 the Republic of Sudan was formally established. It joined the Arab League and United Nations later that year.

Lady Howe did not accompany her husband on all of his tours of office. She spent much time at home in Lostwithiel with her family and son, Peter. She was an excellent horsewoman and very sociable, and took part in many aspects of the life of the town. The couple had learned from their first meeting to cope well with separation. On his retirement, Sir Robert came home to Cowbridge and, together with his wife, entered into the life of Lostwithiel, supporting the Church and community events. He was invited by the Borough Council to become the Mayor in 1958, and he graciously accepted for one year.

He was an excellent and popular Mayor, remembered particularly for insisting on having a telephone installed in the municipal office!

Sir Robert and Lady Howe enjoyed their retirement together. Loveday lived to be 78 and Robert outlived her by 11 years. The tablet in their memory in St Bartholomew's Church records her as being 'Loveday Mary 1892–1970 his wife and comrade'.

PEGGY DOGGETT, NÉE BATTISON

Mrs Peggy Doggett, who at the time of writing lives in Wimborne, Dorset, was born Peggy Battison at Pill Farmhouse in 1912 and lived there until 1919. Her father was the Customs and Excise Officer and rented the house from Mr Nicholls, who farmed the land. Peggy has vivid memories of life in Lostwithiel in those days. She went to 'school' at 'Gilbury' on Rose Hill with her brother Alfred, who was a year older, and a boy from Bridgend, called Ivor Harper. Here they were the only pupils of Miss Ivy Stuart. Miss Stuart was not very fond of boys so Peggy was her favourite, and as a result she was constantly teased by the two boys.

Peggy remembers that walking between the town and Pill, one had to pass the gasworks (behind the houses on Park Road). It was always an anxious moment for the little girl, as frequently 'the geese rushed out with necks stretched and hissing alarmingly' on their way to the river.

She recalls having a photograph taken. On the preceding night her hair was curled into ringlets for the occasion. It was dampened with sugar and water and twisted into ringlets with strips of cloth. By morning it was ready to be brushed and combed. The photographer worked in a wooden hut painted white, on the Bridgend side of the railway crossing.

Just before her seventh birthday the family moved to Hill House, Bodmin Hill, which they rented from a

The teachers whom Peggy remembers at Bodmin Hill School, 1922. Left to right, standing: *Miss Dora Nicholls, F.A. Green (headmaster), Mrs Green, Miss A.M. Neal;* seated: *Miss Kate Nicholls, Joseph Levers, Mrs S. Harris.* (LM)

Miss Nicholls for £30 a year. Peggy became a pupil at Bodmin Hill School. She writes of her experience on Sydney Brewer's wedding day:

Mrs Jenkin next door had a tennis-court where we often played and where a marquee was erected for the wedding of Mary Jenkin to Sydney Brewer. We not only had a view of the bride and groom and wedding guests arriving back at the house, but could see them in the garden! This was a day when the neighbours complained about us. The people from the cottages (across the road) had come across to lean against our railings and watch the arrivals. Alfred and Ivor Harper were as usual tormenting me, so I had locked myself in the bedroom immediately over the front door, to get a good view. Our parents had gone to the wedding. The boys... took a bowl of water to the room above the one I was in... and as I looked out, poured it over me. I ducked in and the water splashed over the windowsill and over Mrs Toms and worse, over Mrs Sandry's best black cape, which she had donned in honour of the occasion. By the time our parents came home they had already been made aware of our bad behaviour and we had to go over and apologise to the neighbours. We were a disgrace! It did us no good when we said that they should not have been on our steps!

When she was ten years old Peggy went to Bodmin Grammar School. Her brother Alfred went away to St Boniface School in Plymouth where he was not happy and where his health deteriorated. He died of TB at the age of 17. Mrs Jenkin gave them a part of the Jenkin's family plot in the graveyard for his burial. Peggy remembers:

There were horse-drawn carriages for the family [at the funeral] and following on foot nearly every man from the town headed by the Mayor, Aldermen and Councillors... we were all dressed in black for six months, then mauve or grey, even Mary who was only ten. Our notepaper was black-edged for a year.

The Battisons were a Roman Catholic family (there was only one other in Lostwithiel at that time), but they never encountered any prejudice, just a little curiosity! Peggy moved away with the family after she left school. She has treasured her memories of childhood days in Lostwithiel ever since and remains in touch with the McPhersons, who now live at Pill.

FLORENCE NETHERTON, NÉE PRYNNE

A lady very active on the local fund-raising committee for Mount Edgcumbe Hospice, Florence Netherton remembers life 'in service' at Pelyn in the 1930s.

In 2003 it would be unthinkable for a young girl of 14 or 15 to leave home, take a residential job and work for 12 hours a day, six days a week. Yet this practice was taken for granted in the 1930s. There were not many other jobs available for the majority of girls leaving school in this part of the world, and it was usual for doctors, solicitors, bank managers, shopkeepers, businessmen and industrialists to employ live-in maids and nannies.

Conditions of work varied a great deal, and girls were lucky if they found employment in well-run houses with kind, considerate employers. To work for 'the gentry' was special.

Florence Netherton (née Prynne) was lucky, although it wasn't all luck, it was her own reputation that secured her position. In 1935, when Florence (usually called Florrie) was 15, her friend Eileen went to work for Mr and Mrs Nicholas Kendal at Pelyn. They soon needed another maid and when Florrie was recommended to them as being honest and dili-gent, they were happy to employ her too. Eileen was able to reassure Florrie that they were good, kind people and that together they would be very happy at Pelyn.

It was, nevertheless, a sad day when she had to say goodbye to her childhood and set off from her home in St Stephen. She made her way by means of train and buses to the big house that was to be her home for over six years. Although having Eileen there made it easier, those early days were difficult. Florrie was homesick, but she came to terms with her situation and settled down to enjoy a completely different way of life.

The Kendal family had lived at Pelyn for many centuries. One of their ancestors had been warden of Restormel Castle for the Black Prince, in the fourteenth century. Since then Kendals had been prominent in local affairs. Mr Nicholas Kendal and his wife were the last of the family to live at Pelyn – they were probably in their thirties when Florrie was there and were childless. The house at Pelyn had been built in the seventeenth century, but a large part of it had been rebuilt following a fire in the 1800s. The large dining-room, drawing-room and ballroom are all part of the new building. The servants' bedrooms and the sitting-room they shared were in the oldest part of the house, approached by back stairs from the kitchen quarters. The ceilings were low and the windows small, but there was a good fire and a wireless in the sitting-room. It was cosy and it was home to them when they were off duty. *(See picture on page 52).*

There was a staff of three living in at Pelyn in 1935 – the cook, an unmarried older lady, Eileen, the parlour maid and Florrie, the kitchen maid. The gardener, Mr Herd, lived at Penknight and came in daily, and a lady came by bus from Par on Fridays to do rough work, scrubbing steps and cleaning grates. Pelyn is a big house in extensive grounds and in those days it was a full-time job for the staff to keep it clean, polished and well maintained, as well as to

see to the daily needs of Mr and Mrs Kendal and provide meals for all the household. The day started early for Eileen and Florrie – taking tea upstairs at 7a.m. was the first job. Breakfast was served at 9a.m. by the maids, spick and span in their starched white caps and aprons. Florrie remembers that while they cleared up after breakfast, Mrs Kendal would be in the kitchen cutting up food for the cats. The Kendals were very fond of animals and had several cats and two dogs. Mrs Kendal also kept a cow that she milked herself and she made butter and cream in the dairy adjoining the kitchen. The Kendals took an interest in the garden and enjoyed walking in their acres of beautifully wooded grounds, but they were not practical gardeners and Mr Herd did all the work himself. One of Florrie's regular winter jobs was to go down to the woods with him and help to load up a cart with the logs that he had cut for fires.

Life at Pelyn was largely uneventful, Florrie and Eileen's days were taken up with routine tasks about the house. Although the house had its own electric-ity generator for lighting, it was not powerful enough to run a vacuum cleaner or a washing machine. (There were very few of these about in those days.) The girls cleaned the carpets with a brush and dustpan. Household linen was sent away to a laundry in St Blazey and came back beautifully laun-dered. The staff of four had plenty of work to fill their days, and none of them had any idea of what their employers' wider interests were, where they went or what they did when they were away from the house. The girls never overheard anything personal being discussed, and never felt any curiosity about any of these things.

Florence Netherton (née Prynne) at the front door of Pelyn with Sally, the Kendals' dog, 1930s. (FN)

The Kendals were gentle, quiet people, they didn't entertain very much, just the occasional dinner party for friends. Very rarely did people come to stay. The beautiful ballroom was always kept immaculate and aired by big fires, but it was never used in the years that Florrie was there. She remembers that Mr Kendal was fond of knitting and spent many happy hours knitting socks, while his wife would read and potter around the house and garden. Neither of them hunted, but during the hunting season they would entertain the hunt to drinks as it came by Pelyn. These were busy days and stand out in Florrie's memory. All the glasses had to be polished in advance, then filled with wine and carried out to the guests. Mingling with the shouting, laughing crowd on horseback in the yard, and being close to the un-familiar noise and smell of so many large animals, was an exciting experience she will never forget.

The Kendals did not attend church regularly, nor was time made for their staff to do so. This was a big change for Florrie, who had attended chapel three times every Sunday before leaving home.

A cooked meal was served at lunchtime and high tea at six o'clock. The cook prepared the same food for everybody, and the staff ate together in the kitchen, kept warm and comfortable by the large aga cooker. After high tea was cleared away and the staff had eaten their meal, they were free to spend the evening as they wished. The girls had by then been working for over 12 hours and were glad to relax in their sitting-room with the wireless. Florrie and Eileen would sometimes go to a dance in Lanlivery, and it was here that Florrie got to know Bruce Netherton, when she was aged 18.

The Kendals enjoyed 'going to the pictures', and would occasionally take Florrie and Eileen with them to the Odeon in St Austell. This was a real treat, they travelled in the back seat of the Kendals' big motor car and sat in the expensive seats at the cinema! On her day off Florrie would sometimes go home for the day. It was an awkward journey, but well worth the trouble. She was indeed well blessed with kind employers, a good friend working beside her, an attentive young man in the nearby village and the opportunity to see her parents regularly.

Then came the war. Everyone knew that an announcement was to be made by the Prime Minister at 11a.m. on Sunday, 3 September 1939. Florrie never knew why, but Mr and Mrs Kendal came up to the maids' sitting-room at that time to listen to the proclamation of war with them. The war brought changes to Pelyn, as it did to every home in the country. Rationing meant that more food had to be produced at home, and Florrie helped in the garden. The need for 'blacking out' in such a big house brought changes to the daily living routine. Mr Kendal served as an officer in the Lanlivery Home Guard. The girls, by now 20, were 'called up' in 1940. The Kendals were very anxious and upset by this,

they didn't want the girls to go, and they managed to get the call-up deferred for a year. Inevitably the sad day came when it could not be put off any longer, and Florrie and Eileen had to leave Pelyn. They were posted together to work in a munitions factory in Gloucester. After six months they were posted to Bath where they made aeroplane parts for the next three years. Their going must have made a tremendous difference to life at Pelyn. It marked the end of an era.

After the war, Florrie and Bruce (who had served in the RAF) were married. Florrie kept in touch with Eileen. Mr Kendal was for a time High Sheriff of Cornwall, and Florrie read pieces about him in the newspapers, but she never again met either of the people in whose house she had lived for six happy years.

CYRIL & BURNESS BUNN

Journalists Cyril and Burness Bunn came to Lostwithiel in the 1960s. They were kind and gener-ous-spirited people, known and loved by everyone and soon made their mark on the town. Burness was an author, poet, playwright and a friend to everyone as well as a journalist. When she died in 1990, a trust was set up in her memory, and each year local school-children compete for the Burness Bunn Award. They submit a piece of creative writing, imaginative, descriptive or poetry, the subject being set by a small committee. A drama group known as the Burness Players was also started, which has since merged with the Church Pantomime Players whose popular performances fill the church hall. Burness would certainly approve.

Right: *Cyril Bunn MBE, 1906–97.* (LM)

Left: *Burness Bunn, 1912–90. This photograph was taken in 1989.* (LM)

Cyril lived on alone, working, attending functions and meetings and reporting local events for *The Cornish Guardian*, into his 90s. The Town Council expressed its appreciation of his services by making him an Honoured Freeman of Lostwithiel in 1996. He was further honoured with the award of an MBE, which he received locally from the Lord Lieutenant of Cornwall, Lady Mary Holborow, on behalf of the Queen. He received these honours modestly, while thoroughly enjoying the social occasions. He died aged 91 in 1997.

Cyril never gave up, he was an optimist and lived every day to the full. In 1978 he had enjoyed writing *The Book of St Austell* and had material for a book on the Boer War. In his 90th year he confided, 'I am looking forward to writing it, when I have the time'. Cyril's photographs of local events numbered many hundreds, they are now in the care of the museum, and some are reproduced in this book. Cyril and Burness were true gentlefolk and it was a privilege to have known them.

MEG & DON BRECKON

The Breckons came to live in Lostwithiel in 1971. One doesn't need to be in Meg's company for very long to realise that she is full of energy, enthusiasm, drive and commitment. She cares passionately about the well-being of the community, and particularly about the education of the young.

As a student she developed a keen interest in educational dance, and this became her main subject when she qualified as a teacher. While in her first post, in Bedford, Meg met Don, Head of the Art Department in the same school. They married and moved to Berkshire. Here Meg became a lecturer in educational dance, in a new College of Education (for teacher training), with some trepidation, having only four years' teaching experience! Meanwhile Don, feeling the need to devote more time to his own painting, took a part-time teaching post.

Meg was deeply affected by her mother's death and it was at this time that she and Don decided to start a family. Meg gave up her post and Don went back to full-time teaching.

Their son Ian was born in 1970, they were happy with their baby, but Meg was not so happy with life on a modern, suburban estate, nor Don with teaching. So they made a decision which changed their lives for ever. Don gave up his job, they sold the house and took off in their VW camper van (with a trailer tent for extra space) to travel around Britain. Ian was just a few months old. This freedom was exactly what they needed. They travelled through Scotland and back into England, finding themselves at Powderham Castle, Lanlivery camp-site by October. They had never been here before, but were enchanted by this area and decided to spend the winter here. They found a cottage to rent in a remote spot between Lerryn and Polruan, and by February 1971, convinced they should stay, they bought 22 Grenville Road and settled in Lostwithiel. Don set up a studio at home and they both taught evening classes to guarantee some income. When Ian started at playgroup, Meg got involved with other mums in running the group. It was her first experience of voluntary work and she was amazed and impressed by what can be achieved by the hard work and commitment of a dedicated group of people. She was soon on the committee and became the local representative at branch meetings of the Playgroup Association, before being elected onto the County Committee of PPA (Pre-school Playgroup Association). This she chaired for the last five years of the 1970s. Meanwhile, two more sons, David and Christopher, had been born and the family had moved to Oak Cottage.

Meg Breckon. (MB)

Throughout these years Meg was heavily involved with fund-raising and became something of an expert. The Lostwithiel playgroup used to meet in the Methodist Hall, which was not an ideal venue, so when the possibility of building a community centre was mooted (spearheaded by the late Rex Stephens and other members of the Town Council) Meg was interested. She joined the steering committee and was invited by Rex to undertake the planning of a fund-raising strategy for the building. A team, which included amongst others Rex, Ralph Broad and Sue Grigg, drew up a long-term programme of fund-raising events. A great deal of money was needed so they had to 'think big'. They worked with Cornish Leisure World who ran the Coliseum at Carlyon Bay, and for five consecutive years organised a Custom Car Show, which was held at the Coliseum over August Bank Holiday weekends. They were thinking big! With the help of Fourways Garage, they also raffled a new car each year.

Rex Stephens was the first chairman of Lostwithiel Community Association (LCA). When the building was up and the organisation of activities became necessary, Meg agreed to work voluntarily as general administrator in the centre. When Rex retired from the chairmanship he became the president, and Meg succeeded him as chairman. Throughout the 1980s Meg worked tirelessly to make the centre a success, and what a difference it has made to the life of the town! There are very few of us who have not benefited in one way or another since it was established.

During all these years Don's career went from strength to strength. He has become an artist of

Don Breckon and Mayor Paul Brewer with one of Don's paintings, 1982. (CBu)

JUDE MARTELLI

Jude Martelli. (JM)

The 28 years that Jude Martelli lived in Lostwithiel she regards as the most fulfilling period of her life. It is only recently that she has had to move away, for health reasons. She came here with Peter, her husband, and five young children from Polruan. Jude was a potter and was looking for a suitable property where she she could set up a pottery and the family could live comfortably. Her father had generously given her the money to enable her to do this.

The Dower House came onto the market and Jude fell in love with the building, mainly Georgian, but with older secrets waiting to be revealed. The Martelli family moved in, Jude set up her studio in the shop, calling it the Lostpot. Jude obviously needed help and 18 months after she arrived in Lostwithiel she was joined by the potter, John Webb. Their first big order was for silver jubilee mugs in 1977, and the Lostpot has continued successfully ever since.

In the 1980s it became clear that the Dower House was in need of some urgent restoration work, which would mean closing the shop. By this time the family had grown up, so Jude closed her doors and went to Bristol for a while. The back of the house was not involved in the restoration, so John was able to continue making pots, finding other outlets for his sales.

The work took two years to complete. When Jude came back she decided to open the room above the shop as a picture gallery, where she could offer exhibition space to local artists. The first works to be exhibited were paintings by James Foot, a young painter who grew up here, but had not had an opportunity to show his work locally. The exhibition was a great success.

national repute and his railway paintings are acclaimed and sought after throughout the land.

Meg and Don's boys attended Fowey School and Meg became a governor. Her continuing deep interest in education led her, in 1990, to stand as an Independent candidate at a County Council by-election (for Lostwithiel and Fowey). The retiring councillor had been on the Education Committee and Meg saw an opportunity to further the causes of education in Cornwall. She won the seat and worked hard on our behalf, becoming chairman of education in 1998.

Since the reorganisation of county councils, there has been an executive of nine councillors responsible for making policy decisions, supported by the rest of the council and local government officers. Meg was a member of this executive, she had the responsibility for the Education/Arts/Libraries and Youth Services Portfolio, with a budget of £200 million per year.

In addition to all this, at national level she was the Independent spokeswoman for education on the Local Government Association. As such she regularly attended meetings and debates in London and Brussels. The opportunity to speak to government ministers and European commissioners about the particular problems Cornwall faces helped towards their understanding of rural deprivation generally. Evidence of this was in the awarding of Objective One status to Cornwall.

On reaching 60 Meg decided not to stand for re-election. In 2001 the Lostwithiel Area Forum was set up. Meg found herself elected vice-chairman, so she has not retired after all. There is still much for her to do! However she and Don have bought another camper van and plan to spend some time travelling again, one day. For over 30 years Meg has worked hard for Lostwithiel and for Cornwall. It was indeed a good day for Cornwall when she and Don stepped out of their first camper van and decided to stay.

Jude at work in her pottery, 1970s. (CBu)

The Dower House Gallery was a much-valued feature of life in Lostwithiel for 12 years, bringing people into the town and giving opportunities to young, talented artists to show and sell their work. Jude was selective in the work she exhibited, regular viewers could always feel confident of the quality of Jude's exhibitions, which ranged over a wide variety of media and styles. She was always happy to see the pleasure experienced by both artist and purchaser when a sale was made.

Jude left the workshop in John's capable hands at the back of the house while she opened the shop to sell his pottery and other local art and craft work. She also devoted some shelves to Oxfam goods. She feels very strongly that we should help underprivileged countries and was proud to be able to send regular cheques to Oxfam. Being a woman who lives by her principles, Jude has been known to refuse to serve customers who have betrayed racist views in her shop.

Her business activities have never been about growing rich, rather she has striven to bring the arts to life and promote work of a high standard. Jude has found great pleasure in all of this and in her involvement in the community.

Jude was instrumental in setting up a live music club, known as 'Hey Jude', in a back room of the Monmouth Inn. This flourished for a while. There were 25–30 regular members who came from all over Cornwall to enjoy the folk and other styles of music, provided by musicians such as Bob Devereux, Clive Palmer and Tony Hazzard.

For two or three years during the early 1980s Jude was the local representative of the Claimants' Union. This was an organisation set up to support and work on behalf of claimants, dealing with misunderstandings and injustices by the DHSS. It will be no surprise to those who know her to learn that Jude found herself championing the needy, with some success. The Claimants' Union was eventually taken over by the Citizens' Advice Bureau. Jude's philosophy has always been to offer help where and when it is needed.

For a time she was chairman of the Lostwithiel Chamber of Commerce. Her best memories of those days are of the medieval market, held during the 800th anniversary of Lostwithiel's first Charter (1989). It was hard work to organise, but great fun and a huge success, and much of the pleasure was again in being part of a co-ordinated community effort.

As one might expect in a town of 2,500 people, Jude has had her detractors. She is sensitive and has been hurt, but she is also very strong in her convictions and has not allowed criticism to deflect her.

In 1993 she was elected onto the Town Council. She was moved by this expression of trust by the people of the town. She took her work as a councillor seriously and did her best to live up to that trust. She is thoroughly honest and unafraid to speak out.

Sadly, however, she became disillusioned and resigned after a few years.

For some years now the Dower House shop has been rented out and it has not been possible to keep the gallery open. This is a cause of sadness to Jude, and to many people in and around Lostwithiel. The Dower House Gallery had its own special ambience, which is missed.

Jude's inspiration was behind the decision to display sculpture in Second Island Park. The Millennium Committee took up her idea and made awards to four local sculptors, whose work is now on display in the park.

Jude was born in Richmond, Surrey and grew up on the west coast of Scotland in a middle class, Catholic, Conservative family. Despite this she has always been a true socialist, believing above all things in 'the brotherhood of man'. She is still Catholic, and attended the churches in St Austell and Bodmin when she could. She also attended St Bartholomew's Church and was involved in parish life. She believes that the God she worships does not mind where she does it!

Jude came back to Lostwithiel in March 2003 for the opening of the new Gallery Eight, a small gallery on Fore Street selling the work of local artists. She was delighted with it, and wishes the proprietor every success with her new venture.

ADRIAN DANIELL

Adrian Daniell celebrated his 91th birthday on 16 July 2003. He was born at 6 Penknek Terrace, the seventh child of Joseph Cyril Daniell and the third child of Cyril's second wife. There were to be two more children after Adrian.

Adrian Daniell in 2002. (BF)

Mr Daniell had worked in the boot and shoe trade in Fore Street but gave this up to become a postman. He was a severe disciplinarian, and Adrian remembers that the family was very strictly brought up. They were 'Chapel people' and every Sunday morning the children, dressed in their best clothes, first attended Sunday school then service in the Bank Chapel immediately afterwards. After a midday dinner, the whole family (except the older ones who had grown up and left home) went for a long walk. The children were expected to walk sedately and purposefully. Adrian's father cobbled (repaired) all their boots and kept a keen eye on the way in which they looked after them. After tea they all went to chapel again.

The new river bridge under construction, 1938. (LM)

Adrian's family in 1917 outside 6 Penknek Terrace.
Left to right, back row: *Ivor, Doris, Carter, Mr Cyril Daniell and his son Cyril, Mrs Daniell, Hadie;*
front: *Enodor, Edris, Joyce, Adrian.* (AM)

Right: *Adrian's great-grandfather,*
Nathaniel Daniell, 1789–1879,
Lostwithiel's first letter-carrier. (LM)

The children attended Bodmin Hill School until the age of 14. Milk was not delivered to the house, so the three eldest children attending the school took it in turns to set off early and take a milk can up to Bodardle Farm, high above the school. At dinner time the can of milk had to be collected and carried home. The two Misses Nicholls, who lived at the farm, would be working in the dairy in the morning, before going on to teach in school. At this time there was a soup kitchen in the old Grammar School, where excellent soup was served at midday for 2d. a quart (1p a litre). This meant that the schoolchildren could have a cheap, tasty, nourishing meal.

When Adrian left school he went to work for Charlie Vine, learning the trades of masonry and chimney sweeping. He remembers two mistakes he made, the first being the time when he cemented up the chimney outlet while replacing a copper basin in a wash-house in King Street. This caused choking smoke when the fire was lit on Monday morning. On another occasion he lost his brush up a chimney at Boseglos House, Fore Street. He had to clear the chimney of both brush and soot using the branch of a holly bush, and wasn't very popular. Considering he was only aged 14, he could be forgiven.

Adrian soon moved on to other work. He learnt carpentry, painting, decorating and glazing and could soon turn his hand to any general maintenance work. He worked for a local farmer, Mr Mitchell at Fairy Cross, and added the craft of hedge layering to his skills. He remembers working with horses too.

During the depression of the 1930s Adrian was in his 20s and kept himself in work for most of the time. When there was no work, unemployed men had to take the train to Fowey to sign on. There was one very bad time during a strike at Fowey docks when these men were sent to load china clay onto the ships. If they refused they received no dole money, yet if they did the work they were labelled 'blacklegs'.

Adrian found work as a lorry driver at the 'milk factory'. In 1938, when the new road was planned to bypass Lostwithiel, Adrian left the milk factory and went back to masonry work, building the new bridge over the river. He remembers his job was to lower the stones into place using a crane, after a man called Carne had spread the mortar. Later, after the concrete undersides of the bridge's arches had been completed, he textured the concrete surface to look like granite, using a bush hammer. It was a long, hard job.

Adrian married Florence on 1 November 1939, just after the outbreak of war. Very soon they moved to a cottage behind Boseglos, which had once been the servants' quarters of that house. When war started Adrian was in a reserved occupation, but he had already joined the Territorials and he joined up in the Parachute Regiment. He was posted to a training camp in Wiltshire where he complained they were 'herded like sheep' and he missed his pasties! The training included Commando work, driving 'ducks' (amphibious American vehicles) and gliding, but his active service was as a corporal with a parachute. He was dropped over Normandy and Arnhem, fought at Osnabrück and survived it all. Meanwhile, Flo worked on the land and then in the milk factory. After being demobbed, Adrian went back to work, driving milk tankers.

He wore his old Army uniform for work and should have taken off all the identifying flashes, but as he drove by Menabilly one day, he came across Sir Frederick (Boy) Browning (husband of Daphne du Maurier) who had been his commanding officer and who noticed the 'flying horse' flash on his uniform! He signalled Adrian to stop and they had a long, friendly chat about the Army days, laughingly criticising the gliders and enjoying reminiscences together. However, Adrian has rarely spoken to his family of his wartime experiences.

Adrian and Flo had two children, John and Janet. The family moved to Barn Park where Adrian took a pride in growing vegetables. At the factory he did a variety of jobs, driving a fork-lift truck, looking after the stores, and then taking on the general maintenance of the buildings and grounds. He also continued to do some farm work in the evenings. He played darts for the Royal Oak team and remembers some good nights at matches in pubs around the town, in the 1950s.

In the 1970s, when the children had left home, Adrian and Flo moved to a bungalow at Mount Pleasant and he retired in 1977. He had worked hard all his life and enjoyed retirement. Since then there has been plenty to occupy him in the garden and around the house. The family has grown to include grandchildren and great-grandchildren. One of them, Andrew, is Lostwithiel's Sergeant at Mace at the time of writing.

Adrian cannot remember when he started to drive – it was around 1930, but he never had to take a test. He gave up his licence voluntarily when he was about 85. He and Florence enjoyed trips out in the car (she was a driver too). After retirement, Flo's favourite outing was to Par beach, and often, as she grew older, she would say that after her death she wanted to be cremated and her ashes scattered there. At first Adrian was shocked, but gradually came to respect this wish. When Florence died her wishes were lovingly carried out, and this continues to give him great comfort.

In 2003 Adrian is being well cared for by his family, who live close to him. His large, extended family and many friends are making sure that he has plenty of company and outings.

HILDA KITTY CHANTER-MENENDEZ

Kitty Chanter-Menendez. (IF)

Cornish through and through, Hilda Kitty Chanter-Menendez grew up in Linkinhorne, a large rural parish, and can trace her ancestry back through many generations of farmers in East Cornwall. She broke the mould when she went to study pharmacy in Plymouth and took up a post at the London Hospital after qualifying. In London she met again a fellow student, Ted Chanter; they married and soon returned to Plymouth where they worked together and prospered. They had three young sons and had just bought a second pharmacy when Ted died suddenly, at the age of 38.

Ted had been active and popular in his professional association, so Kitty had many friends and a great deal of support and good advice from within the profession. When Mr Whiteway, chemist in Lostwithiel for 26 years, retired in 1972, Kitty bought the pharmacy here and came back to Cornwall. Life was not easy, Kitty had to give much of her energy to developing her business. One of her sons was handicapped and it became necessary for him to be settled into a residential care home. The other two boys were educated at Kelly College in Tavistock, none of them too far away.

Kitty had friends and acquaintances in the area, farming people who had known her family for many years, and this helped to ease her into the life of the town. A young, single, female chemist was a new experience for Lostwithiel, but she found she was readily accepted into the community. She set about giving the town an excellent and personal service, developing a mutual trust with her staff and clients.

Her involvement with the community didn't stop there. Kitty was a member of the Parochial Church Council for many years, serving for a while on the Diocesan Synod. As a member of the Chamber of Commerce she was one of the first to see the importance of tourism in the town, and was instrumental in producing a guidebook for the Chamber. She strongly supported the building of the community centre (it is interesting to reflect that this was a contentious issue at the time!) and helped with the breakfasts that the centre provided for early-morning motorists during the summer season.

For 18 years she took part in the carnival parade, trying, hoping and failing to remain incognito! Through the years she has taken part in plays, pantos and poetry readings, being an excellent exponent of the Cornish dialect.

Kitty worked tirelessly for a decade on the Britain in Bloom committee, cutting verges and watering hanging baskets early in the morning and late at night. She encouraged the youth of the town to lend a hand with this. The committee's hard work was rewarded in 1989, Lostwithiel's 800th anniversary year, when it won the trophy.

In 1989 Kitty sold her business, but she has not retired – she is still in demand as a locum pharmacist throughout the region. She takes pride in the fact that she has been on the Pharmacists' Register for 50 years and is still an active member.

Kitty never fails to support the civic parade on Remembrance Day and on the Sunday following

Mayor Choosing and she always makes a point of dressing appropriately for the occasion. She was very moved when a young Girl Guide told her that she had noticed and appreciated this over the years, and thanked her for her support.

In December 1999 Kitty married Tremar Menendez, and they embarked on a new and happy life together at the start of the new millennium.

DEREK TAYLOR

Derek Taylor, 2001. (BF)

Derek Taylor, recorder for the Old Cornwall Society, was born in St Cleer, in the home of his maternal grandmother. His father was away in the Merchant Navy, so Derek's mother went to stay with her mother for the birth of her first child. Derek was home in Lostwithiel four weeks later, in time for Christmas 1929. He grew up at 15 King Street (the old Wesleyan Chapel) where his three younger brothers were born.

Amongst his earliest memories of school was his problem with tying bows. He was teased about this and recalls that, as a result, he learned to fight before he could tie his shoelaces! However, a young schoolgirl called Joyce Vincent helped him and kept him out of trouble. Derek received all his schooling at Bodmin Hill School. He enjoyed learning and when the time came for him to leave (the day before his 14th birthday) he opted to stay on. He was always a good storyteller and remembers that he was often called upon to entertain the class on Friday afternoons with his stories.

Mrs Taylor brought her boys up very strictly and as the wife of a merchant seaman she had to do it alone for most of the time. They were all confirmed into the Church of England and sang in the church choir. During the war the choirboys of St Paul's Cathedral were evacuated to St Austell and Derek remembers with pleasure the occasion when they sang in Lostwithiel Church.

In February 1945 Derek left school and became a Post Office messenger, delivering telegrams. He took this job to get the bicycle that went with it. The pay was 15s.4d a week (the equivalent of about £7 in modern money). The working hours were 9a.m.–7p.m. six days a week, plus two hours on Sundays. The contents of a telegram were confidential, but the messenger always knew if the message to be delivered would bring pleasure or pain to the recipient. In the case of a cheerful message, the clerk would hand the envelope to the messenger, if it contained bad news, it was left in the office for him to pick up. During the war this was an emotionally stressful job for a young boy, as many telegrams carried news of death or injury.

At the age of 16 Derek had to make a decision about the direction of his life, and he joined the Royal Navy to train to be a signalman. For 15 months he endured the ruthless regime of the HMS *Ganges*, a training establishment near Harwich, catering for about 2,000 boys. Here the education was good but the discipline was harsh, and Derek was glad to be assigned to the cruiser, HMS *Newcastle* in November 1947. His early experience was in the Mediterranean, and he was involved with preventing illegal Jewish immigrants from landing in Haifa, just before the establishment of the State of Israel in May 1948. Another mission on which he was engaged was anti-gunrunning and anti-slavery patrols in the Red Sea.

The year 1949 saw him on HMS *St Bride's Bay* sailing to Hong Kong, then patrolling the mouth of the Yangtze River. Until the age of 20 Derek suffered from seasickness, but once he was entitled to his daily tot of rum this problem was overcome!

In 1951 he was back home and he and Joyce were married, but he was soon posted back to Hong Kong to work as a signalman in the British Forces HQ Communications Centre. After the birth of their daughter Dawn, Joyce and the baby joined Derek in Hong Kong. This was a very happy period for the family. They lived in a flat in the Chinese quarter and found their neighbours charming, friendly and helpful. They fitted comfortably and easily into the local way of life. In 1955 the family came home and soon Derek was posted to the Admiralty and the family lived in London, enjoying the theatres, concerts, galleries and museums with young Dawn.

Derek signed up for another ten years in 1959. He sailed again to the West Indies and visited most of the British colonies. This was a particularly happy time, there was a lively social life. Derek was instrumental in starting up a steel band on his ship, the HMS *Ulster*. About 13 men were in the band, including several officers. They taught themselves to play, practised with enthusiasm and dedication and were soon in great demand at parties, concerts and dances, even broadcasting on American and Bermudan TV, wearing their Naval uniforms. On returning to the UK they broadcast on Westward TV and made a recording. (In this country they wore calypso shirts for their appearances!)

For his next assignment, Derek found himself instructing sea cadets on HMS *Raleigh*, Torpoint and, somewhat to his surprise, enjoying the work very much. It was suggested to him at this time that he had the qualities of a good teacher, and that this would be an excellent career move for him. At first he scoffed at the idea as he had no formal qualifications, but when he was later stationed in Singapore he spent his spare time studying for O-level exams and passed without difficulty.

His final posting was as an instructor with the RNVR in Wales, when he was involved with the Naval arrangements for the investiture of Prince Charles as Prince of Wales, at Caernarvon.

On completing his ten years, Derek left the Navy and studied at home through the Wolsley Hall Correspondence Courses for A levels before starting a teacher-training course at St Luke's College in Exeter, where he specialised in Medieval British and European History. Dawn was also studying at this time, so father and daughter encouraged each other and this added an extra dimension to the pleasure of learning.

Derek's first teaching post was at Padstow Primary School. He took up his post at Lostwithiel County Primary School in 1975. History was always his favourite subject and, with his gift as a storyteller, he brought it to life for his pupils. One of these pupils, Corrina Faye Bower, never lost her enthusiasm for history. First encouraged by Derek's lessons, Corrina went on to read archaeology at Cambridge and is now the assistant curator of the Farmland Museum and Denny Abbey in Cambridgeshire. She still expresses her gratitude to him for opening up this world to her.

For many years Derek took parties of children to camp at Gorran Haven, St Buryan and Rame Head, to name but a few destinations. His camps were run with strict rules and the precision of a Naval establishment! This did not always enhance his popularity, but the discipline he maintained enabled the staff and pupils to get the most out of their time in camp and to be ready to deal with any unforeseen crisis that might arise. School parties went to Pleyber-Christ regularly, before the two towns were officially 'twinned'. Derek and Joyce remain close to their friends in Brittany.

On becoming a teacher, Derek joined the National Association of Schoolmasters and was soon made the secretary for the East Cornwall Branch. This voluntary post became increasingly onerous over the years. There were 38 branch members in 1971 and 680 members (including women) in 1990 when he retired. During this time he was required to assist with several difficult court cases. Derek is a man with a strong sense of fairness, and he has never been afraid to stand up for what he believes is right.

He joined the Lostwithiel Old Cornwall Society in 1971 and has been the recorder since 1974. This involves recording everyday life and all that happens in the town, that will be of historic interest to future generations. (The OCS record was started in 1952.)

He has a wide knowledge of local history and a deep love of Lostwithiel. For many years he has been in demand as a lecturer on a variety of local history topics and has conducted guided tours of the town.

Over the years Derek has given a great deal to the community, in many different ways.

His favourite hobby has always been sailing, he and his family and many friends have had much fun on the river and along the coast.

Joyce and Derek celebrated their golden wedding anniversary in 2002. Joyce, who tied his shoelaces when he was a little boy of five, is still caring for him!

THE MITSONS

Graham Mitson and his wife Rosemary are known to half the population of Lostwithiel quite formally as Mr and Mrs Mitson, and to the other half as Mr and Mrs Stick! Their 'shoe shop' at 19 Queen Street, a 300-year-old building, is now passed every day by hundreds of people, rushing through Lostwithiel in cars. Very few are aware of the Aladdin's cave within, full of goods all related in some way to leather or wood. To go into this shop is to enter another world. When you step inside the bell rings and, as you close the door, the traffic noise is blotted out and you are in a dim, quiet and timeless cocoon, smelling of leather and full of 1001 things to see and buy. Graham or Rosemary will then quietly approach to see to your needs. Not many people are aware that Graham Mitson is known throughout the country, and is sought out by clients from far and wide for his very individual and rare skills as a craftsman.

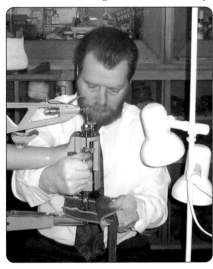

Graham at work. (BF)

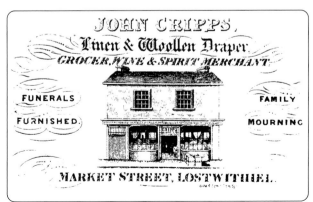

Pre-1846 business card.
This shop is now Stick's at 19 Queen Street. (LM)

Graham was born in South Wales, although his father, grandfather and great-grandfather were all in the shoe trade in East Anglia. Like his grandfather, Graham makes everything by hand. On leaving school, he went directly into the shoe trade, something he knew inside out, having lived, as now, over the shop. Graham and Rosemary met at a local church. Planning for the future, and in order to 'better himself', Graham left the shoe trade and took a post as a travelling salesman. Unfortunately, Graham had an accident which put an end to this career. As soon as he could, he went on an intensive course to train as an engineer, then spent some years repairing and servicing office equipment. It was during this time that Graham and Rosemary were married.

Graham was born to be a craftsman, he realised he wanted nothing more than to work with his hands, to have the freedom to practise his skills and the independence to run his own business. Rosemary supported him in his ambition to return to the shoe and leather trade so, in 1978, when their daughter was just a toddler, they bought the shoe shop in Queen Street and set about building up a very individual business. Keeping the name 'Stick' above the door seemed the obvious thing to do – it was, after all, the name by which the shop had been known for many years. Graham and Rosemary have a gentle sense of humour and are quietly amused that there are still people who think that they are Mr and Mrs Stick.

The business itself has a long history, dating back to the nineteenth century, when a Nathaniel Daniel was listed in Pigot & Co.'s *National Commercial Directory* of 1830 as a boot- and shoemaker. The business stayed in the hands of the Daniell (now two ls) family, in Fore Street for over a century, then Mr Phillips had it briefly, selling it to Mr Tom Stick in 1949. He moved it to 19 Queen Street in 1959. This building was one of the many erected after the devastation of the Civil War.

Graham has a deep interest in history, and since he set up his business he has been developing his own museum of footwear. Two display cases in the shop are devoted to his collection.

In addition to every shape and size of boot and shoe, Graham and Rosemary sell Wellingtons, socks, gloves, straw hats, cloth caps, leather belts, handbags, shopping bags, purses, walking sticks and much besides. They carry the greatest range of walking sticks in Cornwall, and possibly in the West of England, from modern traditional sticks to beautifully carved antique sticks. On one occasion, someone up-country was searching for a blackthorn thumb stick, 4 feet 6 inches long, and with a whistle. This is a farmer's stick with a v-shaped top in which to rest the thumb. The whistle is built into one tip of the v. The agents combed the land and Stick's shop was one of only two in the kingdom that could supply one; Graham got the order. In the shop there is an amazing variety of ceramic and cast-iron

walking-stick stands, enough to keep you browsing for a long time.

Graham will accept any shoes brought to him for repair. He will do the traditional repairs himself. Modern plastic repairs he will farm out to one of several shops that send him traditional leather work. He will undertake to alter the size of a shoe and make it fit. Graham has completely refurbished an old leather suitcase with leather hinges. He had twisted together and waxed eight strands of fine hemp thread to do the hand stitching. The work had been perfectly executed, and must be a source of joy and satisfaction to him. He has always set himself the highest standards and has a deep respect for his craft and for his customers. Graham is prepared to do any small repair work in wood or leather, all to enable us to keep our old favourites.

Among Graham's repertoire are some very unusual items, including leather kneecaps for a goat and leather shoes for a dog. A lady customer once asked him to make a pair of gaiters for her husband, as a surprise present. This presented difficulties, as some precise measurements were required. Undeterred the customer went home and after dinner gave her husband two stiff whiskies. While he slept soundly, she took the measurements… the leather gaiters fitted perfectly and were a complete surprise. Graham was commissioned to repair a pair of bellows, made of tortoiseshell and decorated with silver filigree. These were valued at £800 and he was recommended to the owner, who lived in Surrey, as probably the only person in England who could do such a delicate repair. The lady in question had been looking for ten years to find someone to undertake this work.

Since 1993, Graham has made ten leather cushions (up to 10 feet long and 2 feet wide) for window seats at Lanhydrock, to be found in the billiard room, the prayer room, the nursery and the nursery corridor. He has rebuilt, refurbished and reupholstered the back of a Lagonda motor car, designed and made a cover for a cabin cruiser and repaired numerous rocking-horses, saddles, oars and chairs. He makes bellows, buying old wardrobes from which to fashion the wooden parts, and he also cuts keys. If you have a seventeenth-century lock in your house and have lost the key, Graham will make one for you!

He loves all this work, and feels very privileged to be able to enjoy himself so much while making a living. Restoration is his hobby as well as his livelihood and he can often be seen in the auctioneers' salesrooms looking around for more work! He values his independence, belongs to no union or association and is answerable only to his God, his wife and his conscience. Graham and Rosemary are a strong team, they live and work together 24 hours a day and are the best of friends. Having their own strengths, and sharing their interests and aspirations, they complement each other. Graham and Rosemary's greatest love is for their God. They are members of a church in St Austell and give much of their time to this aspect of their lives. We in Lostwithiel are indeed fortunate to have this talented craftsman in our midst.

JUNE PASCAL

June Pascal closed her small grocery and general store at 12 Fore Street towards the end of 2002. This marked the end of an era in Lostwithiel. June's shop was the last of its kind in the town and is sorely missed by those Lostwithiel ladies for whom shopping at June's was a bright spot in the day. They appreciated the personal service June offered, the time spent attending to their needs and the easy, relaxed conversation as they sat on the chair provided for customers.

The neighbouring business people wish June Pascal well on her retirement, October 2002. Left to right: *John Faircloth, Gill Parsons, Anne Parsons, Rachael Barclay, Bill Perkins, Shirley Nicholls, Alistair Blaxley, Frank Ashton (June's brother), Mayoress Ann Jewels, Violet Ashton (June's mother), Mayor Chris Jewels, June Pascal, Suzanne Shore, Len Parsons, Georgina Rule, Margaret Penhaligan.* (DP)

The shop was certainly a bright spot in Fore Street! Some years ago June took a holiday, leaving her brother-in-law to smarten up the paintwork, and returned to find it yellow, quite an eye-catcher! It caught the eye and the imagination of the watercolour painter Sue Lewington, who featured it in her book *Sketches Around Fowey*, published in 2000.

Gradually, since the late 1970s, small grocery stores have been squeezed out of business by out-of-town supermarkets. June has bravely stayed the course and, although the business has shrunk from the time when her husband Roger delivered large numbers of customers' orders regularly in his van, she has kept going, serving those customers who remained loyal, with her dependable, good-natured, sunny smile and cheery word. June's loyalty to her customers was exceptional – she delivered one order herself, on foot, every week, until she closed the shop.

June was born in North Street, Lostwithiel, in 1938, the second daughter of Frank and Violet Ashton, just one day short of a year after her sister Marlene was born. The family very soon moved to St George's Park, where the children grew up. Her brother Frank was born six years later, and David seven years after that. They all attended Bodmin Hill School. June was happy at school. She remembers that when she was in the top class, classes were held in the upstairs room of the Social Club. (There was great pressure on space in the school at that time, because of the increase in the birth rate after the war.) The girls competed for seats by the windows overlooking Fore Street, especially on Tuesdays, when the lucky ones would smile and wave to the young farmers passing on their way to market. On Tuesdays the top-class girls always spent their lunch breaks in the cattle market.

Aged 15, June left school without having found a job, but very soon Mr Sydney Brewer suggested she came along to see him. He arranged for her to work as an assistant to Miss Winifred Hoskin in Brewer's greengrocer's store on the corner of Queen Street and Bodmin Hill. To June's surprise she loved the work and stayed there for ten years. She enjoyed the social contact with the customers and got on well with Miss Hoskin. When the Brewer's included an off-licence in the business there was much for them both to learn, and together they enjoyed the new experience.

Roger Pascal came to Lostwithiel with his mother by chance in about 1960. They had had a shop in Reading, but after the tragic, accidental death of a son, Mrs Pascal decided to sell up and move on. They were in Cornwall looking for another shop to buy. They stopped in Lostwithiel because the windscreen wiper on their car needed replacing and, while they waited for the work to be done at the Bridgend Garage, they looked around the town. Number 12 Fore Street was on the market and Mrs Pascal promptly fell in love with this Georgian property, especially the staircase! She decided there and then to buy it.

It was at a dance in the Drill Hall that June first saw Roger. He didn't know anybody there and she thought he looked lost and lonely, so she decided that when the 'ladies' excuse-me' dance was announced, she would ask him to dance. Six months later they were engaged. They were married four years later.

On the first day of spring, 21 March 1964, sisters June and Marlene shared a splendid double wedding at the Bank Chapel. The sisters wore matching bridal gowns and the Lostwithiel Band played at the wedding in their honour (their father was a member of the band, although not playing himself on this special day). June moved into 12 Fore Street with Roger and his mother and gradually took over the running of the shop, a job she was well qualified to do. Roger was involved in the business, delivering customers' orders and dealing with reps. He also did

Roger's model circus. (IF)

some taxi-driving and drove the school bus to Fowey for some time.

Apart from the business, Roger had two major interests which took up a great deal of his time and energy, and which strongly influenced June's life too. The first was the fire service. He played a leading role in the development of Lostwithiel Fire Brigade from being a volunteer unit to becoming Retained Station B17 in 1969. Roger, described as 'a man of determination and very high standards' was the officer in charge. June remembers that Mr Wilfred Jeffery and Roger shared a dream that one day a fire station might be built on the plot of land which had once been part of the Jefferys' garden at 'Woodclose' and, later, part of the cattle market. This dream was realised in 1992 but neither of them lived to see it happen. Roger's other absorbing interest was in the circus. This dated from when he was a young boy, but did not diminish throughout his life. He and June had many friends among the famous circus families and artistes, and they visited every circus that came down to the West Country. They would have dinner with the artistes in their caravans after the show and talk 'circus talk'.

Roger was also an accomplished model maker and spent many hours making items for his model circus, on the kitchen table. The model was laid out on the floor of an attic room, eventually measuring three by two metres.

The first time that June and Roger went abroad they delivered a Land Rover from Longleat to Spain for a friend who was a tiger trainer, performing in a circus there. A memorable trip for June!

One night in June 1983, while Lostwithiel Fire Brigade was attending a fire in the pheasant hatchery at Boconnoc, Roger suffered a heart attack and died in the ambulance on the way to hospital. He was 49. June was left alone at the age of 45. It was some comfort to her to know that he died doing what he loved to do. Her family, most of whom are still in Lostwithiel, were a great support and comfort to her and have been ever since. The shop gave her something to cling on to, the regular routine kept her going, and June carried on with her business for 19 more years. She is grateful to all her customers for their loyalty and support throughout all these

years. We, in Lostwithiel, thank her for her dependability and for her example of courage, cheerfulness and optimism.

RACHEL JOHN

Rachel John, 2001. (CRJ)

The name Rachel John is strongly associated with Lostwithiel's Christmas pageant. She was given the names Catherine Rachel at her baptism into the Catholic Church, but has always been known as Rachel. During her earliest years her family, which included an older sister and brother, lived within a community of artists and writers sharing a large, isolated house in the Black Mountains of Wales. Their life was very simple and the children were educated at home. Rachel's father, Donald Attwater, a man of Kent, was a writer and this life suited him. Her mother, who was of Cornish stock, coming from generations of engineers in Hayle, was of a more practical turn of mind and decided that, with three children to bring up, they should move nearer to a town.

In the early 1930s Donald became editor of the national weekly newspaper *Catholic Herald*. The family moved to St Albans and settled down to life in the town.

As a child Rachel was already finding pleasure in words, reading and writing imaginative stories and poems. Then came the war and the whole family moved back to Wales. Rachel attended the Abergavenny County High School for Girls. Tragically, her brother was killed while serving in the RAF.

Rachel was a good scholar and went to Newnham College, Cambridge to read English and the Early History of the British Isles, which included some study of the Celtic and Anglo-Saxon languages.

After graduation, Rachel sampled a variety of jobs. By this time her father was well established as an academic writer, her sister's health was causing some concern and her mother wanted to return to her roots in Cornwall, so the family moved to St Ives and later to Penzance.

Once settled in Cornwall, Rachel took a post as a tutor with a well-known correspondence college, preparing students for O- and A-level English Literature exams. She did this for many years, developing courses and preparing lecture material which went out to students in book form. Rachel describes this as her 'bread' job rather than 'bread and butter' job; it kept the wolf from the door and gave her the time and opportunity to follow a number of different interests. She researched her subjects, wrote plays, poetry, articles for various journals and translated material from French.

In order to make her own way in the literary world, where her father was well known, she stopped using the name Attwater. She took her Confirmation name, John, as her surname. The change was simply made by deed poll, and she had her father's full approval.

In 1970 Rachel was invited to write the script for a musical drama celebrating the life of St Thomas Becket, to be staged in Canterbury Cathedral. She collaborated with Laurence Bévenot OSB, a talented monk, who composed the music. She shocked a few people by describing the work as a 'sacred pantomime', as it included, besides dramatic speech, orchestral music, singing, dancing, poetry and humour. Rachel and her father both felt she had 'arrived' when someone congratulated Mr Attwater on his daughter's work, and called him 'Mr John'!

Another work was commissioned for Canterbury in 1975: 'Seven Branches for Life'. Rachel and Father Bévenot worked successfully together again. A short form of this was produced later in Lostwithiel as 'Seven Candles for Easter'. Rachel came to Lostwithiel in the mid-1970s. She found a small Catholic community here, but no church, and gradually her house, which she called the Lamb and Flag, became a local centre for Catholic and Cornish activities. Here visiting priests would celebrate the Mass in her upstairs study, which overlooked the valley and hills beyond.

Rachel began a study of the Cornish language, as well as research for her book *The Saints of Cornwall*, which was published in 1981. Among her other work is listed a biography, *Adam Schall – a Jesuit at the Chinese Court*, a musical drama, *Keepers of the Light*, a celebration of Celtic saints, and a play, *True Glory*, about Saint Cuthbert Mayne and his times. Her father's best-known work is *The Penguin Dictionary of Saints* and Rachel re-edited and revised this in 1995. It has been translated into a number of languages and has since been reprinted. She has also revised and updated *The Saints of Cornwall* in 2001.

The procession of the Christmas pageant pauses to sing a carol in the 1990s. In the group are: Janet Hayley, Tony Taylor, Heather Turner, Peter Turner, Vanessa Jezzard, Sheila Rich, Richard Bower and others. (JB)

Peter and Heather Turner take part in the Christmas pageant, 1998. (JB)

Over the years Rachel has been involved in broadcasting on Radio Cornwall and on TV, and for her valuable contribution to Cornish culture she was made a Bard in 1982, as was her father in 1960.

In Lostwithiel, Rachel's name is synonymous with the Christmas pageant, a much-loved, living and evolving tradition. On coming to Lostwithiel she was involved in the Chamber of Commerce. At that time the Chamber set up a Christmas tree each year in Monmouth Square. One evening before Christmas, the Town Band played carols in the Square and a few people gathered to join together in singing. Rachel suggested a 'living crib' and the idea was taken up. Two young volunteers were found, and Mary and Joseph with a doll to represent the Holy Infant, together with a real, live donkey, formed a tableau under the tree during the singing of the carols. After that the idea grew, more biblical characters took part, and the venue was moved to the shelter, which then stood in the Parade Garden. This developed into a procession around the town, with stops at various places to sing carols. Adults reacted

Shepherds left to right: *Penny Taylor, Richard Hicks, Ben Knight, 2000.* (JB)

with enthusiasm to the suggestion that they might choose appropriate characters for themselves and join in the procession. The new community centre became the starting point for the pageant and the Cornish carols, plainsong and dancing were activities introduced by Rachel to take place while everyone was assembling. These very soon became an integral part of the programme, as did the participation of the lamb and the donkey, the mulled wine served to one and all en route, and the hot soup on returning to the community centre. From time to time guests, including Lostwithiel Handbell Ringers and the Trigg Morris Men, have taken part. The pageant now takes place on a Saturday, in the afternoon and early evening. Each year more people are involved, and Rachel has around her a strong and reliable team of helpers to carry forward what is now a major event, firmly established in Lostwithiel's calendar. The necessary expenses are mainly covered by grants from Lostwithiel Rotary Club, Lostwithiel Town Council and Restormel Borough Council.

The pageant is a celebration of the true spirit and message of Christmas, and everyone who wishes to take part is warmly welcomed. Rachel insists that this must never change and that there must never be a charge made or a collection of money on the day.

The Christmas pageant and her writings are Rachel's gifts to Lostwithiel, to Cornwall and to us all.

Margaret Wabeke's Story

Margaret's story reminds us again that Lostwithiel is part of a wider world. It covers more than half a century and two continents. Margaret has links with Lostwithiel, with Pill Farm (home of the town's first MP in the 1300s) and with people living here now, that are compelling and fascinating, and she is happy to share her story with us.

Born in Edinburgh in 1944, Margaret is now a Dutch citizen living in Holland. She visited Lostwithiel for the first time in 1998. Her father,

Gerard Krijnen, was born in Batavia (Jakarta) in Java in the Dutch East Indies in September 1921. His family enjoyed an elegant and privileged colonial lifestyle, but when the Japanese invaded Java in 1942 their life fell apart. Gerard, with other young men of serviceable age, many of them not yet 21, enlisted in the Dutch Navy and joined a ship, just in time to sail before the Japanese took over the island. The young sailors had no idea of their destination.

They were brought to England, via Ceylon and South Africa, disembarking in Liverpool. From here they travelled by train to Cornwall, passing through a burning Exeter at the height of the blitz. They alighted in Lostwithiel and were marched up to Pill Farm, where farm buildings had been requisitioned for the use of the Dutch Navy. Here about 100 young men underwent basic training, in readiness for posting elsewhere. The training they received was tough, the discipline strict.

Their billets were in the barns and lofts above the cattle sheds, they dug latrines, washed in cold water, were drilled in the yard and practised military manoeuvres in the meadows. Food was plentiful and good, with lots of potatoes, mutton and gravy, followed by puddings and custard. Life and work on the farm continued more or less uninterrupted. None of these boys knew what was happening to their families back in Java, they must have felt homesick, apprehensive and completely disorientated, but they had courage and the determination to do whatever they could to further the fight for peace in the world.

In the sheds at Pill.
Gerard Krijnen is third from left. (MW)

Lostwithiel took them to its heart. They were quiet, gentle boys, spoke excellent English, which made communication easy, they were intelligent and polite, and quick to adapt to a very different culture from their own. The Lostwithiel girls made friends with them, they met at dances and were soon inviting them home for Sunday tea, games of cards and Monopoly, and meeting them to go to the cinema. It is still part of the folklore of the town that when the Javanese boys had German measles, so had large numbers of Lostwithiel girls!

Gerard made friends with Jean Wevell (now Mrs Hick) and several others who still live here, and when

A party was given in the Drill Hall, Lostwithiel, for the Dutch Naval Cadets. (LM)

Left: *Gerard and Elsie married in Edinburgh in 1943.* (MW)

it was time to move on they corresponded for a while. Gerard was posted to Scotland to train for the Fleet Air Arm. Here, at a dance in Arbroath, he met and fell in love with a young land girl called Elsie Archibald. Soon after this Gerard received his 'wings' and became an officer. He and Elsie were married in Edinburgh in September 1943, when he was just 22. Gerard was posted to Maydown, Londonderry in Northern Ireland to fly on anti-submarine patrols over the Atlantic. Elsie, now pregnant, went with him, full of love, hope and expectations for their future. On 11 January 1944, his Swordfish plane hit a bad storm and had to ditch at sea through lack of fuel. The three men on board all perished. Elsie was devastated, shocked, ill and alone. She needed to get back to her people in Scotland, so she made her way to Larne, the ferry port north of Belfast. Being wartime it was not a straightforward matter to get onto a ferry, and she

was delayed. Elsie was befriended by the Mayor and Mayoress of Larne (the Mayor's work was involved with the port), they took her in and looked after her until she could get a crossing. Meanwhile, word came from the War Office that the young widow of the Dutch airman was to go to London. The Mayor of Larne knew how ill Elsie was, and that she was in danger of losing her baby if put under any more stress, so he took the law into his own hands and, passing Elsie as his niece, he arranged to travel to Stranraer and personally escorted her back to her family. He was not able to take his car back to Ireland, but felt this was a small price to pay for Elsie's well-being and that of her unborn child. Margaret Krijnen was born in Edinburgh on 31 March 1944.

In August 1998 Margaret was standing in Fore Street, Lostwithiel, outside the Dower House antique shop, with a strange, unreadable expression on her face. Pixie Keirle, observing her from inside the shop, thought she might be lost, so went out to offer help. No, the tall lady answered with a Scottish accent, she wasn't lost, rather finding something momentous from her past. She said she had connections with this small town, about which she knew nothing other than its name.

Her father, Gerard Krijnen, had few personal possessions when he arrived in Britain, and had very little time to accumulate any in the short time he was here. After his death, his wife treasured all the keepsakes she had. Amongst some snapshots in a small album were a few pictures labelled 'Pill Farm' Lostwithiel, Cornwall. Elsie was not able to tell her daughter much about these, as all she knew was that it was the first place he stayed on reaching England. None of her Scottish relatives had heard of Lostwithiel, so not much had been made of it.

Margaret told Pixie some of this and Pixie was able to tell Margaret the whereabouts of Pill Farm, and together they wondered if there might be anyone still in the town who would remember her father. Pixie helped Margaret with a few enquiries and Jean Hick's name was mentioned. That day Jean was in the church doing duty as a steward.

Now in her seventies, with children and grandchildren of her own, Jean had no trouble in remembering Gerard and his friends, and talked of the dances, tea parties and evenings at the 'pictures', which were the social round of wartime teenagers, and which they had shared with the boys from Java.

Margaret was truly amazed to find herself talking to someone who remembered her father so well and could give such a vivid portrait of Gerard. The two women, totally engrossed in each other, shared their excitement, tears and laughter as they talked about this gentle young man, full of energy and enthusiasm, who had given Margaret life, and then so tragically died before she was born.

Margaret had made two friends for life that day, Jean and Pixie. She certainly felt her coming here was not just coincidence, but deeply significant, and gradually, as she talked to her new friends and told them something of her life story, they began to think so too.

Elsie was ill for a long time after Margaret's birth and she and the baby were cared for by her mother, in the small, Scottish mining village, south of Edinburgh, where they lived.

When Margaret was four years old, her mother heard from the Red Cross. The letter told her that they had contacted Gerard's family and told them of the existence of his widow and child. After he left Java in 1942, his parents and sister were imprisoned by the Japanese. His father died of starvation in the camp, but his mother and sister had survived, and although in poor health they were now living in Holland. The two women lost everything, Gerard's mother was in a nursing home in The Hague, and his sister, now crippled, was making a living as a silversmith while living with friends near Amsterdam. They both wrote and spoke perfect English, so once the contact had been made, they corresponded regularly with Elsie and Margaret. They all waited for the day when they could meet, but this did not take place until 1955, when Elsie could afford to take Gerard's daughter to Holland. It was a very emotional first meeting.

Meanwhile, Elsie had remarried when Margaret was eight, and Margaret had thought her dreams would come true at last, to be a 'real' family with a dad and a mum and brothers and sisters. However, this was not to last – Elsie died of a brain haemorrhage on New Year's Eve 1957, leaving a seriously ill husband, two baby girls, one aged two, the other just nine months, and Margaret, then aged 13. Her grandmother was a great support and gave Margaret a lot of love, but she was by now feeling very isolated and alien in her village. She was subjected to a lot of sarcasm, teasing and some bullying on account of her foreign-sounding name, and because she was tall for her age. After a holiday in Holland to help her come to terms with losing her mother, Margaret felt that it was in Holland that she belonged, and became determined that she would eventually make her life there.

Just before her 17th birthday Margaret packed her bags and took a boat to Rotterdam. Although not speaking a word of Dutch, she was confident she was doing the right thing. She lived with a family next door to her grandmother's nursing home. They had lived in Indonesia, knew her grannie well, and treated her like a daughter. Her Scottish grandmother often visited her, staying as a guest with her adopted family. Margaret soon learned the language and enjoyed the tales of the exotic, pre-war, colonial world of the Dutch East Indies. It was heaven to be with people her own height, and to have a surname that was no longer foreign! At last she was happy, but often wondered at the twists of fate that started with a father she never knew and brought her to a country he had never visited!

A national newspaper heard about Margaret and published an article entitled 'Margaret Krijnen wants to become a real Dutch girl.' She was later officially adopted, became a Dutch citizen and held both Dutch and British passports.

Margaret married Cees Wabeke, an officer in the Merchant Navy, when she was 23 and they had two daughters, Elisabeth and Marianne. She even visited Indonesia and looked for the house where her father had lived, but it had been demolished and the area redeveloped.

Years later, when she grew up, daughter Elisabeth trained as a graphic designer and came to England to work. In Surrey she met a young man, Parimal Patel, who had been to Cornwall on holiday and was enchanted with it. Parimal decided that if ever he married he would like his wedding to be at the Carlyon Bay Hotel. Parimal and Elisabeth fell in love and planned to marry in August 1998. Elisabeth agreed with her fiancé's romantic idea of marrying in Cornwall, unaware that it might be the strong spirit of her grandfather Gerard influencing their decision. That is how Margaret came to be here. She had never before mentioned her father's photo album or Pill Farm to her daughters, and now they were all astounded at the coincidence of the wedding taking place so close to the first place Gerard had known on coming to Britain.

Gerard's granddaughter Elisabeth, marries Parimal at Carlyon Bay Hotel, 1998. Margaret, Cees and Marianne are standing to the right of the bride. (MW)

Margaret.

and the friends she has made here, and came back in 2000 with Elisabeth to see them again. She met Andrew and Alison McPherson who welcomed her to Pill Farm and hosted a reunion tea party. Now the grandmother of two lovely babies, Margaret looks forward to bringing them here one day, and telling them her story.

Margaret and her family rented a house in Fowey while they were here. It belonged to a Mr Bassett, a member of a Lostwithiel family who lived here some years ago.

So she finally came to this place, alone and with some trepidation, not knowing what to expect. Imagine the joy of finding people with whom she could learn about and share so much of the father she had never known. It was a wonderful experience for her. However, perhaps the greatest surprise of all came when she was telling Pixie her story. As she was relating her mother's sad plight in Larne after the death of her father, Pixie's heart missed a beat. She recalled being told that her grandfather had been Mayor of Larne during the war, and that he had befriended a young, pregnant widow. His trip to Scotland posing as the uncle of the young girl had been a noble thing to do, and the only unlawful act he ever committed! The discovery of this amazing link between the two women was a moment of pure joy, and at first disbelief. Telephone calls to Ireland confirmed that it was indeed true.

Perhaps without the intervention of the Mayor of Larne, Margaret might never have been born, and none of this would have happened.

Margaret's son-in-law, Parimal, is delighted with the part he has played in this discovery of Margaret's history. Had he chosen any other place for his marriage to Elisabeth, none of these revelations would have come to light.

The remarkable coincidence of coming to Cornwall, discovering Lostwithiel, finding people who remembered her father with respect and affection, and not least, meeting the granddaughter of the man whose kindness probably saved both her mother's and her own fragile life, was a profound experience for Margaret. All this coming out of the blue has added a new dimension to her life.

Margaret does not profess to have strong religious or paranormal convictions, but she does feel very deeply that it cannot be merely coincidence. She says, 'It is as though my father had left behind a trail we had to follow, bringing us all together for one glorious day in August.' She feels a strong affinity with Lostwithiel

WHAT DOES THE FUTURE HOLD FOR LOSTWITHIEL?

Since the end of the Second World War, Lostwithiel has moved on. Aspirations and expectations are higher, educational opportunities are greater, the quality of housing has improved, private transport is taken for granted and interests have changed. Some older people look back with nostalgia to 'the good old days', but most appreciate the changes that have made their lives easier, healthier and possibly longer. For many years Lostwithiel maintained an independence and self-sufficiency because it was geographically isolated from its neighbours and had little in common with either the coastal towns or the larger towns of Bodmin and St Austell. Now it finds itself part of a wider neighbourhood and largely reliant on this wider region for secondary education, employment, shopping and entertainment.

However, many of the young people of the town would still prefer to work locally, but, although the number of small businesses on the industrial estate is growing, the town does not generate enough employment for everybody. It is also a fact that a significant number of people come into Lostwithiel to work. This is inevitable in a small town when employers are looking for particular skills. Housing, too, is a problem – houses are being built, but they are generally too expensive for first-time buyers, so Lostwithiel's young people are being forced to move away.

Since 2000 Cornwall has been given Objective One status by the European Union. This means that it is recognised as an economically deprived region and European aid is available for purposes of regeneration. Lostwithiel could benefit from this programme if a commitment to regeneration is demonstrated by the wider community. Ideally local councils will work together with Business and Residents' Associations to agree plans covering all aspects of community life for the benefit of all. These could include work, housing, public transport, traffic management and the care and use of historic buildings, the river and parks.

With this opportunity in mind, a Business Group was re-formed in 2001. Following well-attended public meetings, the townspeople decided to create a Forum and a committee was elected. The Forum committee, chaired by Sir Richard Trant, is composed of representatives of the County Council, Borough Council, Town Council, the neighbouring villages, local businesses and a cross-section of the population. If the three bodies (the Town Council, the Forum and the Business Group) work together positively, Lostwithiel and the surrounding villages, with the assistance of the Restormel Regeneration Partnership, should soon be in a position to devise and put into effect a programme of regeneration. If a well-researched and well-supported action plan is devised by the community, there are many other funding sources which will be available after the Objective One programme has finished.

There will, in the very nature of things, be changes. A meeting of the Area Forum was held in 2003, attended by over 120 people, to thrash out the questions that needed to be asked, to assess the present and future needs of the town. From the findings of this meeting, a survey was devised and delivered to everyone in the town and surrounding villages. This means that every inhabitant has had an opportunity to record his or her views on every topic, and each one of us bears some responsibility for what will happen. Let us hope that together, with the help of the funding agencies, the people of Lostwithiel will be able to improve working and housing opportunities for the next generation, so that those who wish to live, work and enjoy their heritage in this ancient town, may do so.

Come what may, of one thing I feel sure: the heart of Lostwithiel will survive unchanged. The people who live here, who love and cherish the town, will safeguard the community spirit that is the essence of life in Lostwithiel.

'There is history in every stone in Lostwithiel'. This view in 2002 illustrates these words attributed to John Betjeman. The Duchy Palace, built at the end of the thirteenth century, was, for nearly 600 years, intimately involved with the lives of the people of Lostwithiel and of Cornwall. Sold by the Duchy in the 1870s, it has been inaccessible to the public since then. In 2003, as the population becomes ever more aware of its heritage, there is a ground swell of opinion that this historic building should be used appropriately for the benefit of the people of Lostwithiel and Cornwall. (IF)

Continuing Change and Development into the 21st Century

"THE FAIREST OF SMALL CITIES"

A quotation used in the title of the report of a major historic characterisaton study of the town, completed in 2008 by a team from the Historic Section of the Cornwall Council Historic Environment Service.

An Area Action Plan for 2004 to 2024 was formulated for the social and economic regeneration of the town by the Town Forum and the Community Development Trust in 2005. A number of projects were planned some small, requiring minimum funding. Two major programmes initiated by Barbara Fraser and Peter Best secured Heritage Lottery funding. These projects included an historical characterisation study of the town and an environmental focus, involving improvements to the site of the Nature Reserve at Shire Hall Moor. Here essential improvements to the site and the stabilising of part of the eroded banking were crucial. A town Web Site supported by the Business Group was also designed.

Groups of enthusiastic volunteers from the community welcomed the opportunity to become involved with the initiatives and worked tirelessly to achieve positive results. In addition to working with the professionals commissioned to carry out the characterisation study, Heritage Plaques were placed on buildings to mark the sites of historic interest in the town over 800 years. Heritage trail brochures were produced and town guides were trained to continue the town walks programme. Important railings were replaced around the Parade.

The team conducting the major characterisation study explored the previous archaeological and historical work available. In this wide ranging project they also studied in depth specifically significant buildings including the Duchy Palace, the Medieval Bridge, St. Bartholomew's Parish Church and Taprell House. Regular meetings were held in the Church Rooms bringing the community up to date with findings, thus stimulating a renewed community interest in the town's heritage.

The completed report highlights the changing social structure, shape and appearance of the town over time. Photographs, illustrations and maps contribute to this fascinating report, which is available in the reference sections of the town's Museum and Library.

The Town Forum continues to review and update the Area Action plan and support the many activities and initiatives which take place in the community. During this period the town also developed a reputation for quality antiques and good food.

Major restoration work on the historically significant 700 year-old Duchy Palace began in January 2012. This is the first upgrading of the Grade 1 listed building since 1878. The Duchy Palace was purchased by the Prince's Regeneration Trust in July 2009 when its prime importance to the social and architectural history of Britain was finally recognised. During a visit to the town on July 3rd 2009 the Duke and Duchess of Cornwall were able to view the original deed of sale of 1874, when the Duke of Cornwall, later King Edward VII sold the Duchy Palace to local businessman, Marc Thomas. The Deed was lent to the museum for the occasion by Mrs Jenny Pope, the great grand daughter of Mr Thomas. Funding for the restoration and conservation of the building has been generated from a number of sources including the European Regional Development Fund. It is managed jointly by the charity The Prince's Regeneration Trust and their subsidiary, the United Kingdom Historic Building Preservation Trust. The project is being delivered in partnership with the Cornwall Buildings Preservation Trust.

Following the upgrading and adaptation of the building it is estimated that seven jobs, which will be of benefit to the local economy, will be created in the high quality office space. In addition, there will be space for a small retail outlet and an area for heritage interpretation, thus preserving and celebrating the historical significance of the Palace. Carrek a firm of builders specialising in the conservation of historical buildings are carrying out the work, which will enable the Palace to be removed from the Heritage at Risk Register.

On 3 November, 2010 the historic carved wooden Prince of Wales' crest fell from its position on the roof of the Palace. This was spotted by an eagle-eyed pupil from St. Winnow School during a town walk and later rescued by the local fire brigade. The crest, which has been difficult to date, was given to the town by the Prince's Regeneration Trust and is now on display in the Museum. A replica of this fragile

Presentation of the Prince of Wales'
Crest to the Museum. (MRus)

The 250 year old
fire engine following
conservation work. (IF)

crest will be made and returned to the roof of the
Duchy Palace in due course

The Museum celebrated 40 years as part of the
town in 2011. It continues to thrive as a result of the
dedicated voluntary efforts of the trustees, committee, stewards, town guides, the support of the Town
Council, the 200 loyal members, the community and
the visitors.

In 2007 the status of full Accreditation was
awarded to the museum by the Museums and
Libraries Association, now part of the Arts Council.
As a result of this award opportunities became available to access grant funding from awarding bodies.
Conservation work and initiatives to improve the
environment and services available have since been
possible. Over the past 8 years two small grants from
Restormel Council funded an extended reference
section which is very popular with visitors researching their family histories. A major grant from the
Renaissance Fund facilitated the installation of
specialist museum quality lighting which has
enhanced the display area and transformed the environment. Refurbishment of the small office area was
also achieved from the same grant. Two awards from
the Cornwall Council Small Grants Scheme have
provided improved computing and reprographic
equipment and the replacement of an old display
cabinet. Major grants from the Association of
Independent Museums have supported the conservation of the portrait of John Daniels and of the fire
engine, which was given to the town in 1761 by the
Edgecumbe family. After 250 years and careful
conservation work the fire engine is now in working
order once again. Following a generous donation by
the family of the late Derek Taylor, a project and
annual award was initiated by Barbara Fraser to
encourage and nurture the children's interest in the
heritage of the town. The children in year 5 from
Lostwithiel County Primary School, where Derek

was a teacher, continue
to participate each year.
The resulting projects
are placed on display in
the museum window
and generate consider-
able interest in the
town.

As an active member
of the Restormel Mus-
eums Group and the
Cornwall Museums
Group, the museum
participates in joint exhibitions. In 2011 two artefacts
from the museum were chosen to be part of a History
of Cornwall in 100 Objects exhibition and publica-
tion. The two items were the Gorsedd Robes which
belonged to Mr R. Santo and were worn at the 1989
Gorsedd, celebrating the 800th anniversary of
Lostwithiel, and a Crucifiction Figure or Pax, loaned
to the museum by the Reed family. The Pax is a
gilded figure of the crucified Jesus Christ from the
late 12th century and is an important example of
medieval art and religion in Cornwall. It was found
in a field near to Lostwithiel in 1894 and then lost
again until 1994 hidden in a desk.

ROMAN LOSTWITHIEL

At the final presentation of the Heritage Project an
announcement was made regarding the Roman presence in Lostwithiel.

In 2007 a detailed study was published verifying
the presence of Roman settlement on the Restormel
Farm archaeological site. The Cornwall Council
Historical Environment Service were commissioned
by the Duke of Cornwall's Benevolent's Fund
Committee on behalf of His Royal Highness to rein-
vestigate the site. Building on a history of Restormel

Roman Excavation site area near to Restormel Castle.

An example of Lostwithiel Ware pottery. (IF)

from the 2nd Century, with only 24% identified as local ware. Many items were imported Cornish ware rather than locally made ceramics. Evidence from the pottery indicated that the Restormel earthworks were founded at approximately the same time as the military fort at Nanstallon. Facts appear to suggest that the two earthworks may be Roman Military Forts.

The report presented is very well illustrated with maps giving site locations, photographic evidence, detailed descriptions and coloured photographs of artefacts, particularly the interesting ceramic ware. A copy is available in the reference section of the town Museum, together with a historic buildings analysis and landscape survey of Restormel Manor, farm buildings and estate. The Grade 2 listed house was last remodelled in the late 18th Century. In 2006 the Manor became vacant and a restoration programme began. This report contains details of the restoration with photographic records. The Manor and the core farm buildings have been converted to private holiday and office accommodation and provide local employment opportunities.

earthworks and archaeological work previously undertaken, new materials were collected, examined and assessed, in all 726 items. Many of the artefacts were Romano-British in date and covered the period from the middle of the 1st Century AD to at least the 4th Century. The largest number of items were

FLOODS

On Wednesday 17 November 2010 the townspeople awoke to a devastating flood. Torrential rain caused water to cascade down Tanhouse Road. Several

The Derek Taylor Award presentation by the Mayor, Councillor David Robson, to children from Lostwithiel County Primary School. (MRus)

Lostwithiel Bridge in the flood of 17 November 2010.

The flooded Bridal Shop, Queen Street on 19 November 2010. The shop owner Sue Read with the Mayor Councillor Vic May and HRH Duke of Cornwall.

Drill Hall opened 1914. The interior and exterior refurbished October 2010.

houses were flooded and at Mrs Julie Edward's house on Tanhouse Road the water came in the front door out the back and even demolished the garden wall. Homes and businesses were flooded on Queen Street, South Street, Church Street, Quay Street and Monmouth Lane. The historic old bridge was under threat of collapse due to the volume and force of the water flowing down the River Fowey.

On Friday 19 November HRH Prince Charles, Duke of Cornwall came to visit and was shown the flooded businesses in Queen Street by the Mayor Councillor Vic May. The Duke later visited the Fire Station to meet many residents who were the victims of the flooding. Many had to take up temporary accommodation for up to six months before their homes and businesses

were habitable again. Unusually on this occasion Park Road, the lower end of North Street and the Parade were unaffected by this flood.

BOER WAR PEACE MEMORIAL (1899-1902)

A plaque was placed on this memorial in February 2010 instigated by Lostwithiel Town Council and funded by Lostwithiel Forum in memory of the four men of St Winnow Parish who returned home safely. Thomas Henry Maker, William Charles Oliver, Frederick William Stephens and John Wevell.

Lostwithiel Town Council led by Councillor Gillian Parsons and Honoured Burgess Councillor Mervyn Jones in 2010 received a grant from the War

The Old Carriage Works renovated 2011.

Memorials Trust to erect a small railing around the Memorial on Grenville Road to preserve this monument erected in 1903.

BRUNEL QUAYS

The maintenance sheds at the Great Western Railway Yard which were devastated by fire in 1987 were eventually bought by Wombwell Homes. The fire-damaged shed was restored in 2003 to living accommodation whilst new blocks of apartments were built overlooking Park Road and the Parade, all tastefully designed to complement the old existing stonework. The commercial unit was restored to a new dental practice which in 2011 won the award for the best in the South West and Wales. This original, restored 1859 building also accommodates offices, meeting rooms and apartments.

BELLS

Early 2009, after being examined by engineers, the bells of St Bartholomew's Church were silenced as the frames that support the bells were found to be rusting. Fundraising started immediately and with lottery funding, grants and donations approximately £35,000 was raised. On Friday 3 July their Royal Highnesses the Duke and Duchess of Cornwall visited the church to view the newly restored bells. The bells were once more heard around the town on Dickensian Evening December 2009.

JOSEPH BURNETT

Joseph Burnett's gravestone dated 21 August 1814 which was in the churchyard was noticed by members of the Police Historical Society and realised to be the oldest gravestone of a Peace Officer killed on active service. The Police Historical Society funded the cleaning and re-siting of the gravestone into the South Porch of St Bartholomew's Church. The rededication service took place on Sunday 8 June 2008.

MAYOR MAKING

Lostwithiel Mayor Making was held on Friday 11 May 2012. In this historic Diamond Jubilee year of Queen Elizabeth II a lady Mayor, Councillor Gillian Parsons, and a lady Deputy Mayor, Councillor Pamela Jarrett were chosen.

DIAMOND JUBILEE CELEBRATIONS

The Celebrations commenced on Sunday 27 May 2012 with the Beating of the Borough Bounds. Approximately 40 adults and children assembled on the Quay at 8.10am in the presence of The Mayor, the Vicar, The Reverend Philip Conway and the organiser, Councillor John Pegg. A bright and sunny day was enjoyed on the 17 miles walk. At approximately 4pm the happy band crossed the River Fowey at Newham to arrive back in the Church Rooms at 5pm to receive refreshments and certificates. The Mayor and Consort left the walk temporarily to attend the 10am service at Lanlivery Parish Church to say farewell to the Curate the Reverend Sam Denyar and his family who have transferred to a parish out of the County.

Lostwithiel was resplendent with flags and bunting for the weekend celebrations on 2-5 June 2012. On Saturday 2 June the celebrations started with an afternoon tea dance in the Church Rooms followed by a Lostwithiel Town Band and Junior Band concert in the Community Centre.

Shop window Anne's Gallery, Fore Street.

Afternoon Tea Dance, Church Rooms, 2 June 2012

The Big Lunch Sunday 3 June 2012.

Sunday 3 June a Jubilee Civic Service was held in St Bartholomew's Church. Unfortunately due to a dispute there were no church bells rung on this special weekend. The Big Lunch followed but due to the inclement weather was held in the Community Centre where the celebrations in London were simultaneously shown on the big screen. Each participant received a piece of Jubilee cake donated by the Mayor.

On Monday 4 June in favourable weather a Fun Run, family sports and barbecue were held. The sports on the playing field with Jubilee medals for the winners emulated the sports held on Coronation Day 2 June 1953. Jubilee medals and certificates were also given to the pupils of St Winnow School who participated in the Town Council Diamond Jubilee Poetry Competition. Lostwithiel Young Farmers lit a beacon at Polscoe which was visible at about 10:30pm from many points in the town.

On Tuesday 5 June the celebrations concluded with

Fun Run Monday 4 June 2012.

a family disco, free to all, in the Community Centre. The successful weekend was organised by Fowey River Lions, Lostwithiel Business Group, Community Association, Film Club, Rotary Club, Town Band, Town Council and Young Farmers' Club.

The year 2012 has been an eventful year. The community of Lostwithiel has worked well together to celebrate the Queen's Jubilee. That is not the end. We have all had a chance to see the Olympic Flame relay and now the Olympics. What will the future historians make of it all ?

Diamond Jubilee Sports, Monday 4 June 2012.

Bibliography

Barton, Rita M. (Ed.). *Life in Cornwall in the Late Nineteenth Century.* D. Bradford Barton Ltd, 1972.

Barton, Rita M. (Ed.). *Life in Cornwall at the End of the Nineteenth Century.* D. Bradford Barton Ltd, 1974.

Bennett, Alan. *Cornwall Through the Late Nineteenth Century.* Kingfisher Railway Productions, 1987.

Boger, Revd Canon. *Lostwithiel Bridge and its Memories.* 1887.

Borlase, William. *Antiquities of Cornwall.* First Edition, 1754. EP Publishing, 1973.

Brown, H.M. *The Church in Cornwall.* Oscar Blackford Ltd, Truro, 1964.

Brown, H.M. *Battles Royal.* Libra Books, 1981.

Carew, Richard. *Survey of Cornwall.* 1602.

Chadwyck, Healey C.E.H. (Ed.). *Sir Ralph Hopton's Narrative of his Campaign in the War 1642–44.* Somerset Records Vol. XVIII, 1902.

Courtney, W.P. *The Parliamentary Representation of Cornwall.* Thomas Pettite & Co., London, 1889.

Daniel, Revd J.J. (Ed. Peters, T.). *The History and Geography of Cornwall.* Netherton and Worth, Truro, Houlston and Sons, London, 1906.

Foot, Andrew. *History of St Veep Church and Parish, including Lerryn.* 1986.

Fraser, Barbara. *The Book of Lostwithiel.* Quotes Ltd, 1993.

Gillespie, B. Guild. *On Stormy Seas.* Horsdal & Schubart, Victoria, BC, Canada, 1992.

Hamilton Jenkin, A.K. *Cornwall and its People.* David and Charles, 1945.

Hatcher, John. *Rural Economy and Society in the Duchy of Cornwall 1300–1500.* CUP, 1970.

Hatcher, John. *English Tin Production and Trade Before 1550.* Clarendon Press, Oxford, 1973.

Henderson, Charles (Ed. Rowse, A.L. & Henderson, M.I.). *Essays in Cornish History.* OUP, 1935.

Henderson, C. & Coates, H. *Old Cornish Bridges and Streams.* University College of the SW, Exeter, 1928.

Hext, Frances Margery. *Memorials of Lostwithiel and Restormel.* 1891.

Hext, Jean (Ed.). *The Staniforth Diary.* D. Bradford Barton Ltd.

Kop, Hans van der. *The Flying Dutchman.*

Lewis, G.R. *The Stannaries.* D. Bradford Barton Ltd, 1908.

Lyson. *Britannia Magna – Cornwall.* 1813.

McArthur. *The River Fowey.* Cassell, 1947.

Morris, John (Ed.). *Domesday Book – Cornwall.* Phillimore, 1979.

Nicholls, Dorothy de Lancey. *The Black Prince.*

Nicholls, Dorothy de Lancey. *Lostwithiel.*

Nicholls, Dorothy de Lancey. *Gleanings from a Cornish Note Book.* 1974.

Noall, Cyril. *A History of Cornish Mail and Stagecoaches.* D. Bradford Barton Ltd.

Norway, Arthur H. *Highways and Byways of Cornwall and Devon.* McMillan & Co., 1897.

Parkes, Catherine (Ed.). *Fowey Estuary, Historic Audit.* Cornwall Archaeological Unit, 2000.

Payton, Philip. *Cornwall.* Alexander Associates, 1996.

Payton, Philip (Ed.). *Cornwall For Ever.* Cornwall Heritage Trust, 2000.

Pearce, Richard. *The Ports and Harbours of Cornwall.* H.E. Warne Ltd, 1963.

Platt, Colin. *Medieval England.* Routledge and Keagan Paul, 1978.

Polsue, Joseph. *Lake's Parochial History of the County of Cornwall.* W. Lake, Truro, 1867. EP Publications Ltd, 1974.

Probert, John C.C. *The Sociology of Cornish Methodism.* Cornish Methodist Historical Association, 1971.

Rowse, A.L. *Tudor Cornwall.* McMillan, 1941.

Shaw, Thomas. *A History of Cornish Methodism.* D. Bradford Barton, 1967.

Stockdale, F.W.L. *Excursions Through Cornwall.* Simpkin & Marshall, 1824.

Seymour, W.H. *Restormel Castle.* 1911.

Smith, Eleanor. *Lostwithiel 1189–1989.*

Trevelyan, G.M. *English Social History.* Longman, 1944.

Whetter, James. *Cornwall in the Seventeenth Century, an Economic Survey.* Lodenek Press, 1974.

Young, Denham. *Richard of Cornwall.* Basil Blackwell, 1947.

PAPERS

Beresford, Maurice. *The Six New Towns of the Bishops of Winchester 1200–55. Medieval Archaeology Vol. III, 1959.*
The Black Prince's Register, *Part II 1351–65 Cornwall.*
Cornish Archaeology No.14. Irwin, Mary M. *An Earthwork at Restormel.* 1975.
Cornwall Census 1851, *Vol. 4, Part 2.* Lostwithiel Pro. Ref. 110107, 1904.
Lostwithiel Museum. *Lostwithiel Museum Matters.* 1996–2000.
Lostwithiel Museum. *Lostwithiel Past and Present.* 2000–2003.
Minchinton, Walter (Ed.). *Exeter Papers in Economic History No.12.* University of Exeter, 1979.
Pounds, Norman. *The Social Structure of Lostwithiel in the Early Nineteenth Century.* 1979.
Pounds, Norman. *The Duchy Palace, Lostwithiel.*
Radford, C.A. Ralegh. *Restormel Castle, Cornwall.* Ministry of Works, 1947.
Thomas, Nigel & Buck, Colin. *An Historical & Archaeological Investigation of Restormel Castle.* An interim report, Cornwall County Council, 1993.
Toy, Sidney. *The Round Castles of Cornwall.* Society of Antiquaries, London, 1933.

The Parade in winter, during Edwardian times. (DB)

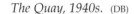

The Quay, 1940s. (DB)

Military Victory Parade along the bypass, Lostwithiel, 1946. (DP)